DURAND

THE MAN AND HIS GLASS

EDWARD J. MESCHI

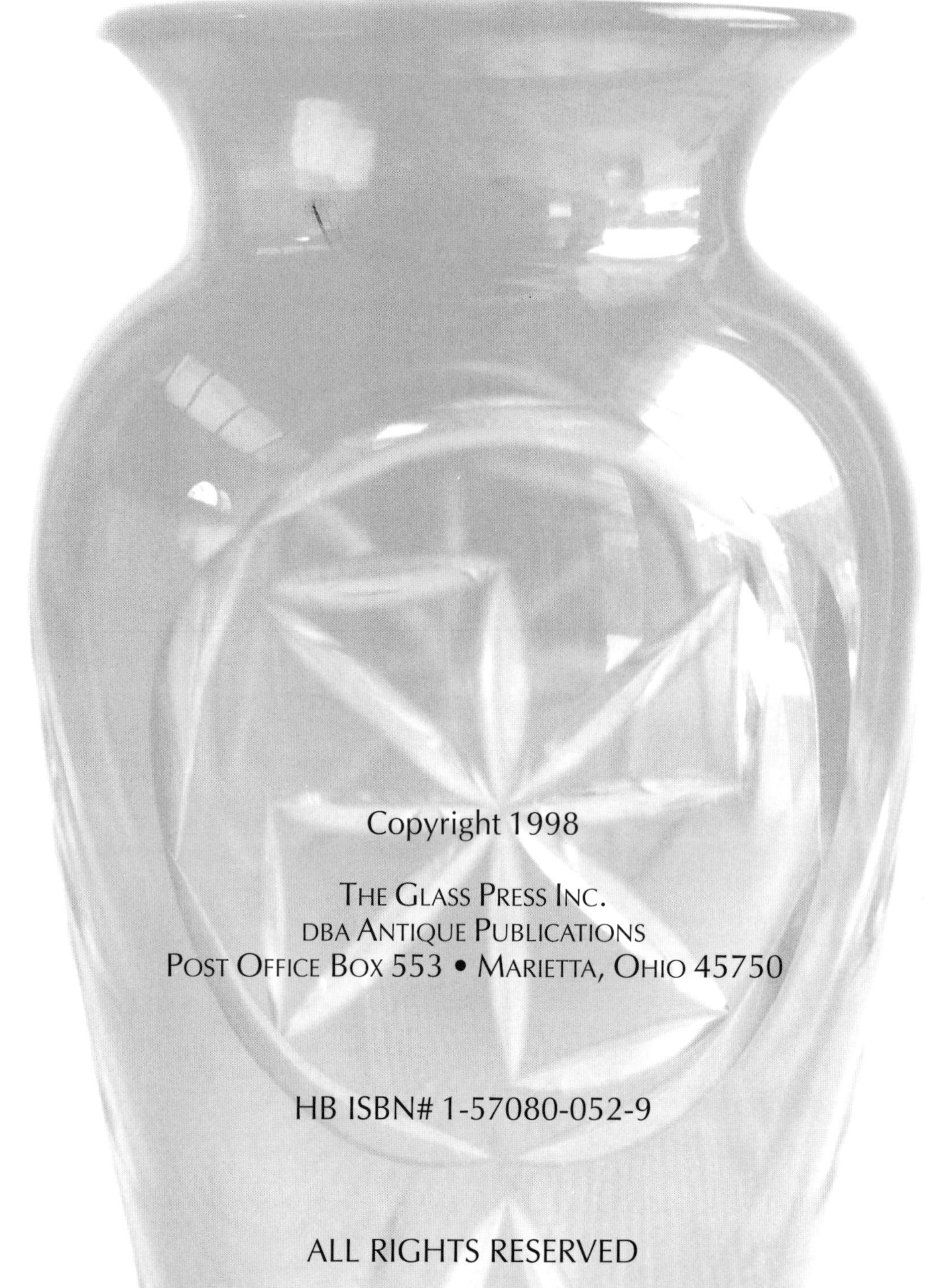

THE GLASS PRESS INC.
DBA ANTIQUE PUBLICATIONS
POST OFFICE BOX 553 • MARIETTA, OHIO 45750

HB ISBN# 1-57080-052-9

Contents

I would like to dedicate this book to my lovely wife Ginny, who has put up with my collecting habits for 30 years.

Edward J. Meschi has been a dealer, collector and aficionado of fine arts for more than 20 years.

He has a particular interest in Durand art glass, having grown up in Vineland, New Jersey, where it was made.

He can be contacted by writing:
129 Pinyard Rd., Monroeville, NJ 08343

In Loving Memory of My Father and Brother

Acknowledgements

I would like to extend my sincere appreciation to the following people, without whose generous support, this project would have been impossible:

My good friend Bill Holland, without whose encouragement I might never have written this book.

Frank Strovel, for allowing us to photograph his extensive collection, and for sharing his library of original catalogs and other references. These materials gave me a solid basis for my research on Durand.

Tony and Donna Matalucci, who gave me access to their original advertising flyers, photos, and other material, in addition to giving us permission to photograph their outstanding Durand collection. They are the most enthusiastic collectors I have ever met!

Adele Cunningham Johnson and Carl Johnson, for providing photographs, information, and memories passed down through the Durand family over generations as well as providing their beautiful Durand collection to be photographed.

The following individuals offered their wonderful hospitality and provided great collections of Durand glass to be photographed:
Isaak and Annette Somershein
Dr. Ken and Mary Izzo
Kim and Dr. Anthony Scialdone

Other individuals who provided hospitality and allowed us to photograph their glass are:
Allan Teal and Dottie Freeman
Linda Link Clark and Charles Clark

Others persons contributing to this book include:
Doris Evy, for supplying original publications on Durand and Quezal used in my research.

Amanda Meschi, whose artistic assistance in photography proved to be important. And for being my cohort in this endeavor.

Dave Richardson, who was willing to go the extra mile to make my dream possible. His knowledge and expertise greatly enhanced this book. Definitely a one-of-a-kind publisher!

Terry Richards Nutter, for her dedication and hard work in the page-by-page production of this book, and for her congeniality and patience in dealing with my fine tuning of each page.

Ginny and Johnny Meschi, for their many hours of typing.

Concetta Meschi, my mom, for stimulating my interest in art glass as a child and always being there to listen.

Bob DiCresenzo of Robert Alan Studios, for making me camera literate.

Hector Bertoia, who shares my passion for art glass, for sharing his glass knowledge.

Jack and Ronnie Cimprich, for navigating me through troubled waters.

Lou and Lena Meschi, for sharing memories of working at the Durand factory.

Mary and Frank Smith, for giving me access to publications on Durand.

And, finally, to the following organizations and their cooperative staff members:

Vineland Historical Society, Vineland, New Jersey
Gloucester County Historical Society, Woodbury, New Jersey
Rakow Library, Corning Museum of Glass, Corning, New York
The Free Library of Philadelphia, Philadelphia, Pennsylvania.

Introduction

When I was asked to write the introduction to this book I was very excited and quite flattered. I did not know (Victor Durand Jr.) my grandfather, who died before his time. What I do know about him came from things that both my grandmother and mother as well as others who knew him well have told me. Having read this book I feel a sense of remembering childhood stories and amazingly I found many interesting things about my Grandfather and the production of his glass, that I was not aware.

Growing up, I was surrounded with his lovely art glass. Many pieces were those that he created himself for my Grandmother or Mother. These pieces are now my most treasured possessions. My three children grew up with all of this art glass, and have developed a keen interest in reading and learning about their Great-Grandfather. I'm sure that they, as I, are very proud to be a direct descendant of the orchestrator of such beautiful art glass.

My congratulations to Ed Meschi for having compiled this wonderful history of Victor Durand, that includes the marvelous illustrations of his art glass. This book should be in every glass lovers library.

—Adele Cunningham Johnson

Adele Durand and her sister, Lorraine, both daughters of Victor Durand, Jr.
They were aunt and mother, respectively, of Adele Johnson.

Introduction

I have always been convinced that Durand should be in the company, of Tiffany, Steuben and Quezal as the epitome of American art glass. I hope after reading this book you will also be convinced. I have compiled photos of more than 500 pieces, from some of the finest collections known, in an attempt to give everyone who reads and views this book an exhilarating voyage into the seldom seen beauty of Durand art glass. The classic shapes, beautiful decorations and extensive colors, along with many rare, one-of-a-kind, and experimental pieces should make this publication the most complete of its kind.

I have documented more than 170 shapes with the corresponding numbers used to identify them. I have shown all of the basic signature types, along with variations and paper labels in order to familiarize you with what is authentic. I have compiled a list of terminology used by Durand and clearly defined those terms in order to achieve a more uniform language amongst collectors and dealers alike. I have explained how the many types and decorations of glass were made. I have shown most of the cuttings used on cased and uncased glass and devised a simple but effective cataloging system so that they can be described without having to be an expert in cut glass. I have paid homage to a group of artisans that were second to none and to their founder, Victor Durand. My attempt here is to help put Victor Durand in his proper place in the history of glass making and bring Durand art glass to a higher level of appreciation in the art world.

—Edward J. Meschi

Historical Time Line

1870 Victor Durand Jr. was born in Baccarat, France.

1882 Victor Durand Sr. immigrated to America.

1884 Victor Durand Jr. and other family members immigrated to America.

1897 Victor Durand Jr. and his father opened the Vineland Flint Glassworks in Vineland, N. J.

1899 Victor Durand Jr. purchased his father's interest in the Vineland Flint Glassworks, becoming the sole proprietor.

1901 The Quezal Art Glass and Decorating Co. was established in Brooklyn, N. Y.

1904 The Vineland Flint Glassworks was destroyed by a fire. A completely new factory was built where the old one had stood.

1909 The New Jersey Clay Pot Co., of Vineland, N. J. was formed.

1912 The Vineland Flint Glass Co. merged with Kimble Glass Co. forming the Kimble-Durand Glass Co.

1917 The Vineland Scientific Glass Co. in Vineland, N. J. was formed.

1918 Durand ended the merger with Kimble Glass Co.

1918 The Newfield Glass Co. of Newfield, N. J. was established.

1924 The Quezal Art Glass and Decorating Co. went out of business.

1924 Durand began production of artistic glass.

1926 Durand art glass won a medal of honor at the Sesquicentennial International Exposition in Philadelphia, Pennsylvania.

1928 Durand began the production of artistic glass lamps.

1931 The Vineland Flint Glassworks merged with Kimble Glass Co. for the second time, keeping the name the Kimble Glass Co.

1931 Victor Durand Jr. died from injuries sustained in an automobile accident.

Durand — The Man and His Glass

Durand art glass stands among the finest in the world for its beauty and innovation, in large part because of a team of artisans who worked together with all the precision of a symphony. Most of the credit however, must go to Victor Durand Jr., who created a haven for glass artisans to practice their craft and develop their artistry. He had the foresight to allow these men to express their creativity without having to worry about the pressures of financial gain as their driving force. Durand art glass may be the only major art glass that was created for artistry first and only secondarily for profit.

Victor Durand Jr. was born In 1870 in Baccarat, France. An area renowned for its glass making. At the age of twelve, he went to work in the local glassworks, as several generations of Durands had done before him. Victor's father and grandfather had worked at Cristalleries de Baccarat, a factory long noted for its exquisite glass making. The privilege of working at this famous glass factory was handed down from father to son. The factory was established in 1764, and its glass was often referred to as the glass of kings, of czars, of popes, and of presidents.

Victor Durand, Sr.

Victor Durand, Jr.

The Durand Family

In 1882 Victor's father, Victor Durand Sr., immigrated to the United States. Armed with nothing more than an ability to blow glass, he settled in Millville, New Jersey. That he settled in Millville was no coincidence, for this area of New Jersey was known for its glass making. While there, Durand worked at the Wheaton Glass Works and at Whitall-Tatum and Company. Both of these glass factories were located in Millville. In 1884, Victor Durand, at the age of fourteen, along with the rest of his family, joined his father in Millville. It was at Whitall-Tatum and Company where Victor would first work in the United States. At first, he took on odd jobs but eventually he became a glassblower. He worked at Whitall-Tatum for several years before taking a job at Wheaton Glass Works.

Whitall-Tatum and Wheaton Glass were only the first of the many glass-making houses where Durand would work over the next decade. His passion to learn all that he could about glass making led him to several glass factories in Pennsylvania, Ohio, West Virginia, and Canada. He would stay at a factory long enough to learn their glass-making methods and then move on. The experience he gained in each factory

Marie Durand, wife of Victor, Jr.

was an important factor in his success as a glass maker and no doubt helped mold his character. He formed a bond with fellow gaffers and glassworkers that would remain with him for his entire life. His vision was clear. All of his hard work and his hard-earned glass making knowledge would lead him to his own glass manufactory one day.

In 1897 Durand returned to Vineland, New Jersey. With the help of his father, he leased a small glassworks, formerly occupied by the Vineland Glass Manufacturing Co. Founded in 1892, this company manufactured ordinary bottles and jars. The Durands built a new furnace and engaged in making glass tubing, rods, and clinical and thermometer tubes. The Durands named their newly-formed company, which started out with twenty-five employees, the Vineland Flint Glass Works. Victor's father was president of the company and Victor was its secretary. Periodically, Victor would list the articles his factory made. The company's funds were so limited that he could not afford train fare to New York City. Instead, carrying his list he would ride the caboose of the Jersey Central freight train into the city. There he displayed his samples and took orders from prospective customers, telling them how much his factory could produce, at what price, and at what quality.

Victor remained frugal not only out of necessity, but he knew that his twenty-five employees and their families were depending on him. Meeting the company's payroll was important to him. He continued these jaunts to New York for some time, and he put every cent he made back into the company either for improvements or to hire new employees.

In 1899 Victor purchased his father's share of the company and became sole owner. Victor Sr., now semi-retired, stayed on for several years to teach the men how to make various items. Victor's brothers—Henry, Paul, and Charles—were employed by the Vineland Flint Glass Works. They worked in various capacities but never in any executive position. In 1916, Charles and Paul Durand ventured out on their own and, with Louis Koering and George Delruyelle, formed the Durand-Koering Glass Company.

On February 26, 1904, what had happened to the typically wooden structure glass factories across America unfortunately happened to the Vineland Flint Glass Works. The glassworks burned to the ground. The loss was complete and totaled more

From the *Vineland Evening Journal* (May 4, 1897):

Our New Industry.

The Vineland Flint Glass Manufacturing Company commenced business yesterday morning with twenty-five hands. The day was a successful one throughout, and the good beginning has greatly encouraged the proprietors, who are all practical men and will undoubtedly succeed. The company is now manufacturing tubing. . . The process of manufacture is quite interesting. The first part is the melting of the ingredients, after which skilful men take blow pipes and gather from the seething furnace the exact amount of this liquid mass necessary to make the required length of tubing. This blow pipe with its bunch of molten glass on the end, goes into the hands of another artist who rolls and puffs it up with wind until it is ready for the next expert. After going through several hands, the last man takes it and, reheating the mass, has a helper attach an instrument to the hot glass and, running backward, draw the liquid mass out in a tube about two hundred feet long. While this drawing out process is going on, the expert at the end of the blow pipe supplies the necessary amount of air to make this tubing just about so large all the way from the pipe to the end of the run. The tubing is then cut up in convenient lengths and packed in boxes for shipment. The firm are all expert workmen and are looking closely after the most skilful part of the work.

From the *Vineland Evening Journal* (July 27, 1904)

A Substantial Building.

The fire fiend will find himself baffled if he ever tries to burn down the Victor Durand Glassworks again. The new building that is going up is one of the substantial structures in South Jersey. Iron, brick and stone are the main components, making fire almost an impossibility. There is nothing to burn except the window frames and they are braced with iron so that the wall would not be effected should the frames burn out. The building is an immense one. Over four hundred and fifty thousand brick have been used and iron by the tons. The furnace building is 120 feet in length and 69 feet wide. The lower floor is all iron, brick and cement. The upper floor is iron and cement and the roof iron. The rear part is 100 feet long and 65 feet wide, making a factory 220 long and of fine workmanship. New pots are being put in the furnace, which will keep 24 blowers busy and drying fires may go in today. Although the brick work is not quite done and the roof not quite on, Mr. Durand is making arrangements to commence work about September first. The young blood of the town has been prominent in the building of this factory. The brickwork has been in change of George W. Stewart and was the largest job he ever undertook. He mastered every detail without a mistake. Gus Charlson looked after the woodwork with approved skill. Cox & Sons of Bridgeton had the contract to do iron work. When finished this factory will be one of the finest 24-blower tube works in the State.

Workers at Victor Durand's first glass plant in Vineland. Back row, left to right: Victor Durand, Jr., Charles Hankins, unidentified, Joe Coupler, Charles Durand, unidentified, Bob Ramsey, Joel Hankins, and Winnie Corson. Middle row, left to right: Joe Zonack, Henry Durand, unidentified, Victor Durand, Sr., Harry Fenna, Mike Kain, and Jacob Schlagel. Front row, left to right: Joe Zonack, Jr., Doc Koering, Swain Thompson, Joe Schlagel, Dan Jost, and Dan Wheeler.

than $30,000. Victor Durand would not be discouraged, and within months of the fire he rebuilt his factory using more than 450,000 bricks! This iron and brick state-of-the-art building would make the threat of a fire less likely.

Because of Victor's strong work ethic and persistence, the Vineland Flint Glass Works became one of the most successful privately owned glass factories in the country, as reported by the Vineland Chamber of Commerce. By 1920, the Durands' interests included: the Vineland Flint Glass Works, of which Victor was sole proprietor, the Vineland Scientific Glass Company, of which he was president, the Newfield Glass Company, and the New Jersey Clay Pot Company, both of which he served as president and majority stockholder. The New Jersey Clay Pot Company boasted that it was the only manufacturer of German Clay Pots (used in glass

Above: Durand's glass plant in Vineland, New Jersey, c. early 1900. The paymaster's building is the small one on the left.
Below: Card showing the Vineland Flint Glass Works.

CRYSTAL AND OPAL TOWEL BARS
BATHROOM ACCESSORIES

VACUUM BOTTLE BLANKS, BEAKERS
FLASKS AND CHEMICAL
GLASS WARE

GLASS TUBING AND ROD OF ALL
DESCRIPTIONS

VINELAND FLINT GLASS WORKS
VICTOR DURAND, PROP.
DURAND ART GLASS
CONSISTING OF
IRIDESCENT AND FANCY VASES, TABLEWARE, NOVELTIES, ETC.
LAMP VASES AND ELECTRIC SHADES

Vineland, N. J.

Sample of a Vineland Flint Glass Works letterhead and an invoice.

OFFICES, VINELAND, N. J. FACTORIES, VINELAND, N. J.

VINELAND FLINT GLASS WORKS

VINELAND, NEW JERSEY

VICTOR DURAND, PROP.

DATE

SOLD TO

ADDRESS

SHIPPED TO

SHIPPED VIA

TERMS STRICTLY % 10 DAYS:
30 DAYS NET

YOUR ORDER NO.

IMPORTANT: No discount allowed on containers. ¶ This shipment was packed by EXPERIENCED PACKERS, has been delivered to the Transportation Co. in good order, and we hold receipt for same to that effect. Should it not reach you in like good order, you can make CLAIM FOR DAMAGES AGAINST TRANSPORTATION CO., as we positively refuse to allow any claim for damage caused while in transit. Be careful not to receipt for same as being in good order if any damage is apparent. ¶ Goods shipped as ordered cannot be returned. NOTICE—GLASS CANNOT BE GUARANTEED AGAINST BREAKAGE. Glass returned without permission will not be accepted for credit.

QUANTITY	ARTICLE	PRICE				
	No Allowance for Breakage Interest Charged on Overdue Items F. O. B. Vineland, N. J. The goods herewith invoiced have been manufactured in compliance with the Federal Child Labor Law.					

making) in the United States. The combined factories employed more than seven hundred workers and turned out forty thousand thermos bottles, and ten thousand to fifteen thousand pounds of glass tubing every day.

The outbreak of World War I and thus the supply stoppage of scientific glassware, glass instruments, and x-ray bulbs, which were imported mostly from Austria and Germany, stimulated American ingenuity and Victor Durand had plenty of that. The Vineland

DURAND ART GLASS

We take pleasure in presenting a very artistic line of

IRIDESCENT and FANCY VASES, TABLEWARE, NOVELTIES, Etc.

LAMP VASES to harmonize with any color scheme and *ELECTRIC SHADES* that will beautify any room. Also *GLASSWARE* for fixture breaks and any other uses.

See our line without fail. Catalogues issued upon request. We are represented in every large city in the United States. Write us and our representative will call.

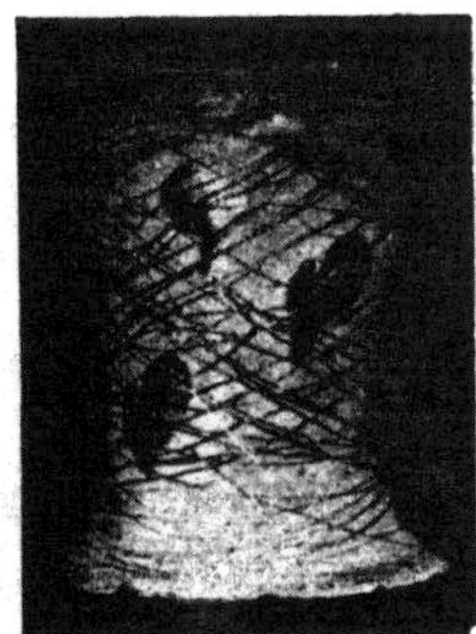

VINELAND FLINT GLASS WORKS

VINELAND N. J.

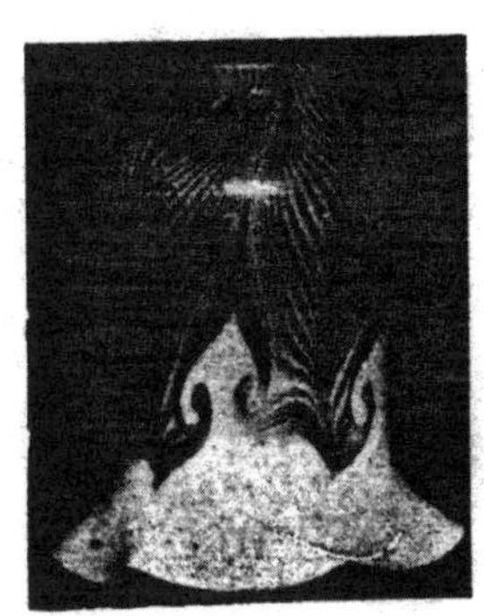

Ad from the December 21, 1925 issue of *China, Glass and Lamps.*

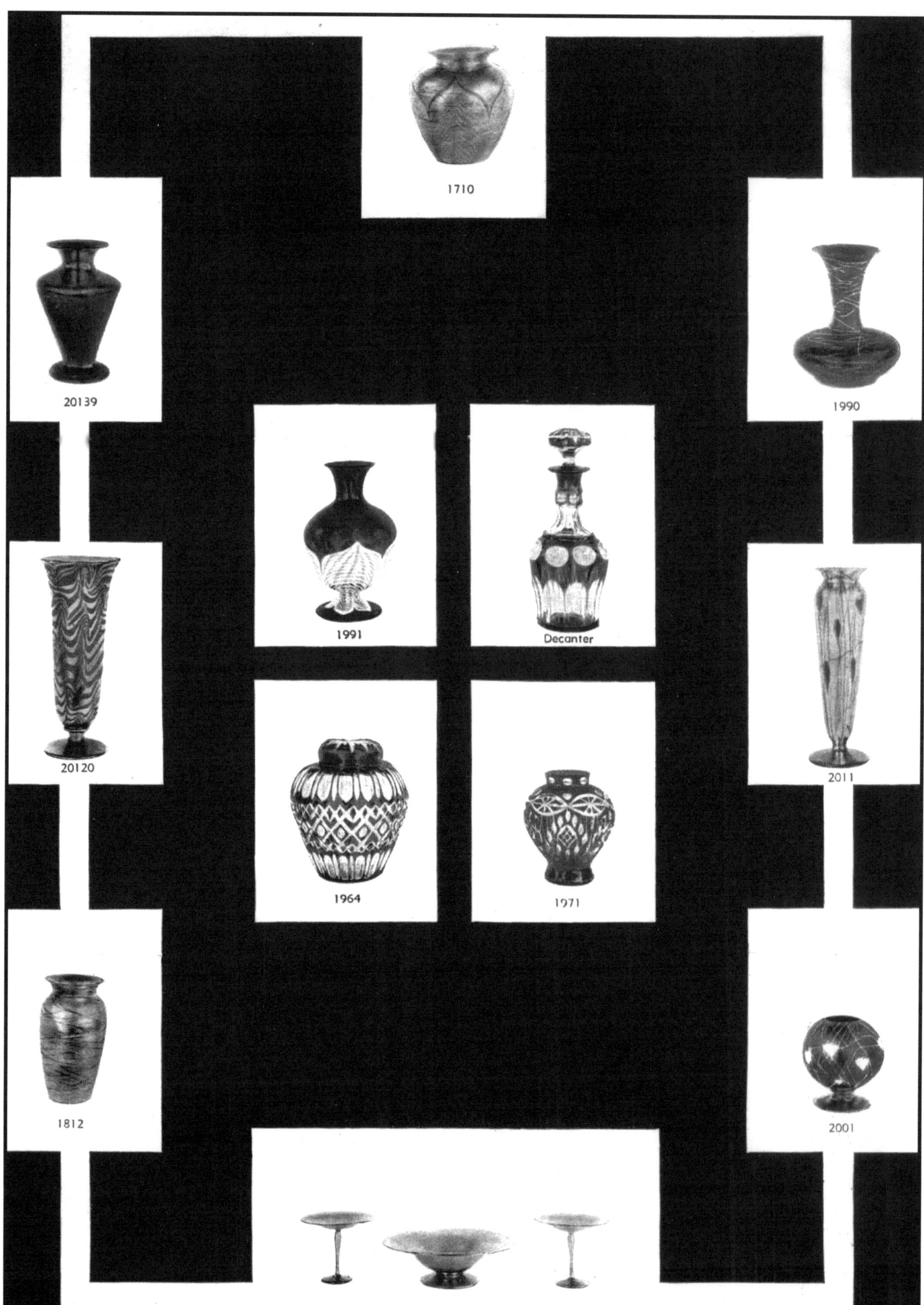
1710
20139
1990
1991
Decanter
20120
2011
1964
1971
1812
2001

DURAND ART GLASS

offers the choicest of fine glassware at a reasonable price. From the raw ingredients to the finished piece, perfection prevails. The highest grade of materials and great care in shaping with infinite exactitude in decorating create a remarkable line of blown glass for home use. Apart from the cased glass, there are twelve regular Iridescent designs and many special designs, some of which are illustrated on the other side, with notations after the design descriptions below.

CASED GLASS IS

the highest achievement of the glassmaker's art. It consists of casings or layers of various colors of glass, one above the other. As an example of double casing, a sapphire blue layer may be entirely imposed over crystal, and then in regular design the sapphire cut away till the crystal is reached, thus giving a double tone effect. It may be had in Crystal with Ruby, Emerald, Topaz or Sapphire, with or without an extra casing of Opal on the outside. (See Four Center Items.)

DECORATIONS

The following Decorations have the Iridescent Effect Glass.

REGULAR DECORATIONS

A.—Gold Lustre Body Semi-Transparent. No design. (See Console Set.)

B.—Silver Blue Body with White Hearts and Vines. (See No. 2001.)

D.—Silver Blue Body. No design. (See No. 20139.)

C.—Golden Yellow Body with Blue Hearts and Vines. (See No. 2011.)

E.—Golden Yellow. No design.

D. Spider—Silver Blue Body with Gold webbing. (See No. 1990.)

E. Spider—Golden Yellow Body with Gold webbing. (See No. 1812.)

K.—Golden Yellow Body with Blue Coiled Design.

M.—Opal with Gold and Blue Hearts with Gold Webbing.

SPECIAL DECORATIONS

AA.—Golden Yellow with White Feather or Peacock Design with a Blue Band and Gold Webbing. (See No. 1710.)

XJ.—Opal with Blue or Green Feather or Peacock Design with a Gold Band to trim the Blue and Gold Webbing.

LGR.—Lady Gay Rose body, with Gold Coiled Design.

KK.—Green Body with Gold Coiled Design. (See No. 20120.)

SIZES AND PRICES

List prices per each for all regular decorations. Special decorations 10% additional. Cased glass prices on application.

No. 1710—Vase
- 4" .... $ 3.50
- 6" 7.00
- 7" 8.00
- 8" 10.00
- 10" 18.00
- 12" 25.00

No. 20139—Vase
- 8" .... $ 8.50
- 10" 11.00
- 12" 18.00
- 14" 25.00

No. 20120—Vase
- 10" .... $ 8.50
- 12" 10.00
- 14" 13.00
- 16" 20.00

No. 1812—Vase
- 6" .... $ 5.00
- 8" 8.00
- 10" 10.00
- 12" 13.50

No. 1990—Vase
- 6" .... $ 5.70
- 8" 8.00
- 10" 11.00
- 12" 25.00

No. 2011—Vase
- 8" .... $ 6.00
- 10" 8.50
- 12" 10.00
- 14" 13.00

No. 2001—Rose Bowl
- 4" .... $ 7.70
- 7" 13.00

No. 20150/5002
- Bowl and Compotes $38.00
- Bowl and Candlesticks 34.00
- Bowl separate 20.00
- Compotes separate, each 12.00
- Sticks separate, each 10.00

No. 1991—Vase
Peacock design as shown
- 6" $12.00
- 8" 15.00

No. 1971—Vase—Cased
- 6"
- 8"
- 10"

No. 1964—Cased Jar with Cover
- 6"
- 8"
- 10"

DECANTER—12" high

GENERAL INFORMATION

Prices quoted are per each—List. All merchandise is shipped F. O. B. Vineland, N. J. Prices subject to change without notice. Packing charges are at cost.

No goods must be returned without notice and permission to do so. In case of breakage in transit, notify your carrier. All merchandise is inspected and carefully packed before leaving plant. Terms on Glassware 1/10 and 30—List.

DURAND ART GLASS DIVISION OF KIMBLE GLASS COMPANY

Factory: Vineland, N. J.

New York City Showrooms

EMIL S. LARSEN & CO.

225 FIFTH AVENUE

Left and right-hand pages: Ad for Durand Glass when part of the Kimble Glass Company.

DURAND ART GLASS

Decorated and cut.

VINELAND FLINT GLASS WORKS

VINELAND - - - - - - - N. J.

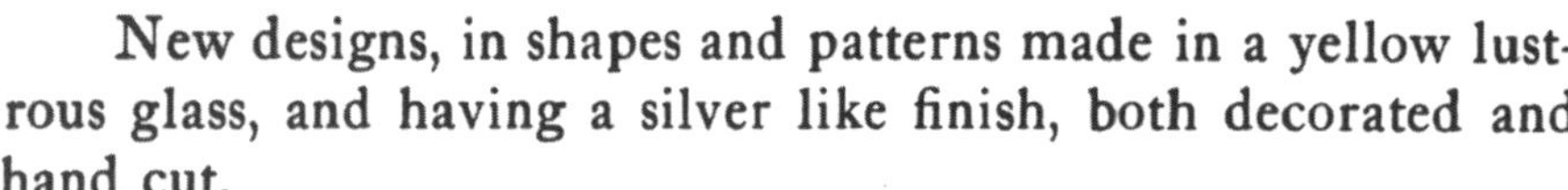

New designs, in shapes and patterns made in a yellow lustrous glass, and having a silver like finish, both decorated and hand cut.

A line of beautiful glassware, that can be retailed from one dollar up.

The line must be seen to be fully appreciated. Write, and we will have our representatives call, or you may stop in at our showrooms.

DELA CROIX & MONROE,	WILCKEN & FRESE,	P. W. WAGENSELLER,
19 Madison Avenue,	103 East Pine Street,	536 Lake Shore Drive,
New York, N. Y.	Orlando, Fla.	Chicago, Ill.

Vineland Flint Glass Works,

MANUFACTURERS OF

PRESCRIPTION WARE PLAIN OR LETTERED.

OUR SPECIALTIES

BEER BOTTLES, AND MILK JARS.

GLASS TUBING AND GLASS RODS OF ALL SIZES AND COLORS.

V. DURAND, JR., Proprietor,

VINELAND, NEW JERSEY.

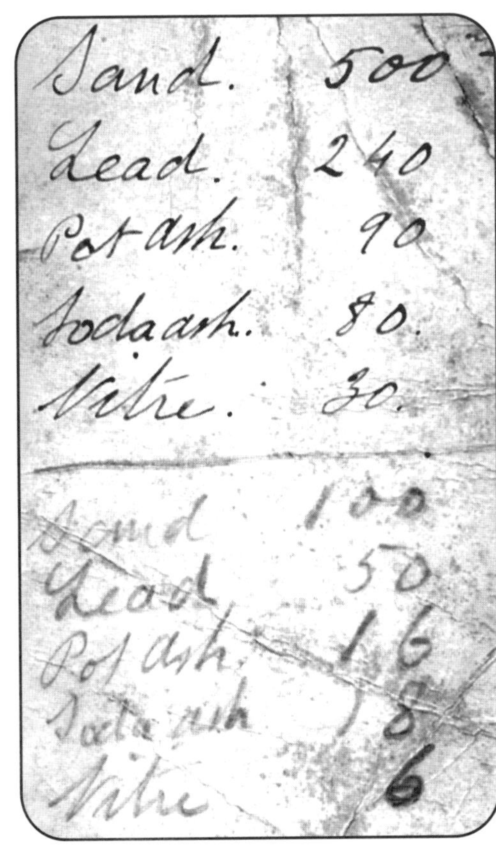

Front and back view of Victor Durand, Jr.'s business card. The items listed on back apparently are a listing of elements for making glass. Right hand page: Ad from *The Jeweler's Circular*, January 5, 1928.

Scientific Glass Company began producing chemical, medical, pharmaceutical, and surgical glassware. General Electric summoned Durand to produce the first x-ray bulbs blown in America.

With all of Victor's accomplishments and financial success there was still one more thing that he needed for his fulfillment in glass making. He had always wanted to produce artistic glass. In 1924, he began a correspondence with Martin Bach Jr. He offered Bach employment if he would come to Vineland and establish an art glass shop. Martin Jr. had grown up in his father's business, the Quezal Art Glass and Decorating Company, in Brooklyn, New York, which was started in 1901 by Martin Sr. and Thomas Johnson. Martin Bach Sr. had been an employee of Tiffany Furnaces. He worked as a batch mixer and as a result shared in Tiffany's secret formulas for producing various colors of glass needed for art work. When Martin Sr. died in 1924, the Quezal Company was already in financial difficulty. Martin Jr. made several attempts to keep the company solvent, but he failed. In 1924, the Quezal Art Glass and Decorating Company closed its doors forever.

Bach, and some of his workers had gone to work for the Imperial Glass Company in Bellaire, Ohio. Martin Bach Jr. accepted Durand's offer to establish an art glass shop at the Durand factory. Production began in December of 1924. The team of the "fancy shop," as it was called, was made up entirely of men who had worked at the Quezal Company. Martin Bach Jr. became superintendent, formula maker, and art director for the fancy shop. Emil J. Larson was the gaffer, that is, the master glassblower and foreman of the shop who also designed prototypes. William Wiedebine was the decorator, Harry Britton was the servitor, and his brother Percy Britton was the gatherer. Ralph Barber, famous in his own right for Millville Rose paperweight making and glass blowing, was a plant superintendent of the Vineland Flint Glass Works. Even though he was not an employee of the fancy shop, occasionally he blew some art glass. Bach brought with him a catalog from the Quezal Company showing shapes and decorations. He also brought Quezal's formulas for making colored glasses. In the beginning the artisans at Durand's factory made art glass that resembled Quezal glass in color and decoration and at times even shape. One early Durand catalog notes that "Martin Bach Jr. was now associated with this company and continuing to manufacture Quezal Glass as well as other glasses known as Durand Art Glass."

Soon this team of artisans, who had blown glass together for so long, began to reach new heights of artistic accomplishment. Martin Bach and his staff of artist assistants developed a new, unique style of designs and color effects that would become distinctively Durand Art Glass.

In 1925, Durand began selling cut-glass wares. Jack Trevethan was in charge of the grinding and polishing shop. Charles Link, previously the owner of the Acme/Aetna Cut Glass Company in Bridgeton, New Jersey, was their most renowned

Gold Medal
Award
First Prize

DURAND ART GLASS

MEDAL OF AWARD

Sesqui-Centennial
Philadelphia
1926

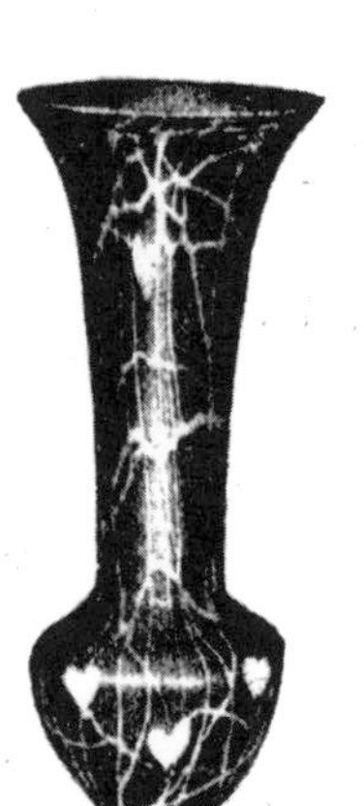
No. 2022

No. 1716

Do not fail to see our new Line for 1928 including Lamps and Tableware.

On display at
The Eastern Manufacturers and Importers Exhibit
February 6th to 17th, 1928
Palmer House, Chicago, Ill.
Rooms: No. 742-43-44

Also

At the Annual Glass Show, Jan. 9th to Jan. 21st,
Wm. Penn Hotel, Pittsburgh, Pa.
Rooms 458-60.

SPECIAL INTRODUCTORY OFFER

To the Jewelry Trade ONLY

In order to introduce this beautiful Line of Glassware to Jewelers that are not able to visit our Exhibits during the coming Spring, we offer to send to any rated firm from fifty to one hundred dollars' worth of the Glassware on consignment for a period of ninety days F.O.B. Vineland, N. J.

Art Division,
Vineland Flint Glass Works,
Vineland, N. J.

Exhibit Sales Manager and Eastern Distributor
Emil S. Larsen & Co., Inc.
225 Fifth Ave., N. Y. City

No. 1710

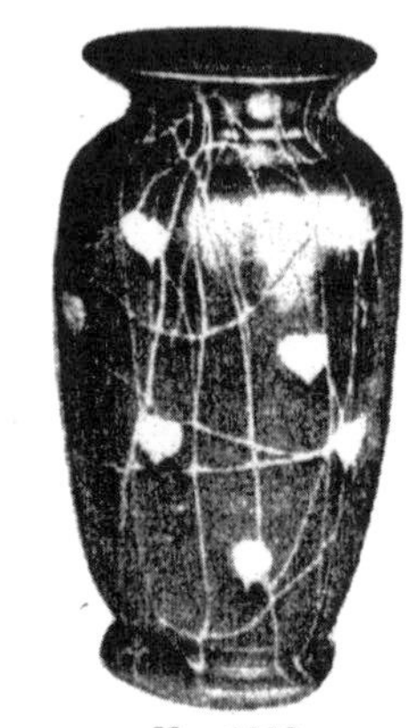
No. 1803

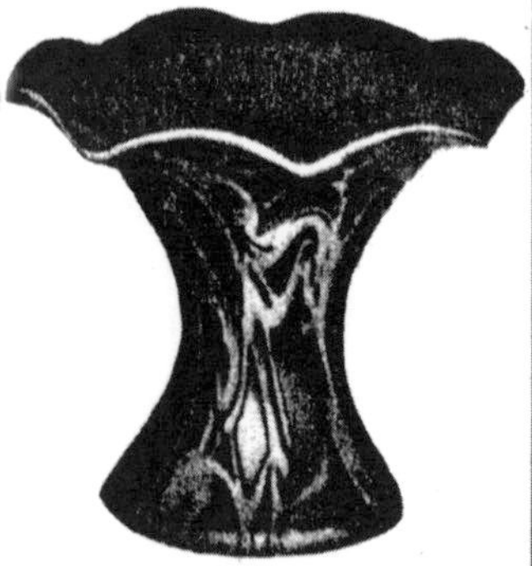

5014/2044

No. 2001

No. 1723

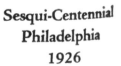

workman in the cutting department. Link was well known for his Bridgeton Rose cutting, which he continued to produce, while working for Durand. In 1926, within two years of the inception of Durand Art Glass, the company reached a pinnacle when it was awarded a medal of honor at the Sesquicentennial International Exposition in Philadelphia. No doubt this was a very rewarding accomplishment for Victor Durand and his team at the "fancy shop." Many of the pieces exhibited were beautifully cut cased glass, probably influenced by Charles Link. Durand art glass was by now being distributed throughout the United States. The fancy shop, although a commercial venture, was not always profitable for Durand, and had been supported primarily by the other divisions of the Vineland Flint Glass Works. What would be regarded as bad business by today's standard, could be called a heroic act. Durand preserved a tradition, even at the risk of financial loss, to keep the fancy shop up and running. His respect for the artistic craftsmanship of the hard-working glassblower allowed the company to persevere and stay in business in New Jersey. By 1924, however, machines had made the craft of glassblowing obsolete. Surely Durand identified with these men and their struggle to pursue their craft. By the standards of the times, these artisans were very well paid. Victor Durand was the unsung hero of the glassblower. He gave this division free rein to experiment and create. That artistic freedom is certainly obvious today: Durand's shop produced one of the finest and most unique artistic glass forms ever made.

The fancy shop continued to produce beautiful art-glass vases, lamps, lamp shades, and dinnerware for almost seven years. Not long, compared to their predecessors, Tiffany, Steuben, and Quezal, but long enough to make a significant mark in the world of artistic glass. It has been said by Sam Farber, an antique dealer who was familiar with the fancy shop, that they never stopped experimenting until they closed the doors for good. During all that time and to the very end Victor Durand had no intention of closing the fancy shop.

Durand was a man who loved the automobile, and he drove the latest and most high-powered

EVAN E. KIMBLE
PRESIDENT
VICTOR DURAND, JR.
VICE PRESIDENT
HERMAN R. DOERR
SECRETARY

KIMBLE-DURAND GLASS CO.

SUCCESSOR TO
KIMBLE GLASS COMPANY
VINELAND FLINT GLASS WORKS

GENERAL OFFICE
CHICAGO
BRANCH OFFICES
VINELAND, N. J.
NEW YORK
FACTORIES
CHICAGO
VINELAND, N. J.
MILLVILLE, N. J.

VINELAND, N.J. October 7th.1915

Mr.R.P.Tuller,

Vineland,N.J.

Dear Sir:-

Enclosed please find Check for $16.00 to cover the rent of the Bungalow corner of 8th. & Wood Sts.,from September 10th. to 30th. inc.

Youre very truly,

[signature]

Left-hand page: Ad from the January 4, 1926 issue of *China, Glass and Lamps*.
Above: Letterhead from the first merger of the Kimble-Durand Glass Co.

models. On April 24, 1931 he drove his Pierce Arrow to Philadelphia to keep a dentist appointment. On his way home, he lost control of the car and ran off the road near Runnemede, New Jersey. Durand's face and neck were badly cut from the shattered glass from the windshield. He was taken to Underwood Hospital in Woodbury, New Jersey. Once notified, his physician, Dr. Charles Cunningham Jr., rushed to the hospital. Durand needed a transfusion and Cunningham gave his own blood for the procedure. In a wonderful show of affection, several of Durand's employees also arrived at the hospital to donate blood to their fallen boss. Unfortunately their efforts were futile because Durand had already lost so much blood. On April 25, 1931, twenty hours after the auto accident, Victor Durand died at the age of sixty.

At first the doctors thought that Durand had had a stroke while driving, but an autopsy revealed that the paralysis on his left side after the accident was a result of shock and injury. The cause of the accident was believed to have been the effects of anesthesia from his dental appointment that had not yet worn off. Ironically Durand, who had dedicated his life to glass production and had become wealthy because of glass, lost his life in an accident in which he was cut by glass. Durand had previously issued orders to his workers to replace the conventional windshields in their cars with safety glass. His car was only three days old and he had not yet had safety glass installed.

The glassblowers and workers of the fancy shop had lost their hero. All of his employees had lost a benevolent boss. Durand was a man who helped organized unions at other companies as a young worker and as a boss he still carried a union card. This boss knew all of his forty-odd glass blowers by their first names. He was a man who mingled with his employees and at times would reward them for a job well done with an immediate pay raise. The community as well had lost a generous man—a man who provided funds for the Newcomb Hospital, helped organize the local YMCA, and, not least had provided more than seven hundred people with jobs, which of course added to the prosperity of the community.

At the time of Durand's death, the Vineland Flint Glass Works was in the process of merging with the Kimble Glass Company, also in Vineland. These two firms had merged before in 1912 and then separated in 1918. Colonel Evan E. Kimble was to be president, Victor Durand was to be vice president and Herman K. Kimble the general manager.

Buy Now! Charge Purchases Payable January 1st.

GIMBELS

Above and next page: Advertisement from the Tuesday, October 31, 1933 edition of *The Evening Bulletin* in Philadelphia for Gimbels Department Store for Durand Vases.

The second merger was left to be completed, sometime in 1931, by Durand's widow, Marie. The two companies would become the Kimble Glass Company. The Vineland Flint Glass Company would be known as the Vineland Flint Division of the Kimble Glass Company. Without Durand's support, the fancy shop stayed operational for only a short time, under the management of Kimble.

As the Great Depression took hold in the country in the 1930s, few people could afford expensive art glass. (Colonel Kimble had all but decided to discontinue the fancy shop, when one of his employees brought him a sample of what the workers called "powder glass." This glass was similar to the Cluthra glass produced by Steuben. The Kimble Cluthra production continued for only about a year. Although some of the early pieces of Kimble Cluthra glass were signed with a Durand signature, it is uncertain if the production of this glass did involve any of the men of the fancy shop.) By 1933 the remainder of stock from the fancy shop, along with the Kimble cluthra, was either sold for a fraction of its original cost or was broken up and carted off to the dump. On October 31, 1933, Gimbels department stores ran a large ad in the *Philadelphia Evening Bulletin* claiming to have bought the entire stock of Durand vases, 1900 pieces in all. The vases were to be sold on the fourth floor at less than half the wholesale cost. It is ironic and sad that Durand art glass ended on such a tragic note, as had its brilliant creator Victor Durand.

Sale of Durand Vases
"Finest in America"

So said America's finest stores for Forty Years.

$1.50

$2.50

$2.95

At Less Than **1/2** Usual WHOLESALE Cost!

1900 Pieces, 85c to $5.95

Only America's finest stores stocked Durand vases—and never sold except at standard (and almost prohibitive) high prices. This is the first sale—and the *last*. Gimbels bought the entire stock of these enchanting vases; seventy styles, thirty shapes, ten sizes, all of a shimmering beauty that makes further words futile, that beggars more description. Please remember, these are the finest quality crystals in America — entirely hand-moulded and fabricated. Hundreds of them—made unique by adding gold and silver and other precious metals in the colors, resulting in tints and tones never before achieved and never to be duplicated.

Gimbels—Fourth Floor—Market

$1.95

$1.50

$2.50

$2.50

DURAND ART GLASS

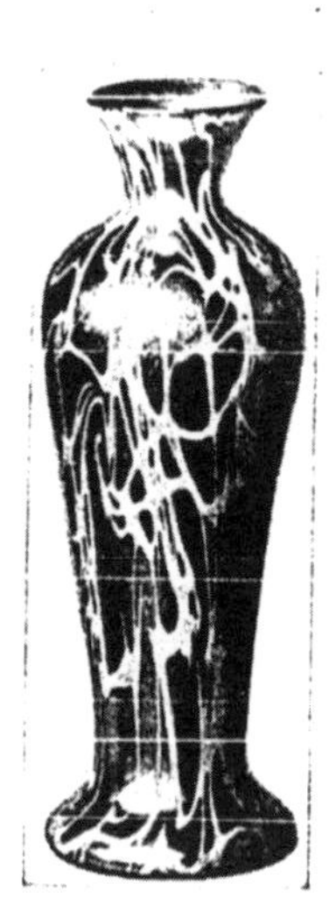

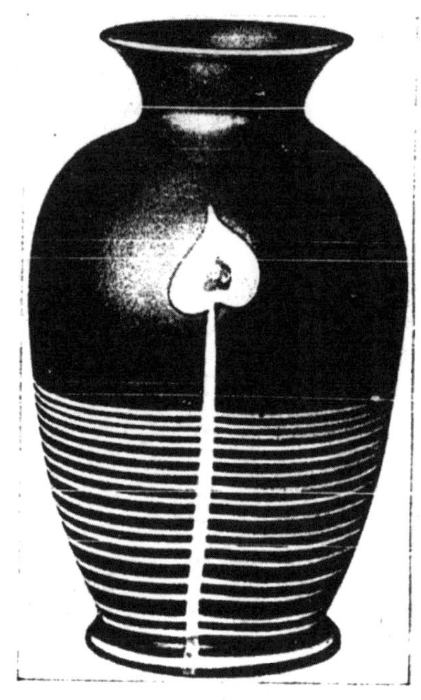

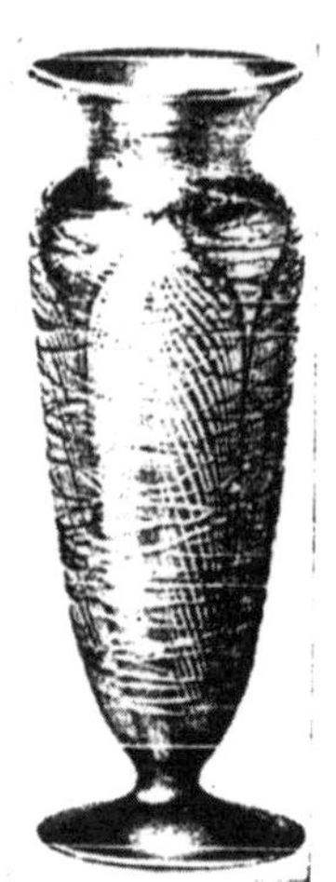

DURAND Art and Fancy Decorated Glassware is the real home beautifier. It is made up of a line of Vases, Compotes, Tableware, Lamp Vases, Electric Shades and Fixture Breaks. It is not a hand painted article, but an inlaid decoration made with colored iridescent glass and worked into the original body, while in a molten state. It is impossible to destroy the beautiful color and decorated effects, and the more it is handled, cleaned and polished the brighter the iridescent color effects will become. It is not a common doped ware such as is seen daily and made by the thousand, and appearing nice on the surface, but is a hand made article of a tedious nature to produce, and therefore we guarantee the color effects for a lifetime.

If you are not acquainted with our line, write us and we will forward catalogue upon request.

To our trade, we take pleasure in wishing you the Season's Compliments and to thank you for your hearty co-operation in the past.

VINELAND FLINT GLASS WORKS

Durand Art Glass Dept.

VINELAND N. J.

Ad from the January 11, 1926 issue of *China, Glass and Lamps.*

FORMER DISTRIBUTORS

I have compiled a list of former distributors taken from flyers and other publications. As you can see Durand art glass was distributed coast to coast. From New York City to Tacoma, Washington and from Orlando to Los Angeles. They boasted of being represented in every large city in the United States.

Not included in this list were many fine department and jewelry stores which partook in the sale of Durand. The more famous of which were Macys, Bambergers, Marshall Fields, Neiman-Marcus, Wanamaker's, and Bailey Banks and Biddle.

EAST COAST
Emil S. Larsen & Co., Inc.
225 Fifth Avenue
New York, N.Y.

Dela Croix & Monroe
19 Madison Avenue
New York, N.Y.

Louis Carter
Commonwealth Building
Philadelphia,Pa.

SOUTHERN
C.L. Wilcken
700 Harwood Avenue
Orlando, Florida

Joseph P. Krukin Company
Arcade Building
Norfolk, Virginia

Wilcken & Frese
103 East Pine Street
&
509 Oscola Street
Orlando, Florida

WEST COAST
Roy C. Youngstone
839 E. 31st Street
Los Angeles, California

F.E. Wolf
3205 N. 28th Street
Tacoma, Washington

Shaw-Newell Co.
Los Angles,California

CENTRAL
P. W. Wagenseller
536 Lake Shore Drive
Chicago, Illinois

Ernest Bersback
402 Boston Block
Minneapolis, Minnesota

NEW ENGLAND
Robert W. Corey
2 & 9 Parker House
Boston, Massachusetts

Dictionary of Glass Terms

Annealing: Tempering glass through a gradual cooling process to prevent stress and breakage.

Applied glass: Pieces of molten glass, such as handles or decorative elements, that are added to the object during the manufacturing process.

Batch: Raw materials for making glass that have been carefully mixed together in preparation for melting in a crucible.

Blank: A piece of glass intended for cutting, enameling, or some other means of decoration.

Block: A cup-like piece of wood that is dipped in water and used to shape the molten glass.

Blowpipe: A hollow iron tube, roughly four to six feet long, used to gather molten glass for the purpose of blowing an object with or without a mold.

Clay Pot: The heat-resistant crucible in which a glass batch is melted.

Copper Wheel: High-speed disk used for the fine cutting of intricate designs on glass.

Cracking Off: After scoring the glass, the partially cooled object is separated from the pontil rod with a sharp tap, usually just before carrying it to the annealing lehr.

Crucible: A container, usually a clay pot, for melting glass.

Crystal: Brilliant, clear glass containing lead oxide.

Cullet: Cleaned and broken glass added to a batch in the melting process.

Fire Polishing: Reheating a nearly finished object in the glory hole in order to remove blemishes and add brilliance.

Flint: An early name for lead crystal or glass containing lead oxide.

Foot: The bottom flare of a glass object, sometimes built in during tooling. At other times, the foot may be applied..

Free Blown: Glass formed without the use of molds, although tools may be used to shape the piece on the blowpipe.

Gaffer: A master glassblower who heads a shop of glass workers.

Glory Hole: A small furnace used for reheating or fire polishing the wares. It may be part of the large central furnace or a separate unit.

Hooked Decor: Feathers or other designs created by pulling glass threads with a hook-shaped tool.

Hydrofluoric Acid: A corrosive chemical used in the glass industry to etch glass. Sometimes it is used in combination with other chemicals to frost, gloss, or brighten the surface of the glass.

Iridescent: A rainbow-like effect on glass, usually produced by spraying the object with a metallic salts solution.

Lehr: A long furnace containing a slow-moving conveyor belt, which allows glass to cool gradually, thereby relieving stress and preventing breakage.

Marver: A metal slab used by a blower to smooth and shape a glob of glass.

Metal: A term used in the trade for glass that is either in a molten or hardened state.

Metallic Oxide: The oxides of several different metals are used as a coloring agent in a glass batch.

Mold Blown: Glassware made by blowing a gather of glass into mold, which may be plain or engraved with a pattern.

Opaque: A solid glass in various colors that will not transmit light.

Parison: The gather on a blowpipe after it has been blown in a small bubble.

Pontil: A mark that remains on the base after a piece has been struck from a pontil rod. A finished item often has the rough edges of this mark ground off.

Punty Rod: Another name for a pontil rod, which is attached to the base of a vessel before the piece is struck from the blow pipe. This allows the object to be reheated in the glory hole and further shaped in the finishing process.

Resonance: The ringing quality of lead crystal glass when lightly tapped on the rim.

Servitor: The person in the shop who directly assists the master glassblower.

Shop: A crew of glass workers, usually from four to six men, who work as a team to manufacturer glass.

Threading: The application of glass threads for decorative purposes, done either by hand or by machine.

Tooling: A general term for a variety of decorative techniques applied to glass in the manufacturing process.

Translucent: A glass that transmits light, but not so that one can see clearly through it.

Transparent: Any glass that allows light to pass through, so that objects can be clearly seen.

Viscosity: The state of glass when it is still pliable, so that it can be shaped into its intended form.

Dictionary of Durand Art Glass

Acid cut back: This was done by applying a stencil onto the surface of lustre glass which would outline where the acid resistant wax would be applied. Acid was then used to cut away that area that was not protected by wax. When the wax was removed, a raised iridescent pattern would remain. The patterns were usually floral or rococo design. Very few pieces of acid cut back were done by Durand.

Ambergris: A transparent yellow glass called "oil glass" by the workers. It was used mostly as a base glass in production and can be found in most of the pieces that were made. It was a very integral part of producing lustred glass. It would also vary in intensity of color and, at times, was referred to as topaz or Spanish yellow.

Applied Coil: A thick and iridescent coil applied to the surface of an object in an ascending spiral. The coils were usually very evenly spaced. This was a seldom-used process.

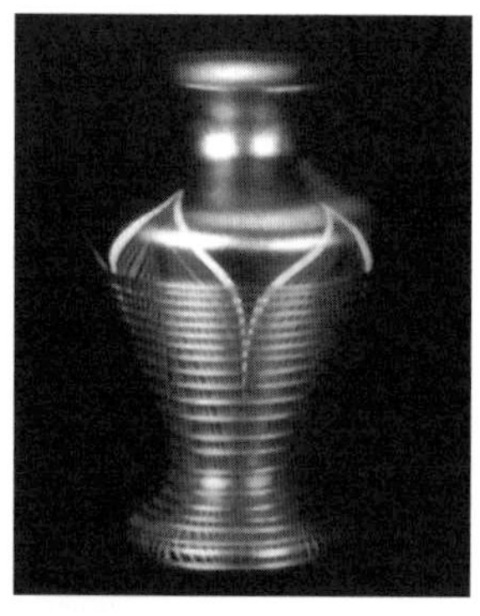

Band: Refers to an applied contrasting color of glass pulled into an arched shape, mimicking the outline of a pulled feather decoration. Commonly seen as an opal band on ambergris base.

Bubble: A bubble mold was used by Durand to produce controlled vertical rows of bubbles in the glass. Actual size of bubbles would vary, but uniformity is a noted characteristic. This process was used to make vases as well as bubble balls for lamp production. Sometimes bubbles would be combined with optic ribbing.

Cameo: Done in the same manner as acid cut back but on double and triple cased opaque glass. By cutting away the top layer and exposing the contrasting color below, a two-tone effect with a raised design on the surface of the glass was produced. Most of this glass was done in a floral or neoclassical pattern. Like the acid cut back, very few pieces were produced.

Cased or plated glass: The process of applying from two to four colors of glass one over the other while in a molten state. Much of this cased glass was used for cutting. By cutting away the top layer or layers, it would expose the contrasting base color which was almost always transparent.

Coil pattern: Made by placing heavy threads of a contrasting color of glass on a parison and pulling those threads all over the surface of the object in a random manner. Called King Tut in early catalogs, it became known as Coil, as another more refined pattern was developed.

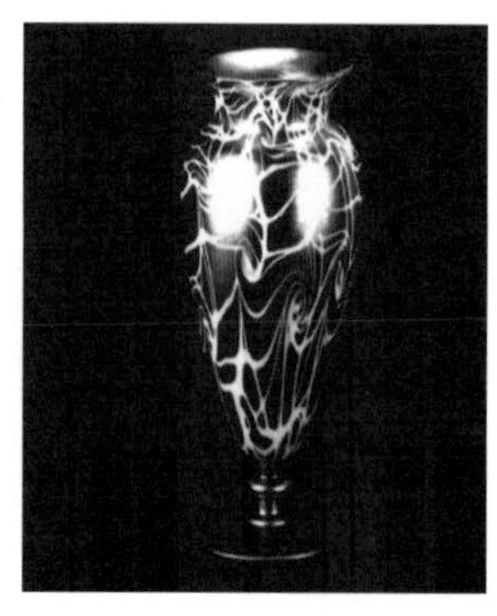

Crystal: Leaded glass sometimes used as a base; especially in the Peacock Feather decoration, Crystal Crackle and layered glass. Unlike pure clear lead crystal glass, there was a very slight tint to this glass. It often appeared like a very pale ambergris.

Golden Orange: A dull orange, almost pumpkin colored, lustre glass that has been included in the golden yellow category, although it does not truly fit in that category. Often referred to as marigold.

Crystal Crackle: A crystal parison would have another transparent color cased and threaded over it. After the parison was formed, and while still hot, it would be dipped into a container of water, fracturing the outside layers. Then the glass would be reheated and blown into a shape. This caused the fractures to spread apart creating a rough texture to the surface and exposing some of the crystal base.

Golden Yellow: A bright golden yellow iridescent glass that could sometimes vary to a golden orange with golden yellow highlights, all within the same piece.

Egyptian Crackle: A term used synonymously with Moorish and Mutual Crackle. Made in the same manner as all of the crackle glass at the Durand factory, but referring more often to crackle glass using an opal base and layered with colored glass or glasses.

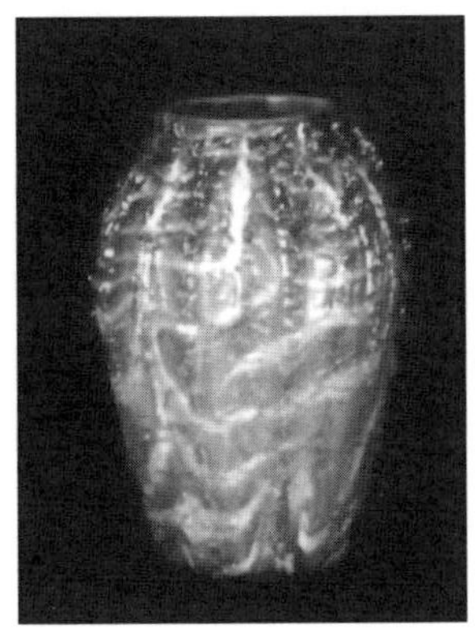

Hard Ribbed: Glass blown into a vertical ribbed mold which creates protruding, evenly spaced vertical ribs on the surface. The ribs comprise the darkest shade, and lighten as they move out from the center. The exception to this would be ribbed pieces that are iridized.

Flashed: This was really not flashed, but rather thinly cased glass. Most often it was a term used in referring to red, blue, and green stemware, dinner ware and table settings.

Heart and Clinging Vine: Made by placing a small amount of a contrasting color of glass on a parison and pulling it with a hooked tool into the shape of a heart and connecting those hearts to each other with lines that resemble vines. This was done all over the surface and usually on lustre glass.

King Tut: Made by placing heavy threads of a contrasting color of glass on a parison and pulling those threads all over the surface in a controlled manner. Applied somewhat more evenly than for the Coil pattern. Sometimes referred to as the Coil King Tut pattern.

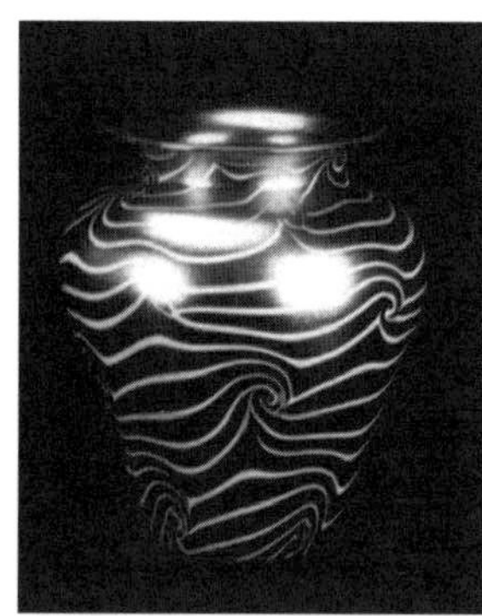

Lady Gay Rose: A thin casing of red glass over opal glass, creating colors that vary from a pale pink through a deep pink to a red color. The color obtained was dependent on the thickness applied and the color intensity of red glass used. It was not a popular color in its time.

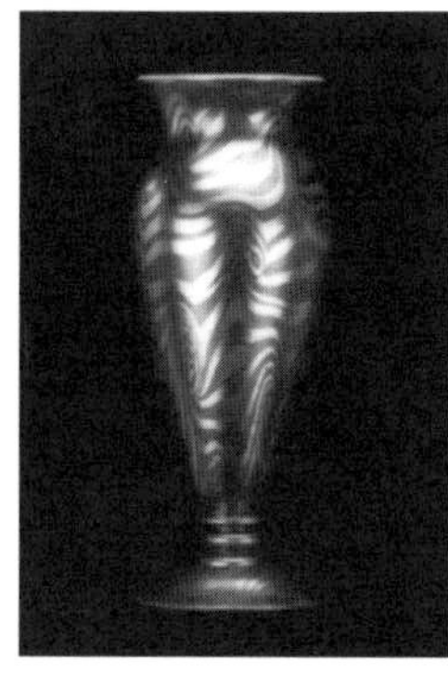

Lava: A crackle glass with globular portions of glass at the top, as if flowing from the opening onto the outside of the vase. Resembling lava spilling from the rim of an erupting volcano.

Lustre or iridescent glass: Done predominantly on an ambergris (transparent yellow) glass. The glass was sprayed, while still hot, with a liquid containing a metallic solution that would permanently color the surface of the glass. The effect achieved depended upon the color of the glass used, whether or not it was cased, and the metallic solution used to spray the glass. Silvery blue, dark blue, golden yellow and golden orange were classic lustre colors produced by Durand.

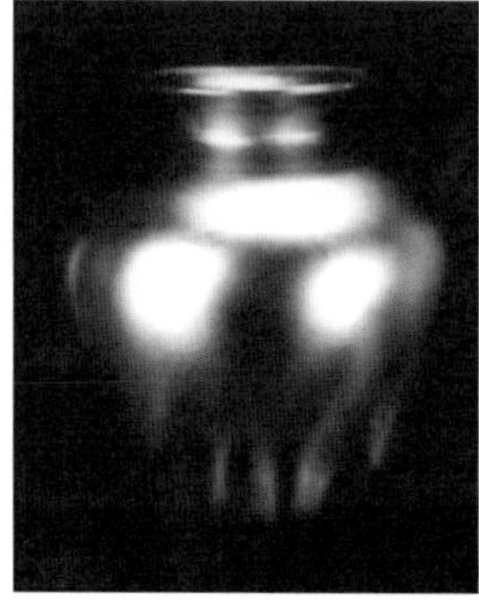

Moorish or Mutual Crackle: Also referred to as Egyptian Crackle. An ambergris or crystal parison would have opal plated over it and another color threaded or plated over the opal. While still hot it would be dipped in water, fracturing the outside layers. Then the glass would be reheated and blown into a shape, causing the fractures to spread apart and expose some of the base color. Then this glass would be lustred. Sometimes these pieces would be blown into a vertical rib mold and/or iridized in various colors. Crackle glass was costly to make and prone to breakage. It was originally made as lamp shades and bases, but as its popularity grew, production of vases in many shapes began.

Opal: A white opaque glass used sometimes in cased glass and other times as a base glass. Along with ambergris and crystal glass, it formed the base for fancy glass production at Durand.

Optic Ribbed: Glass blown into a mold creating evenly spaced vertical ribs. Similar to hard ribbed but rather than protruding ribs, it has a vertical rippling effect which creates color variations within the same color.

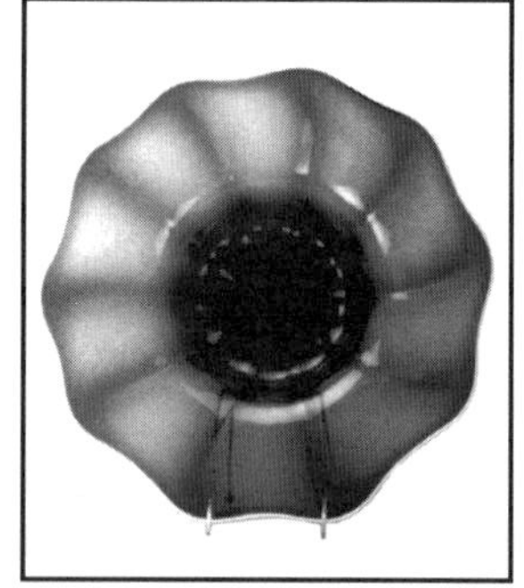

Peacock, Feather Design or Pulled Feather: Made by winding a thread of glass (in most cases opal) around a parison. Threads were pulled with a hooked tool into a pattern resembling a feather. Sometimes a contrasting color would be applied over the feather in a looping manner for a two-color effect.

Ribbon glass: Also known as latticinio, it was made by placing lengths of glass cane, which already had a criss-crossing pattern of lines in the cane, adjacent to each other in a vertical manner onto a glass parison. A mold was probably used to hold the cane in place while the parison was blown into the mold. Then these glasses were blown and heated until they became one. This was a very time-consuming process and therefore rarely done by Durand.

Silver Yellow, or Yellow Lustre: Terms given to ambergris glass which was lustred to produce a shiny or mirror-like finish, but still showing its deep yellow transparent color.

Spanish Yellow: A more marketable name used to describe ambergris glass. This term was used in their catalogs in reference to the stem of stemware, compotes, candlesticks and even complete sets of dinner ware.

Spider or Spider Webbing: Also called threaded glass, this is a fine glass threading applied around the main body. In most cases spider webbing was an ambergris glass that was gold lustred. The threading was not rolled into the surface of the glass, but rather left on the surface in a very delicate manner. For that reason, the threading is seldom found in perfect condition.

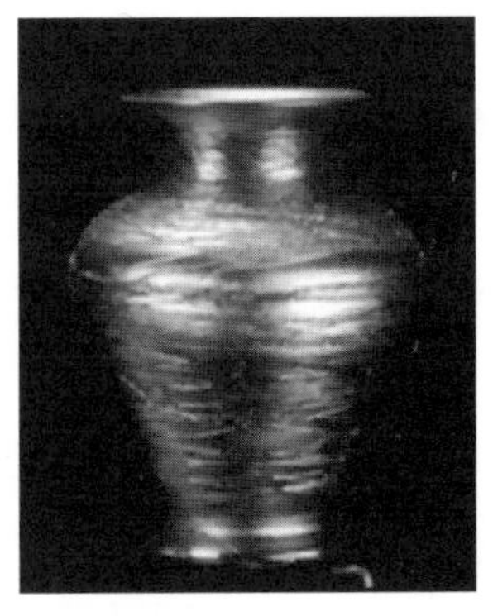

Venetian Lace: Made by applying fine threads of opal and/or blue glass on an ambergris base. These threads were spiraled and sometimes criss-cross throughout the piece. With reheating, the threads would be joined to the base glass. In most cases a thin line of blue glass was applied to the rim of the item. This decoration was primarily done on compotes, plates and bowls.

Wavy pattern: Made by placing threads of a contrasting color onto a parison and usually pulling those threads in a diagonal manner. The decoration resembled continuously connected "C" shapes or waves. It was also referred to as the Zigzag pattern. This method was used often on the final applied threaded color to Moorish Crackle prior to crackling the glass.

Front and back views of the medal of honor award Durand Art Glass at the Sesquicentennial International Exposition held in Philadelphia in 1926.

Heart & Vine

1

Heart & Vine

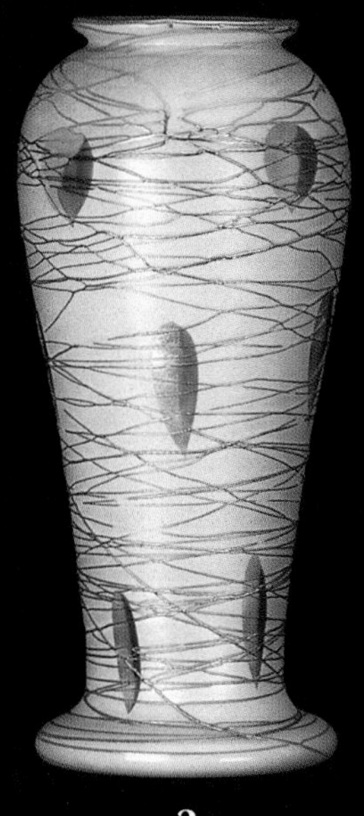

2

3

4

5

6

Heart & Vine

Heart & Vine on Blue Lustre

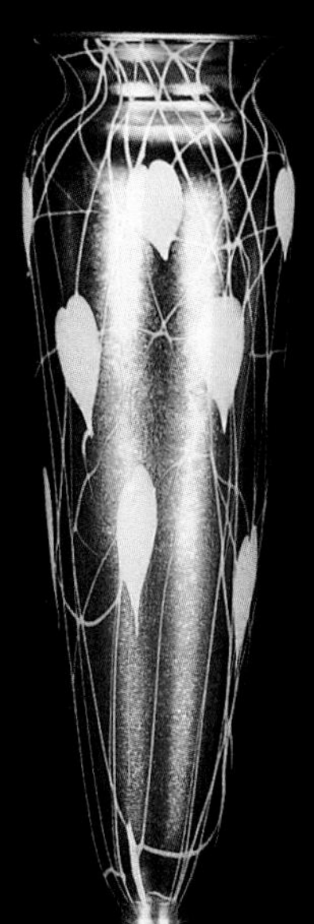

12

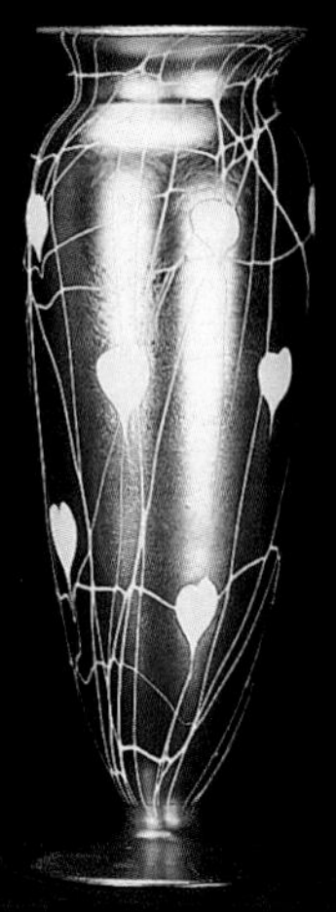

13

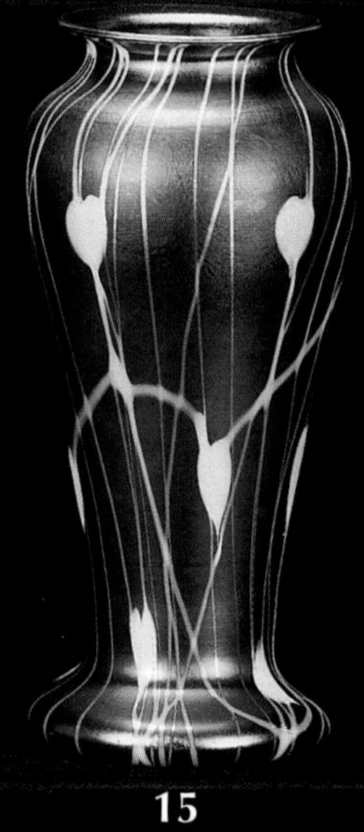

15

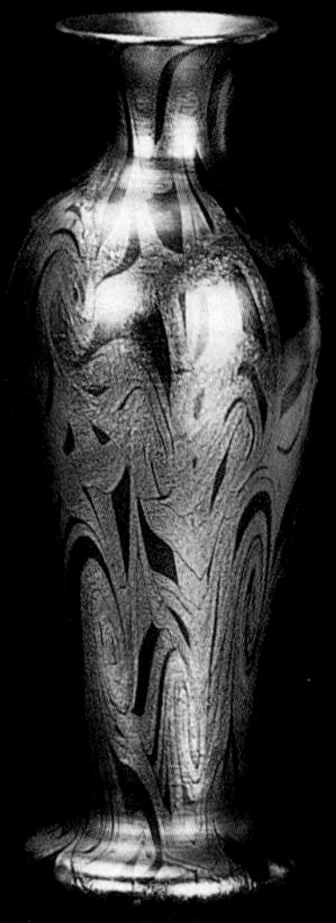

14

16

17

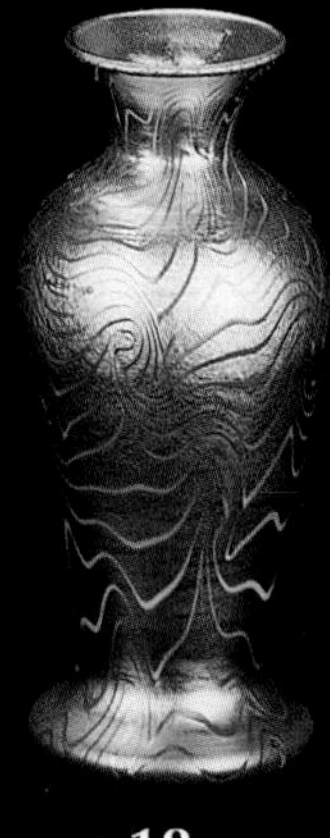

18

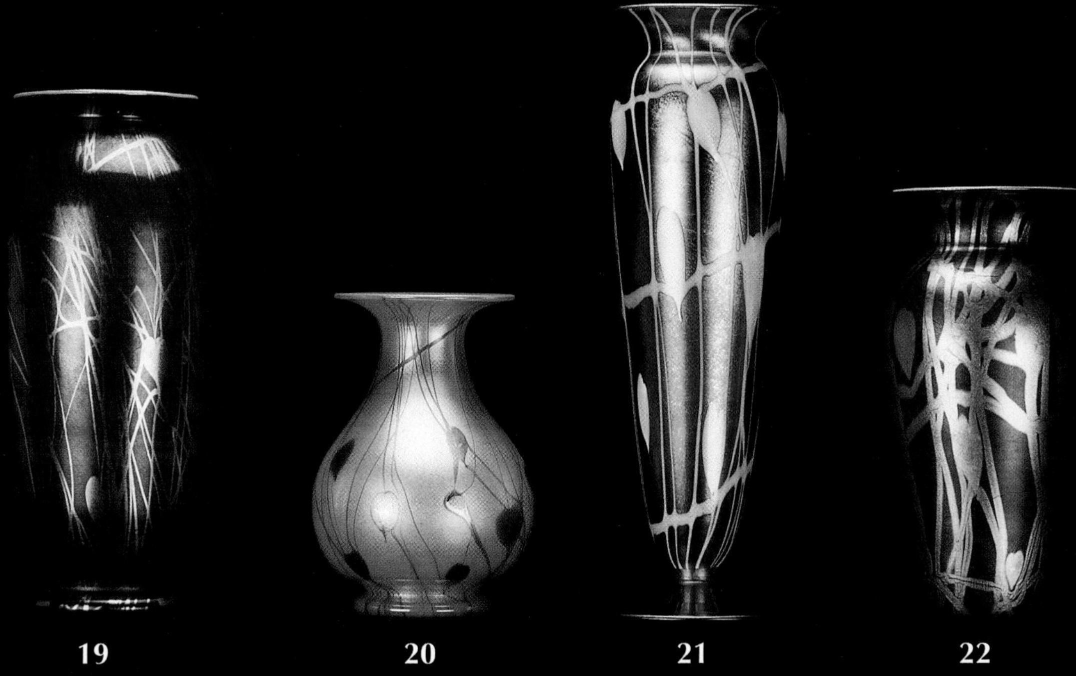

19 20 21 22

Heart & Vine

23 24 25

26 27

Blue on Gold

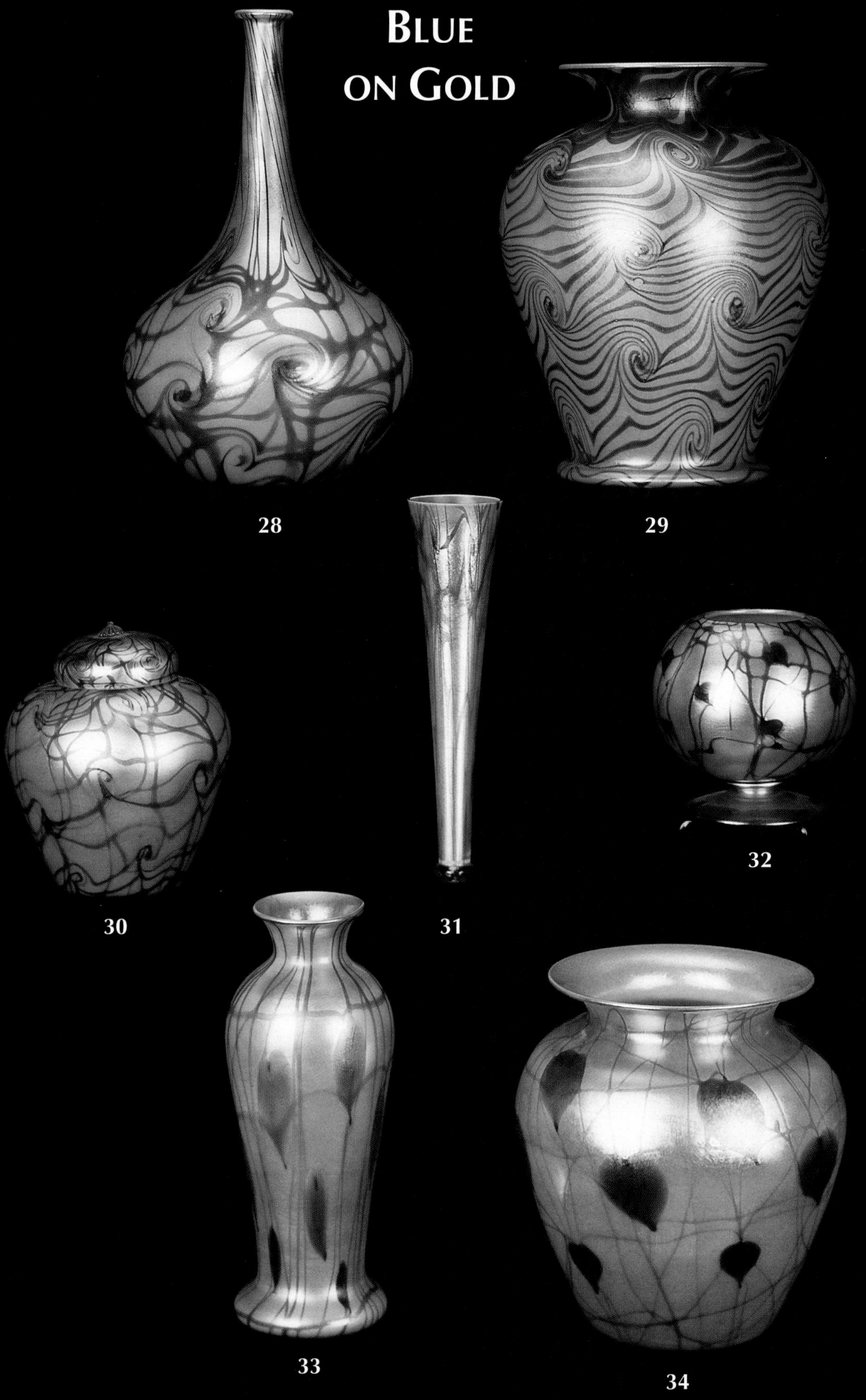

28

29

30

31

32

33

34

Heart & Vine

35

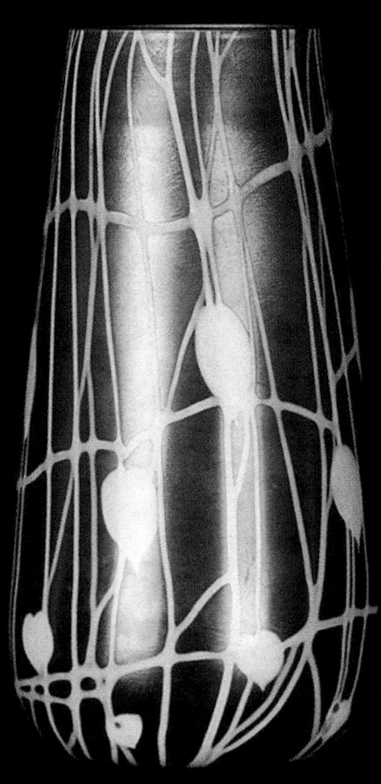

36

37

38

39

40

41

42

Rose Bowls

44

43

45

46

47

Pulled Feather

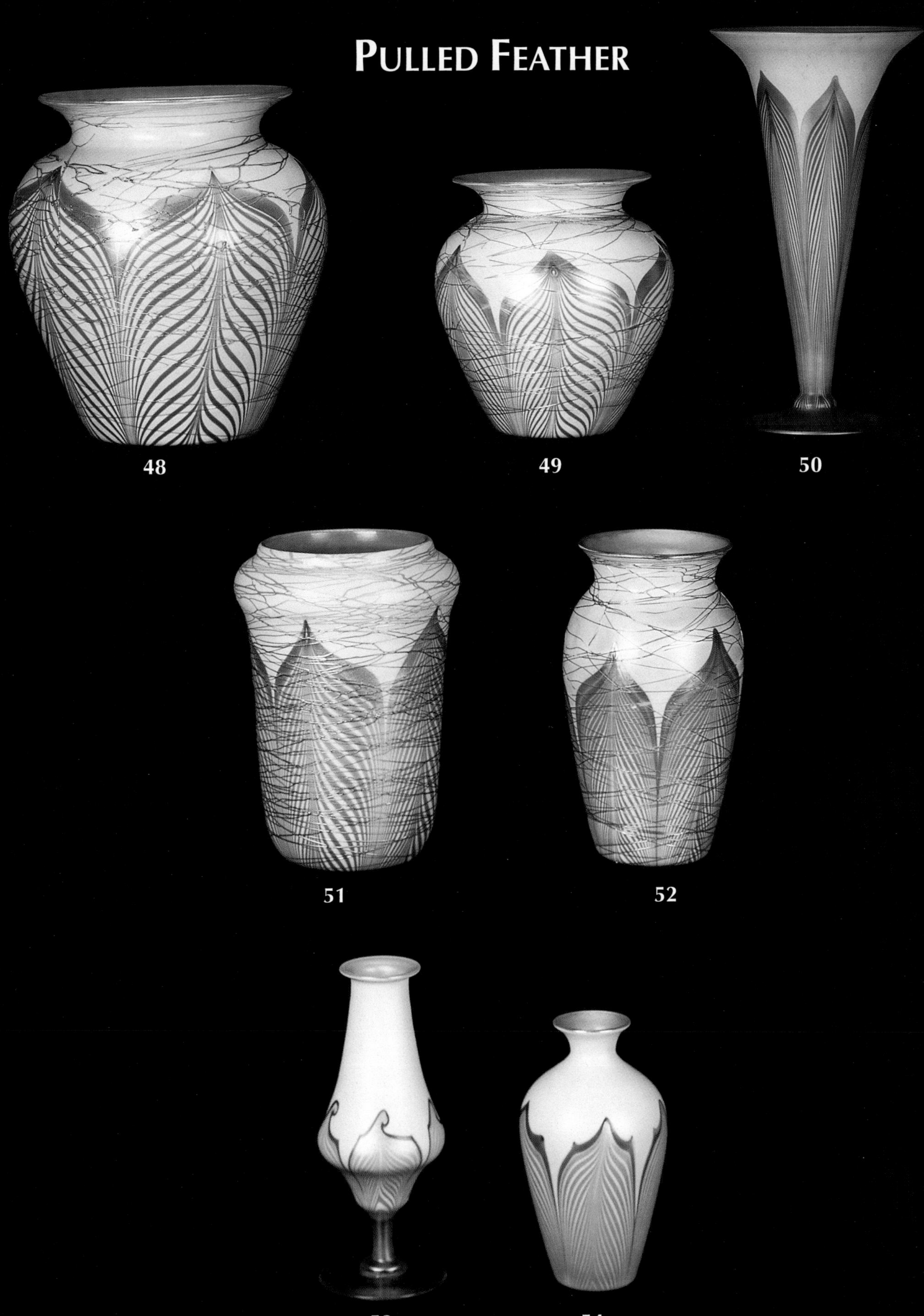

48 49 50

51 52

53 54

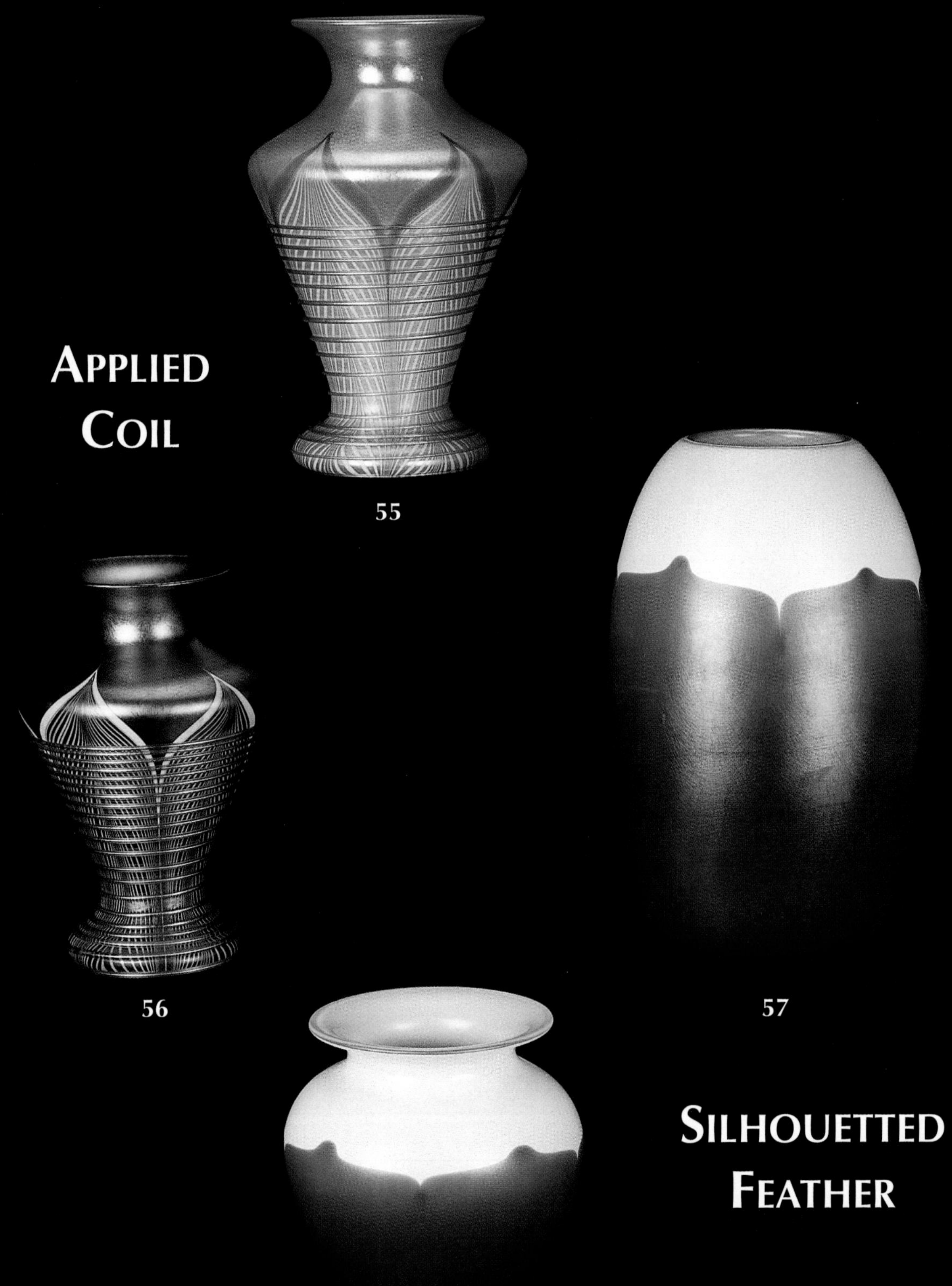

APPLIED COIL

55

56

57

SILHOUETTED FEATHER

58

Spider Webbing

COIL
65
66
67
68
69
70
SPIDER
WEBBING

Coil

71

72

73

74

75

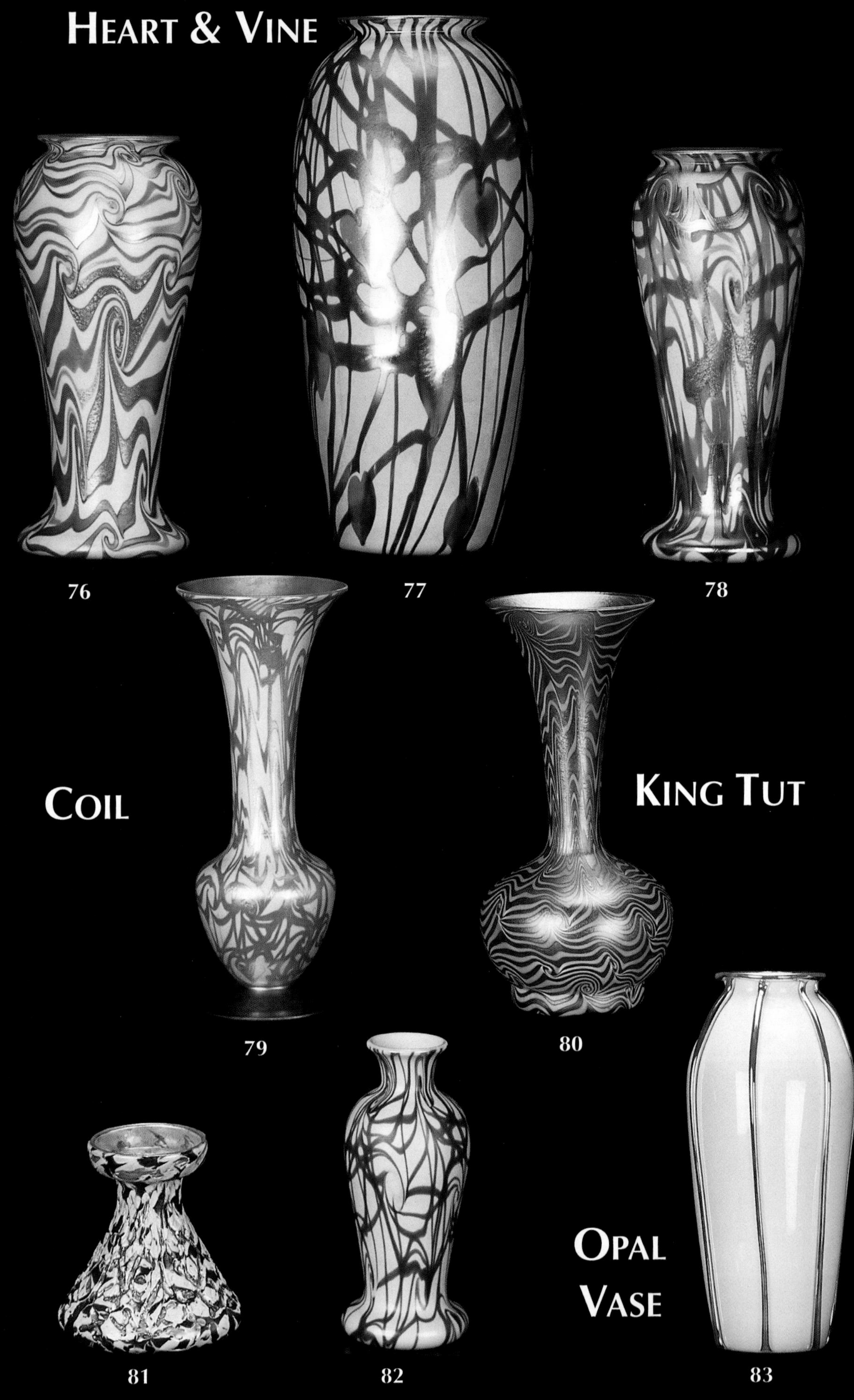
HEART & VINE
76
77
78
COIL
KING TUT
79
80
OPAL
VASE
81
82
83

Crackle Pulled Feather

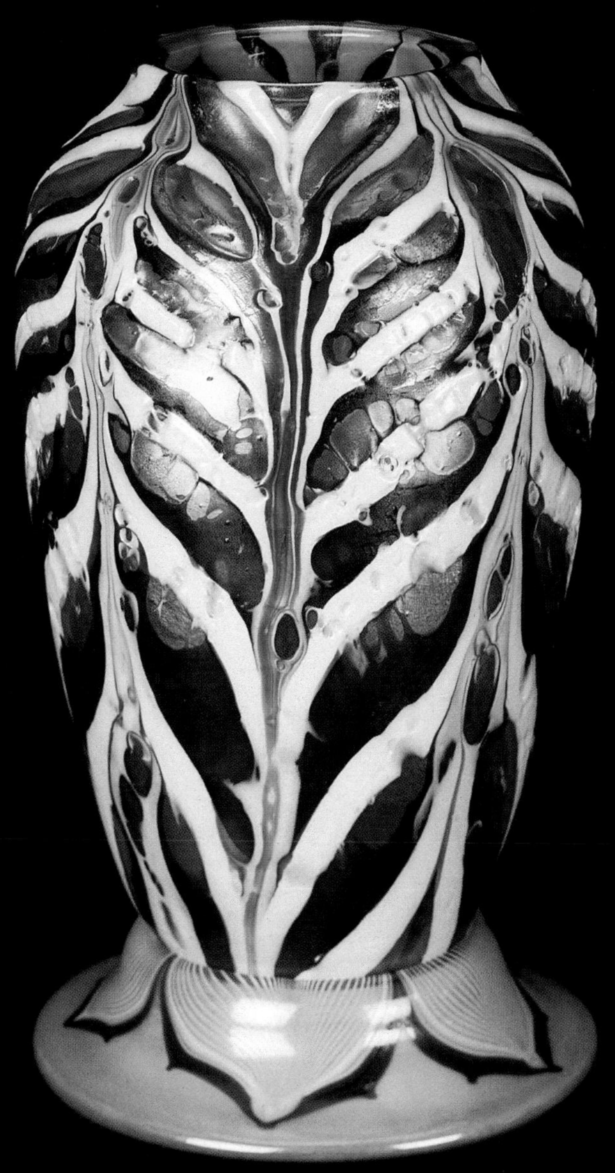

84

CAMEO

85

Cameo

86

Lady Gay Rose

87

88

89

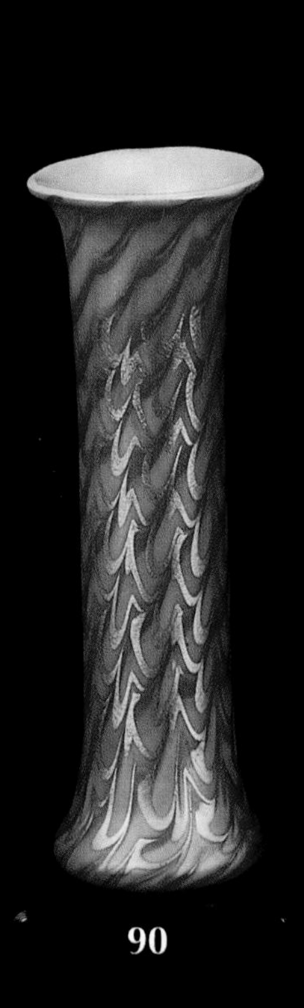

90

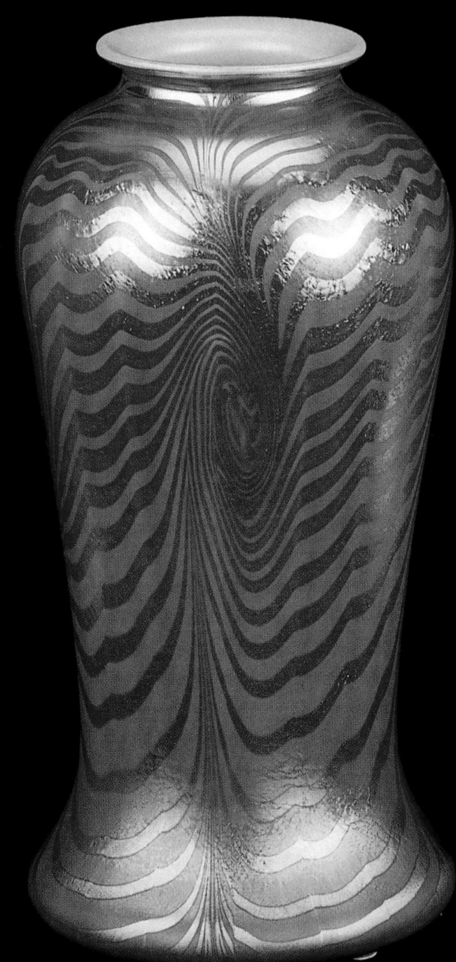

91

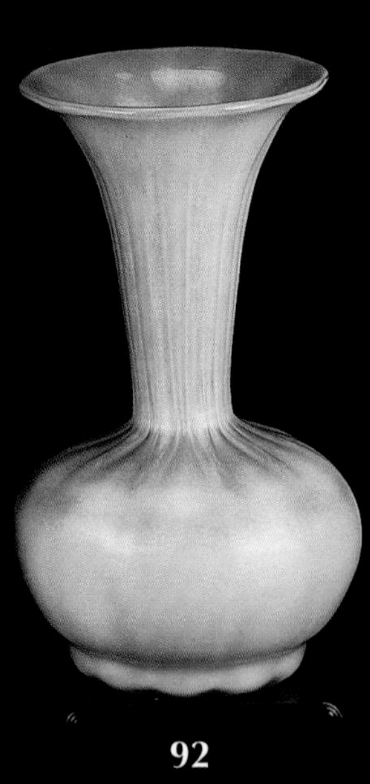

92

KING TUT

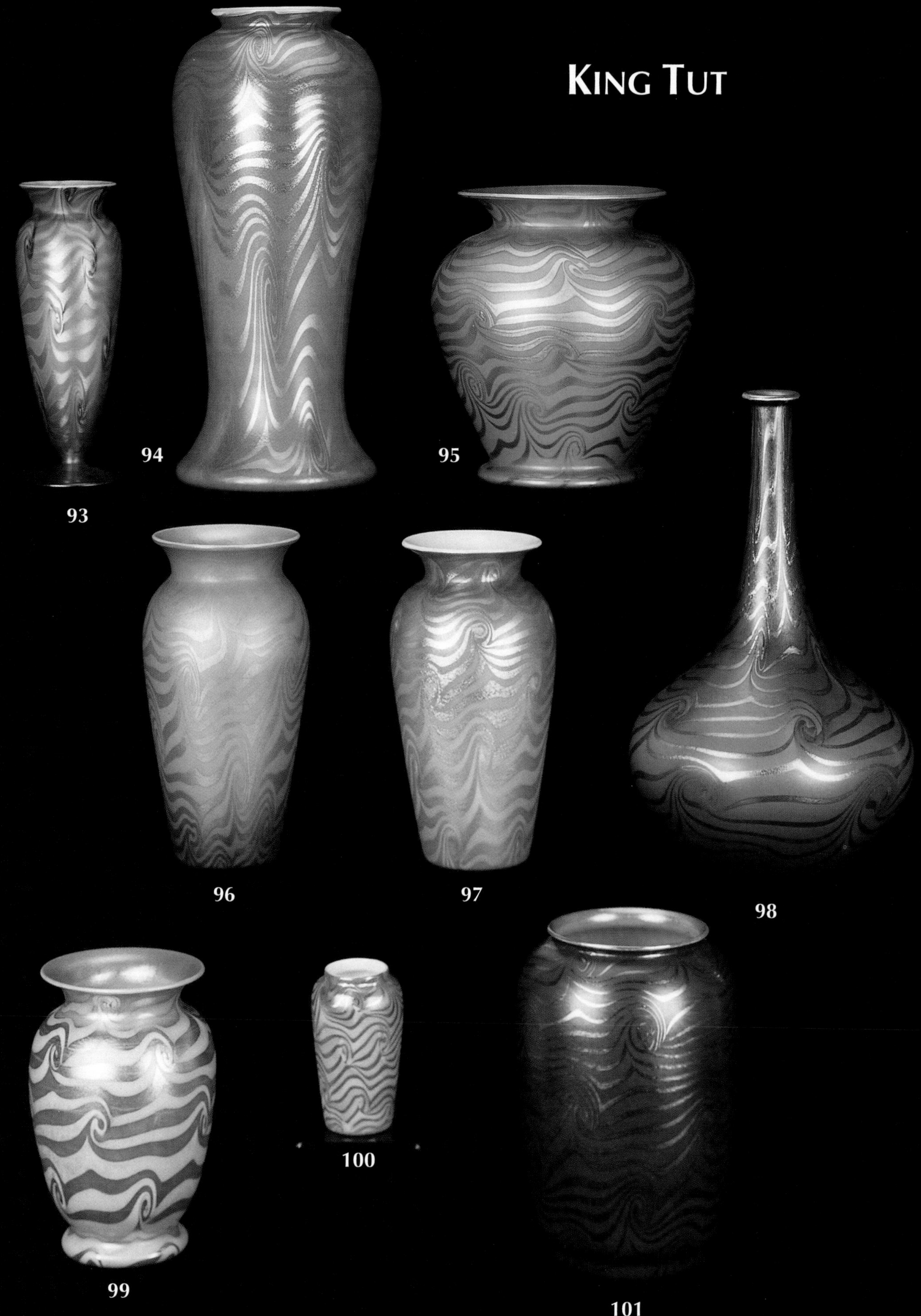

King Tut

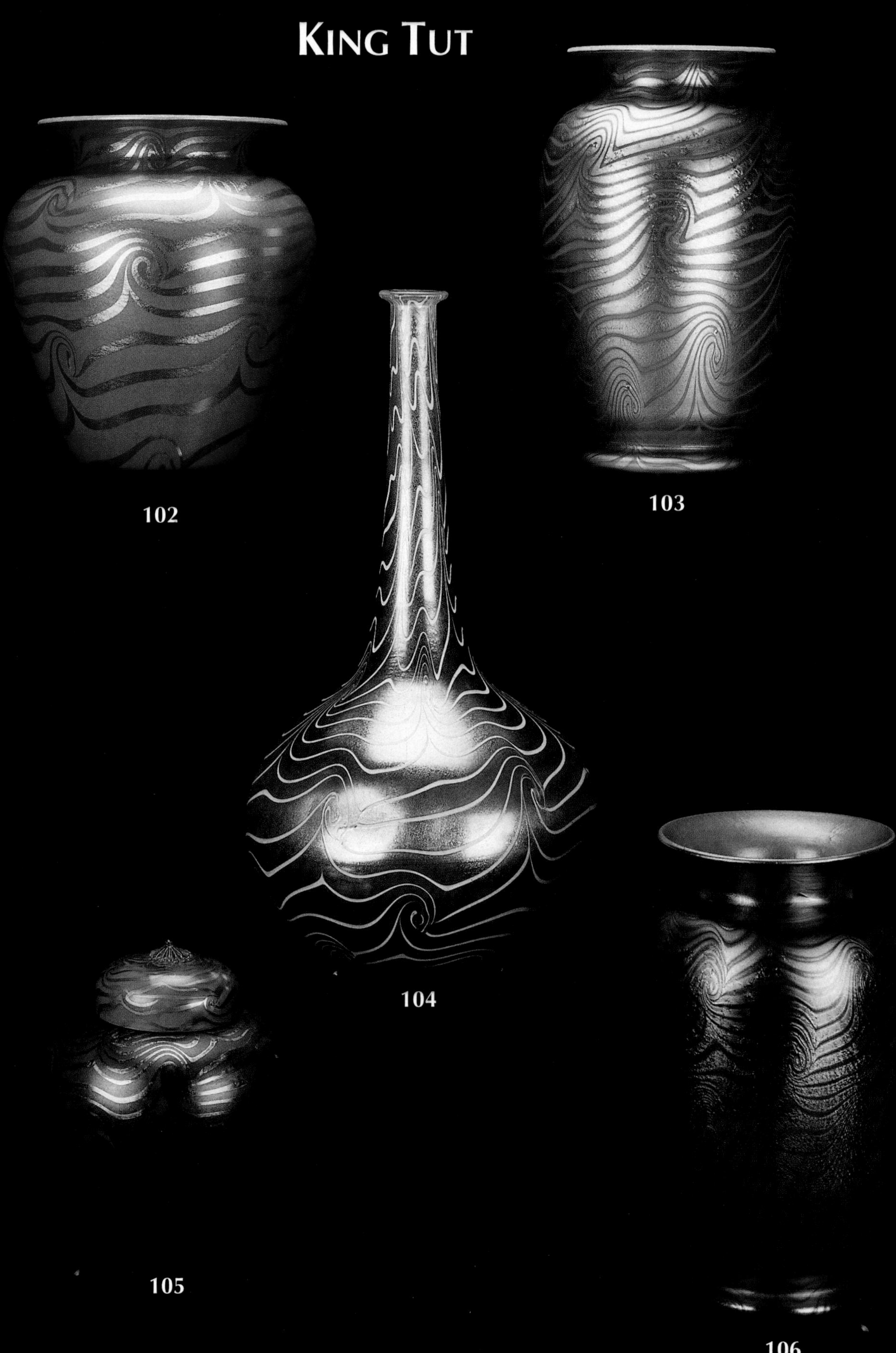

102

103

104

105

106

King Tut

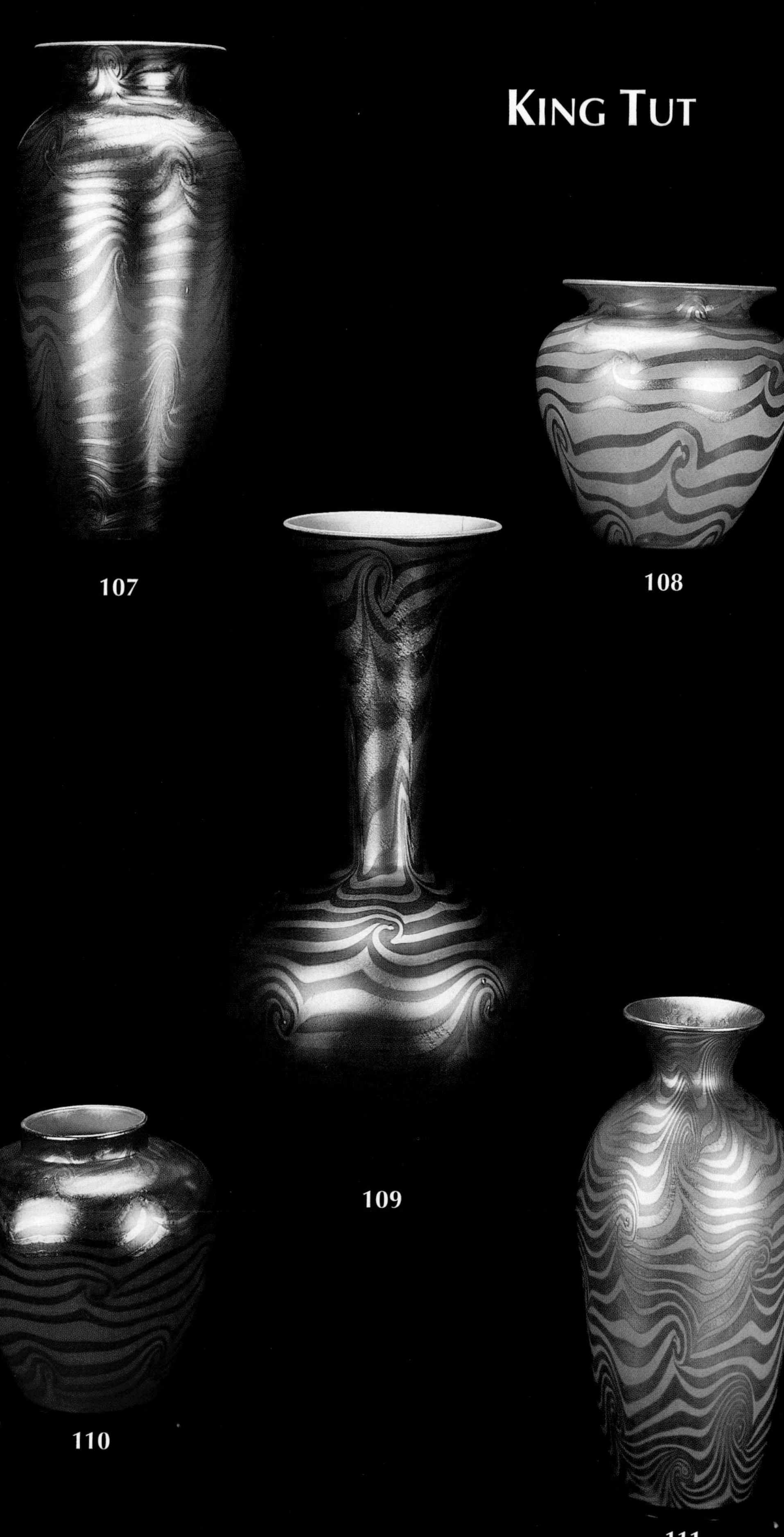

107

108

109

110

111

King Tut

112

113

114

115

116

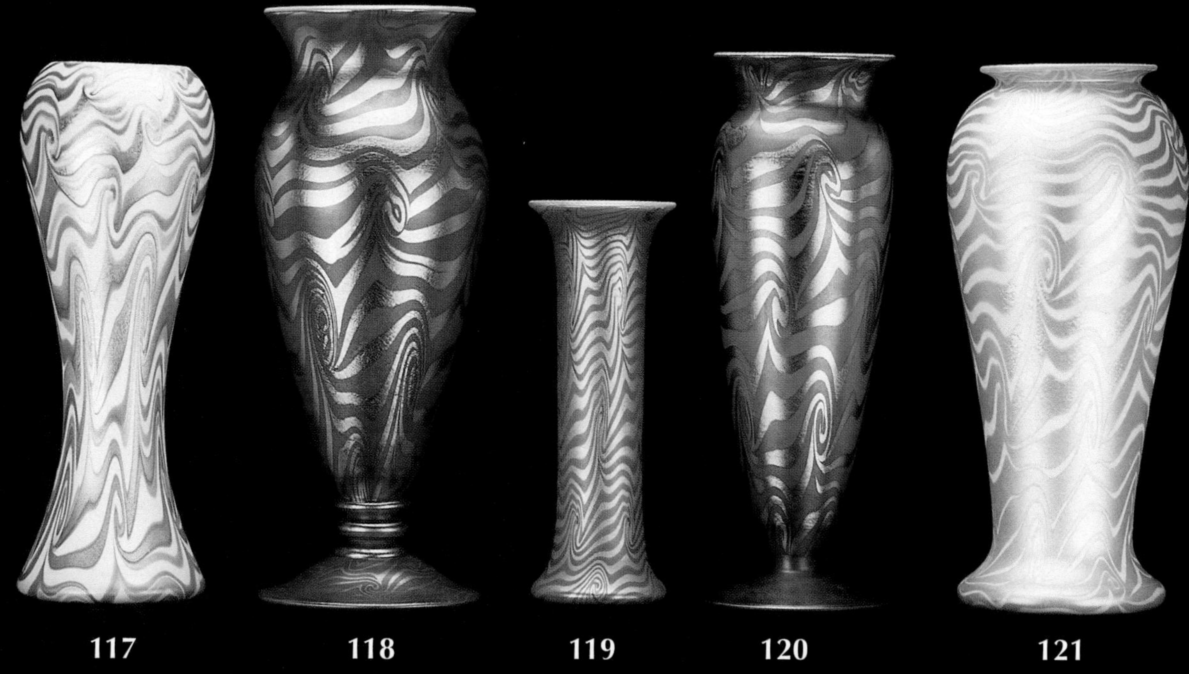

117 118 119 120 121

King Tut

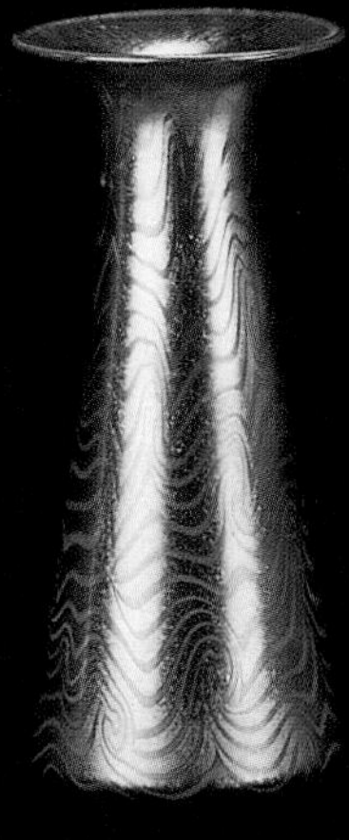

122  123 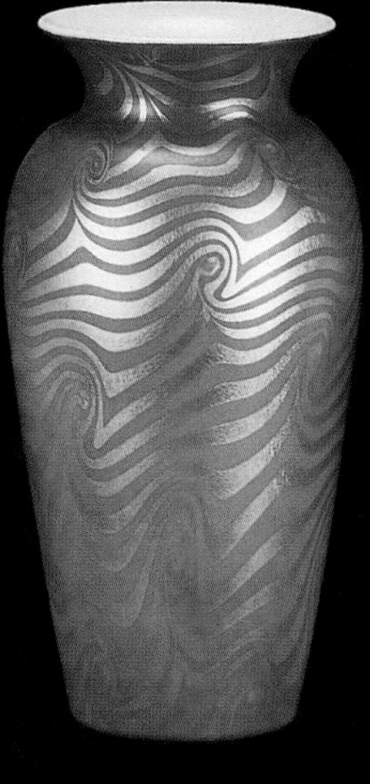 124  125

126 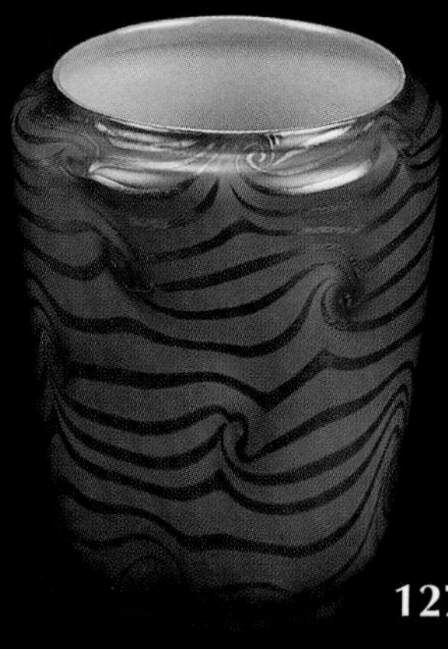 127

PERFUME ATOMIZERS

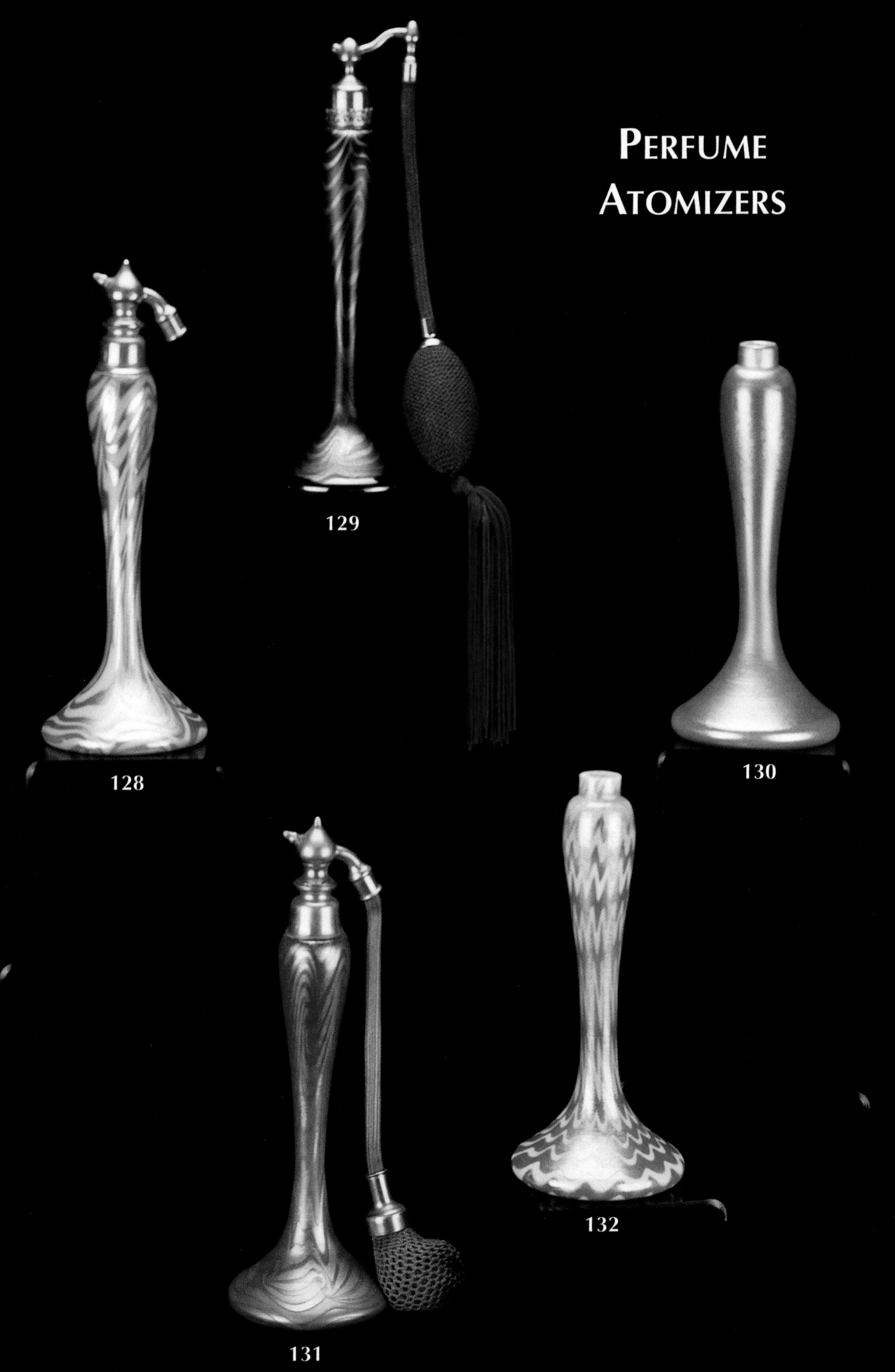

129

128

130

132

131

AUTOMOBILE VASES

133

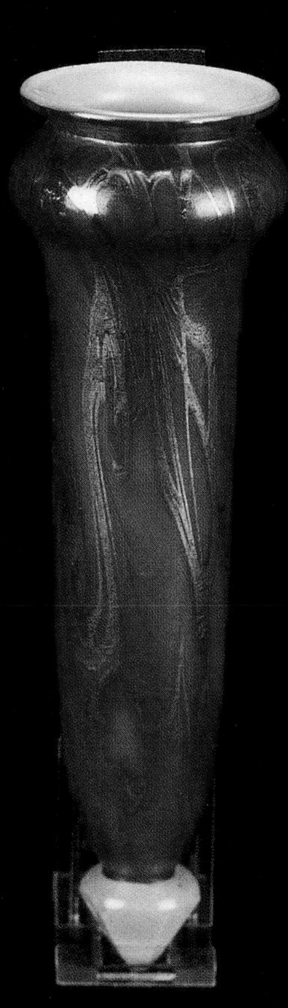

134

King Tut

135

136

137

138

Coil

139

Triple Pulled Feather Decoration

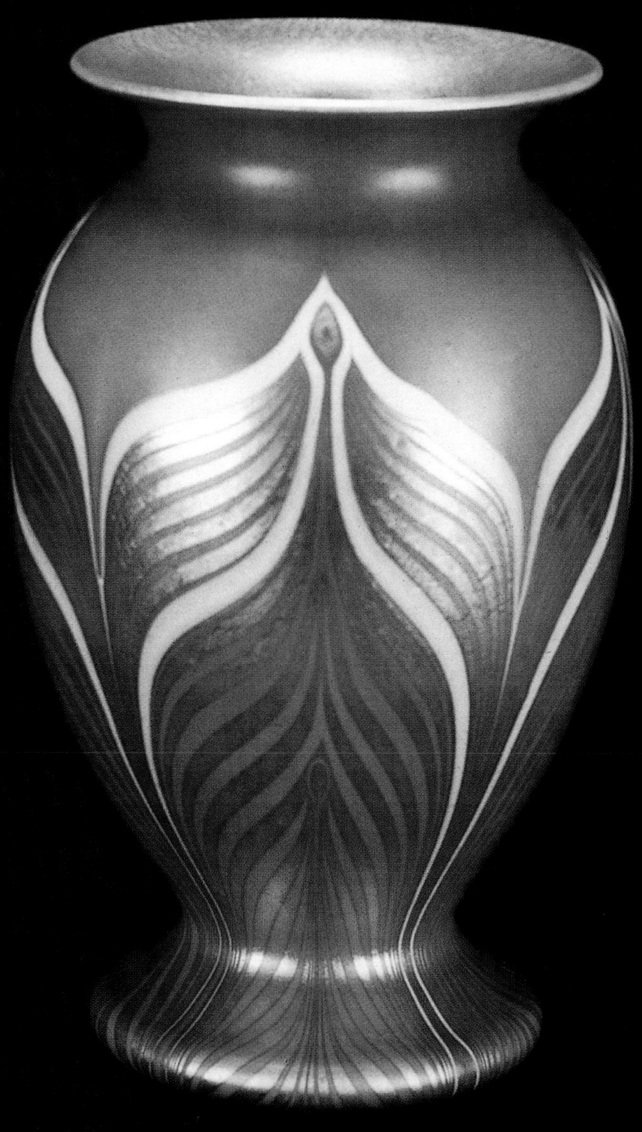

140

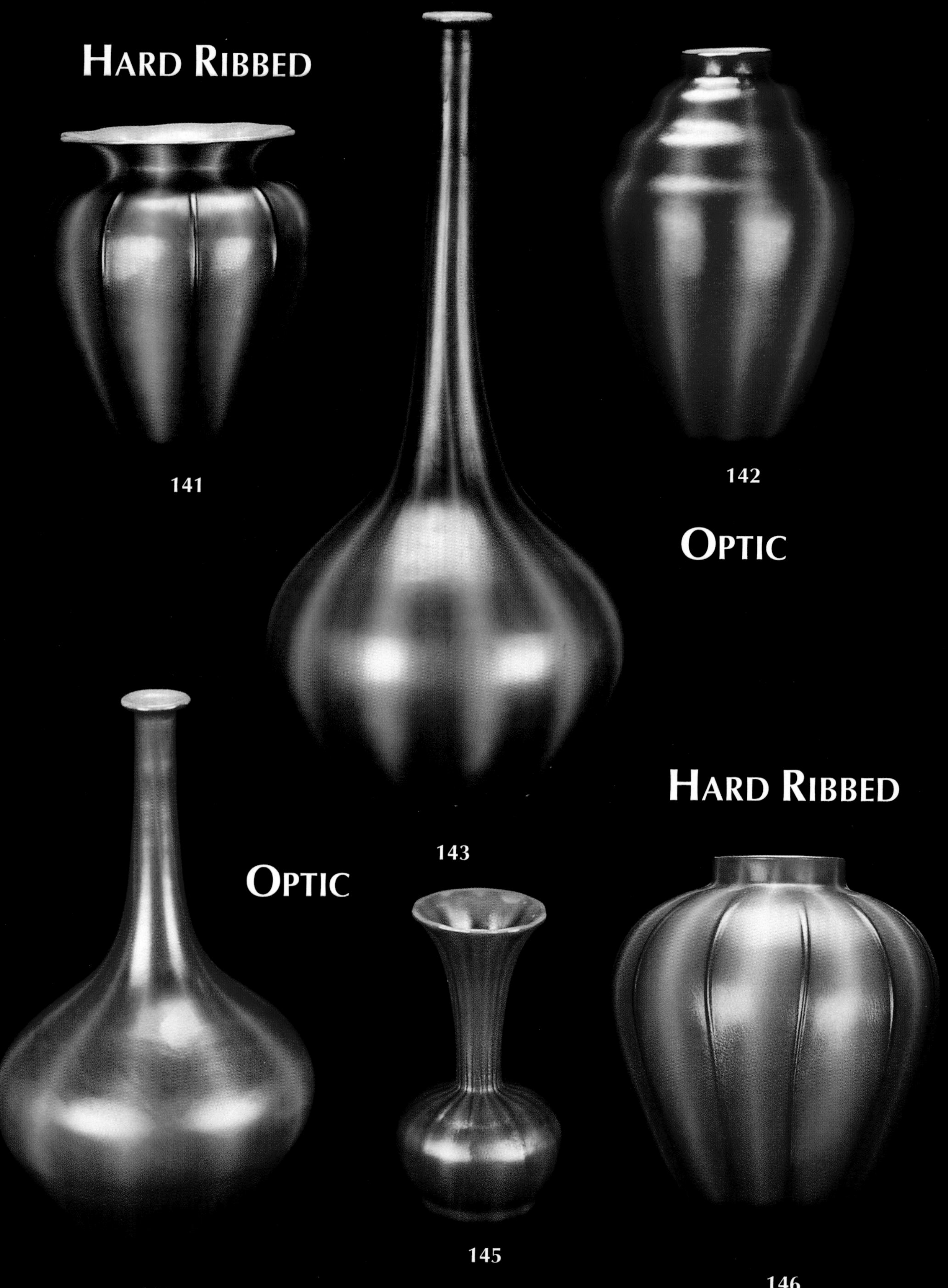

141

142

143

144

145

146

BANDED WITH APPLIED COILS

147

Grotesque
Ribbed Crackle

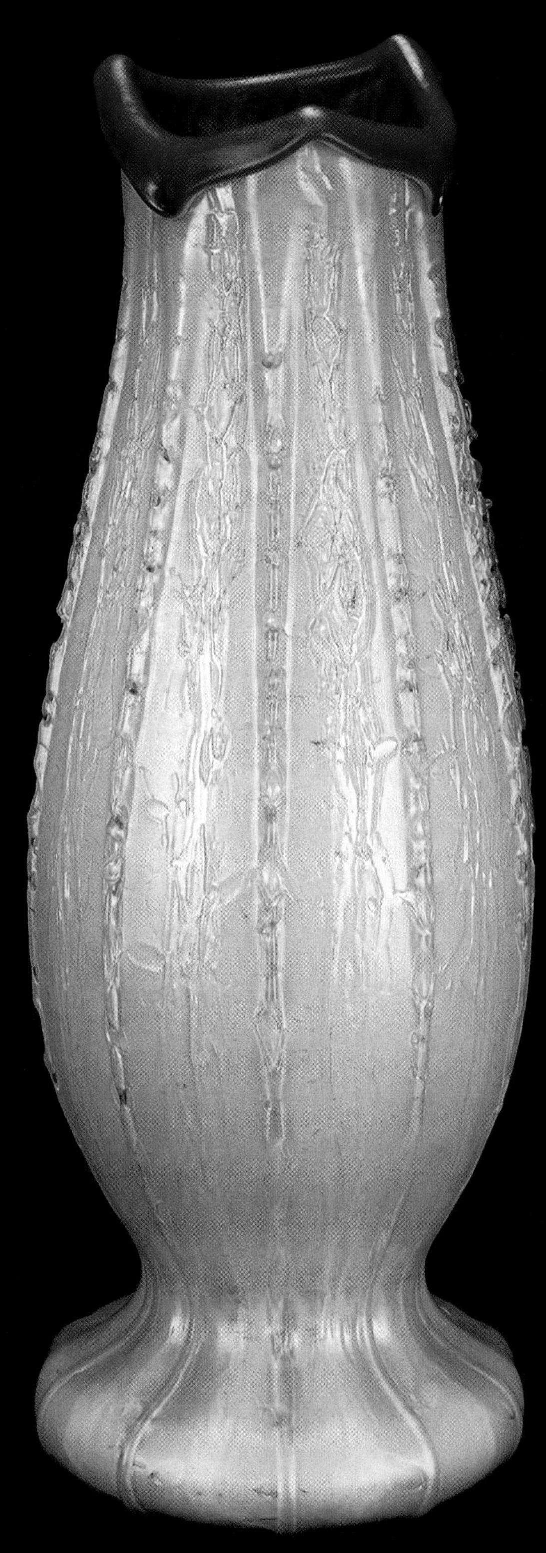

148

CRACKLE WITH LAVA DECORATION

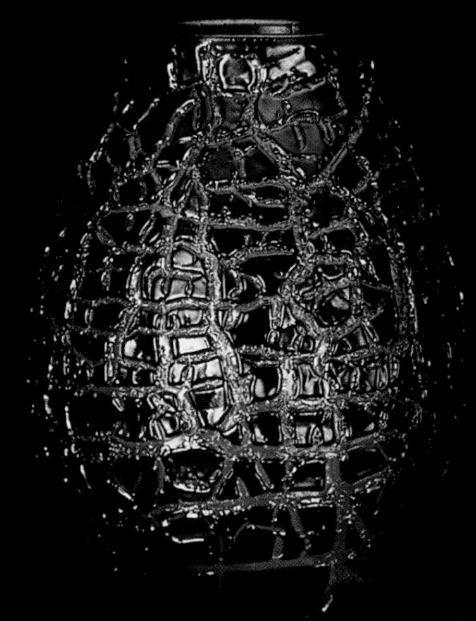

149

150

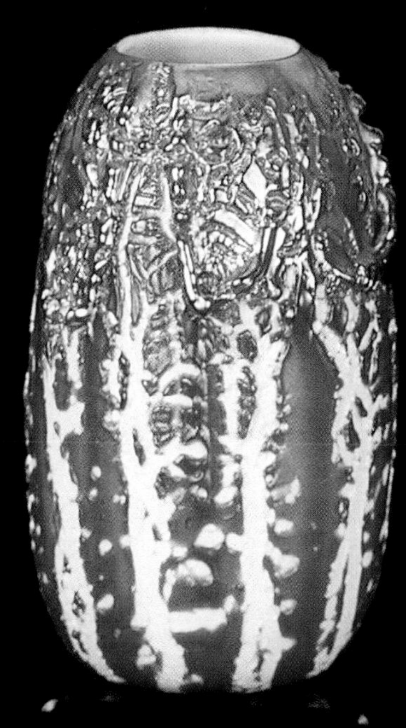

151

Moorish Crackle

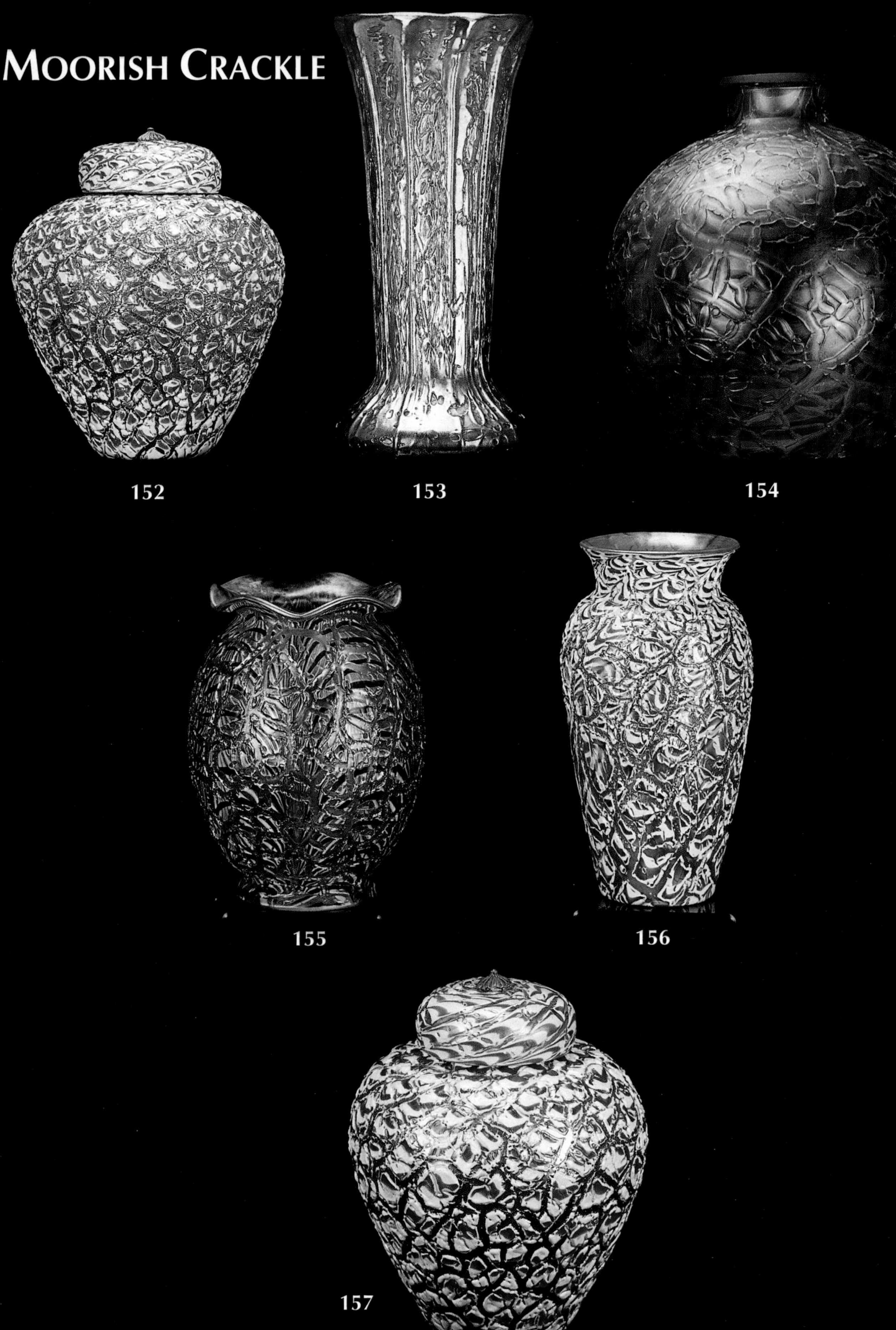

152

153

154

155

156

157

158

159

Moorish Crackle

160

161

162

163 164 165

Crystal and Moorish Crackle

166  167  168

169 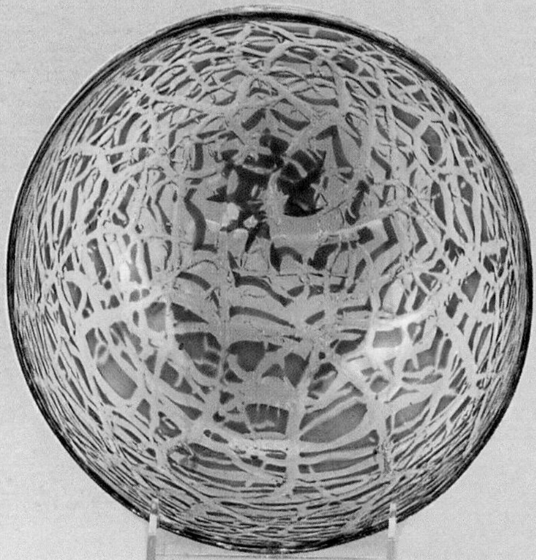 170  171

Crystal Crackle

172 173

Venetian Lace

174

LAVA
CRACKLE
175
176
177

178 179 180

Covered Jars

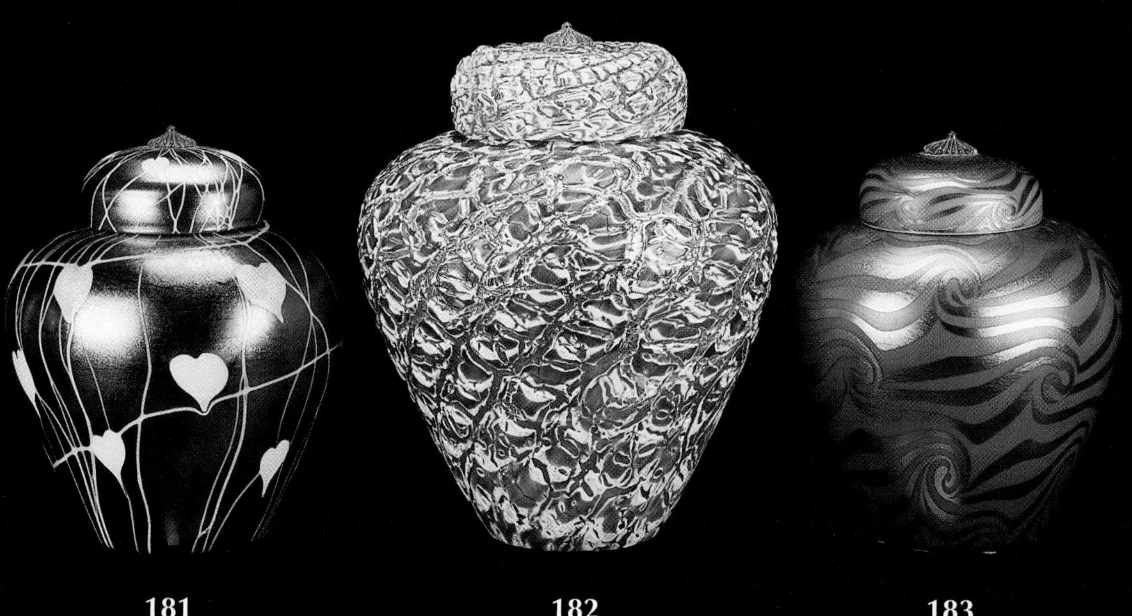

181 182 183

184

185

Lustre Ware

186 187 188

189 190 191 192

193 194

Lustre Ware

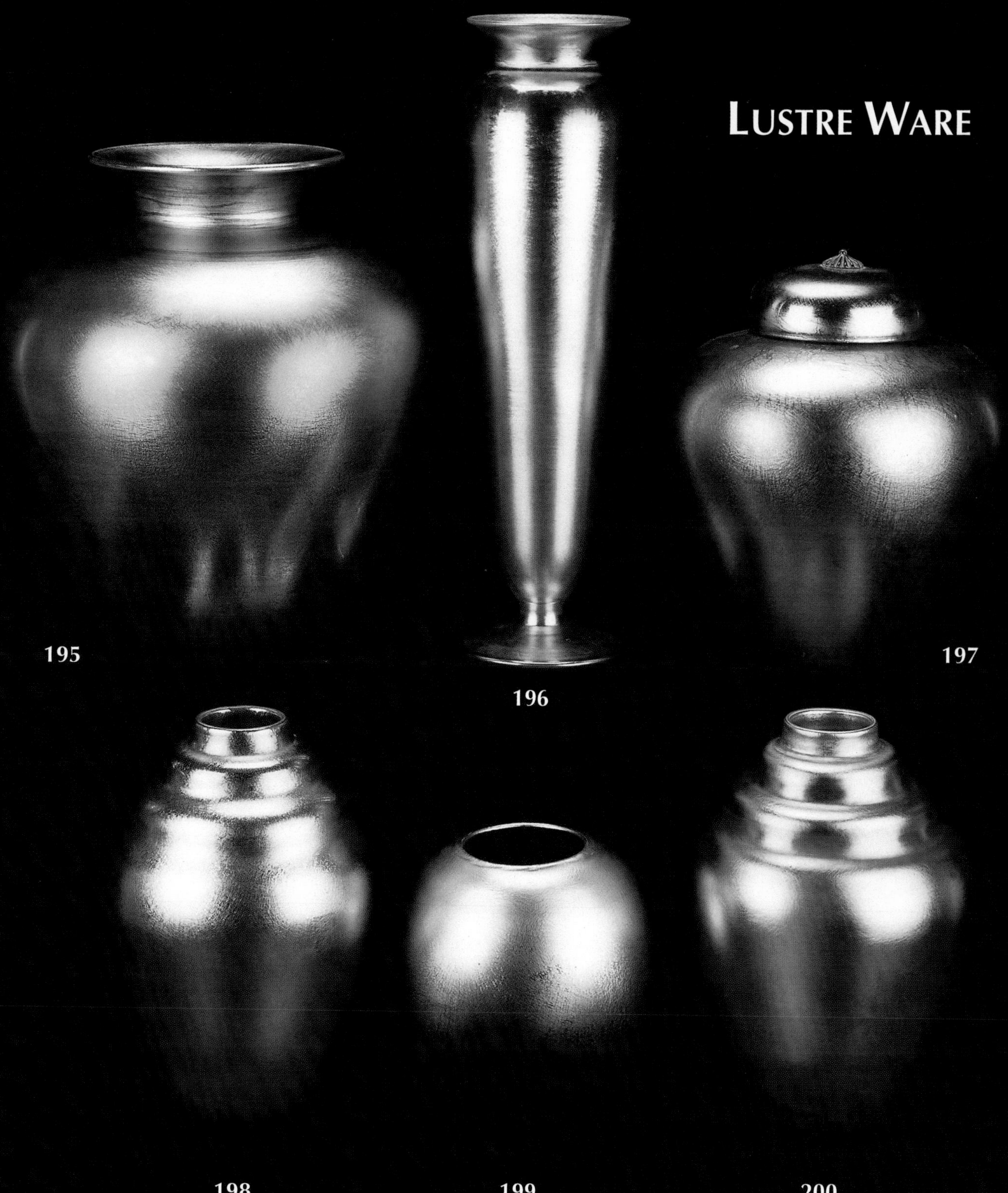

Lustre and Cased Glass

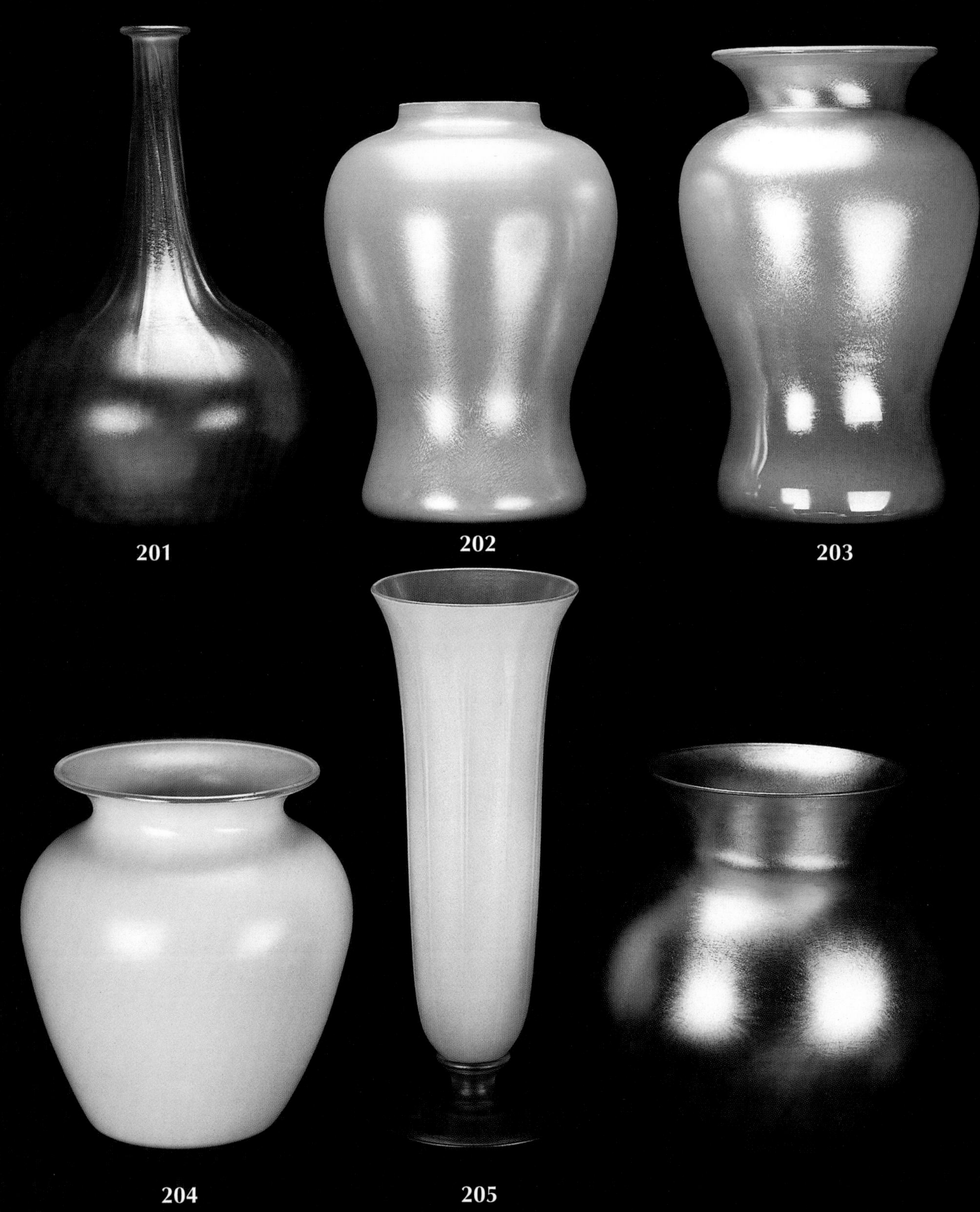

201 202 203

204 205 206

King Tut and Lustre

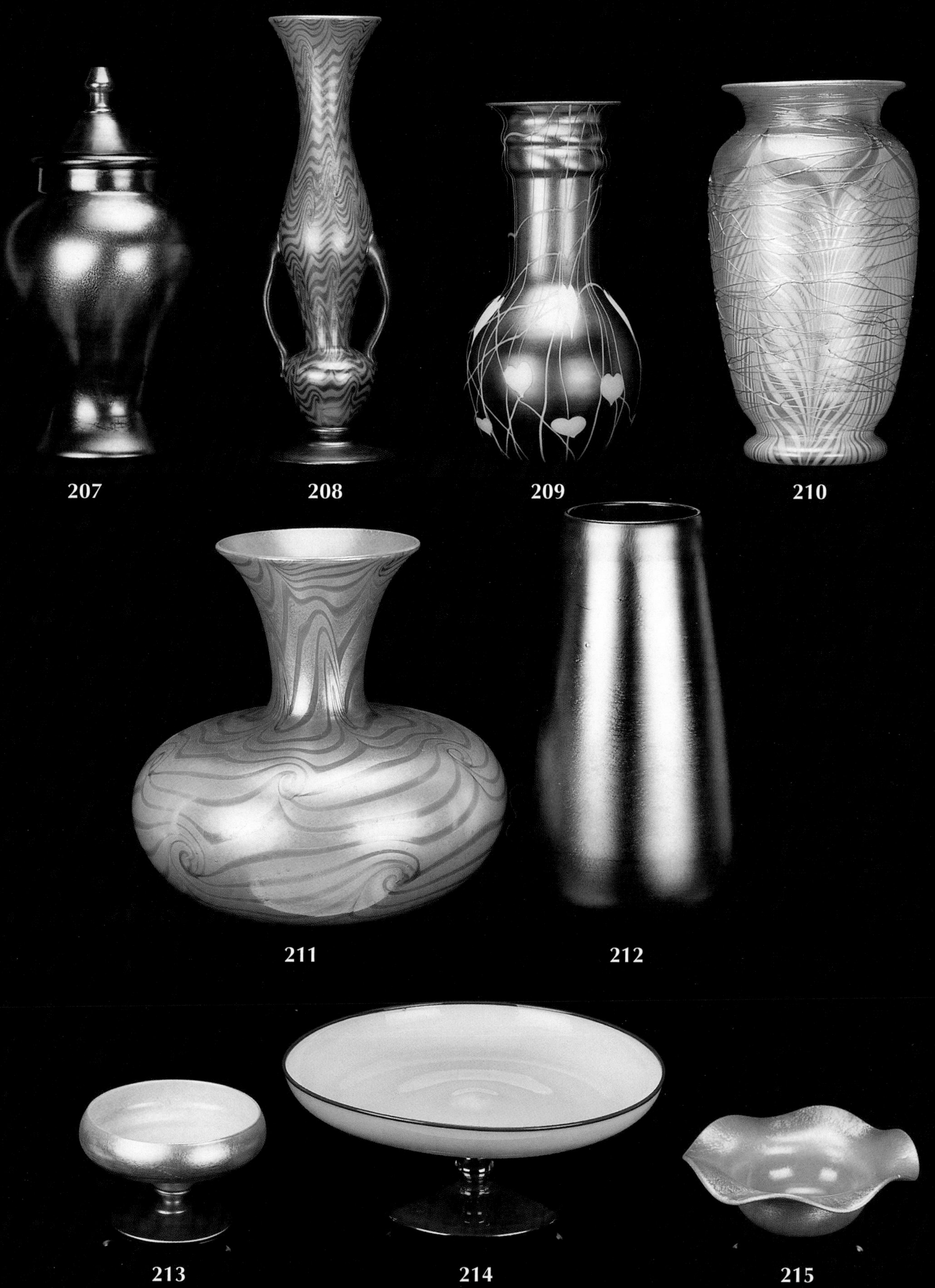
207 208 209 210

211 212

213 214 215

216

ACID CUTBACK

217

Peacock Feather

219

218

220

221

222

223

Ruby Dinner and Stemware

224 225 226 227 228 229

230 231 230 232

233 234 235

236 237

Peacock Feather

238 239 240 241 242

243 244

245 246 247

Stemware

248 249 250 251 252 253

254 255 256 257

258 259 260 261 262

263 264 265 266 267

PEACOCK FEATHER

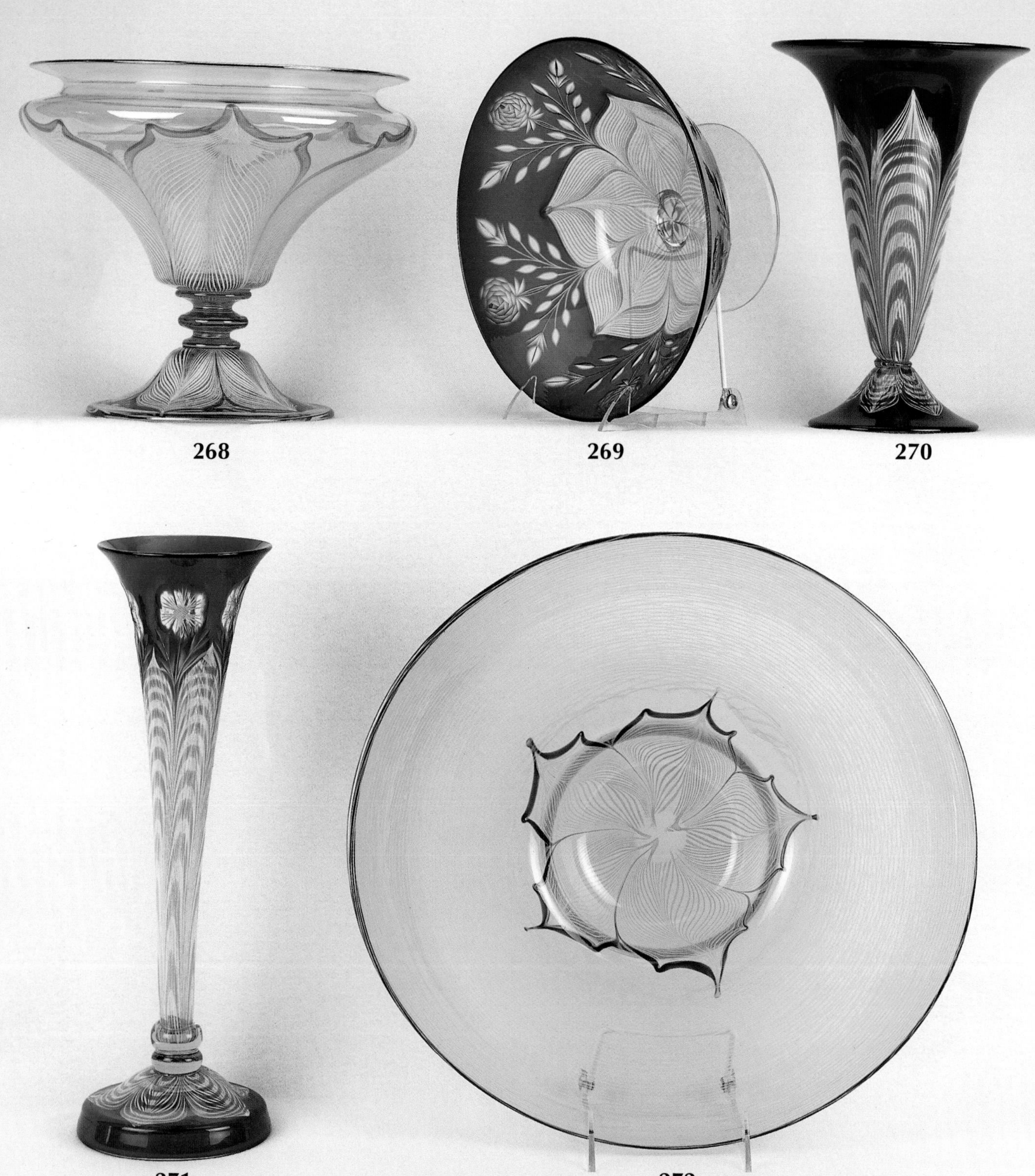

268 269 270

271 272

273
274
275
276
PEACOCK FEATHER
277
278
279
280
281

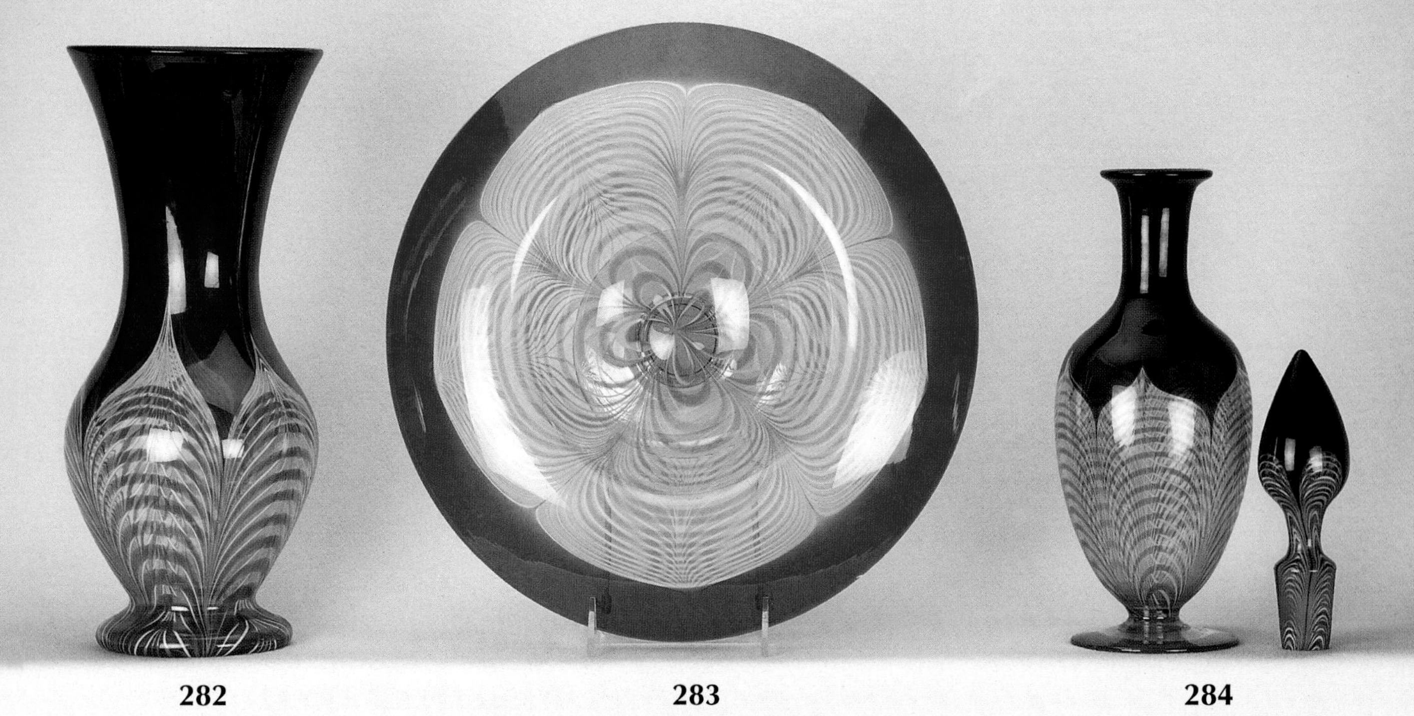

282 283 284

Peacock Feather

285 286 285

287 288 289

Peacock Feather

290

291

292

293

294

Dinner Plates

Pulled Feather

303

304

305

Yellow Lustre Dinnerware

306

307

308

309

310

311

Amethyst Optic Ribbed

312

313

314

315

316

317

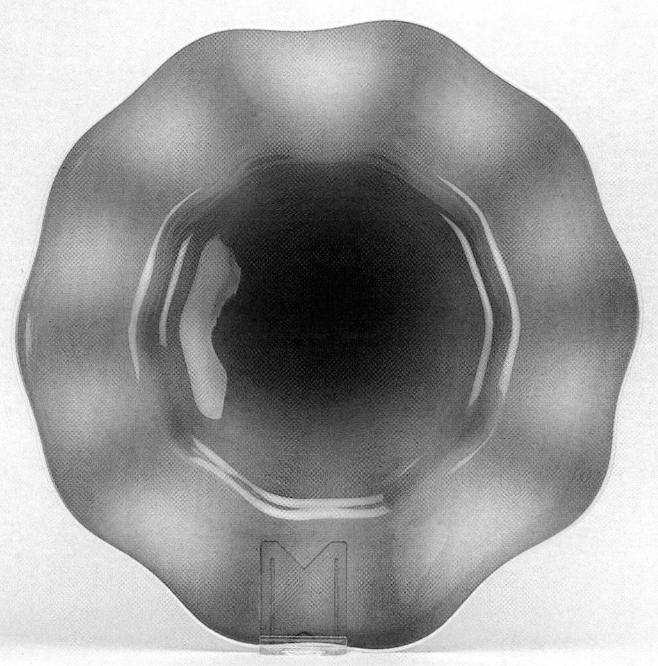

318

319

Blue Optic Ribbed Dinnerware

320

321

322

323

324 325 326

Dinnerware Plates

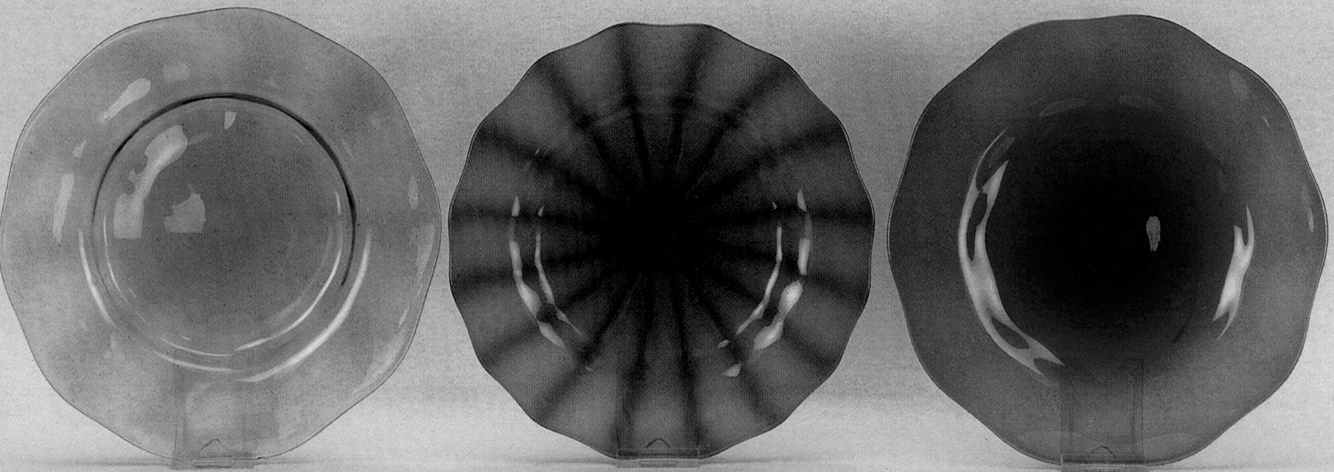

327 328 329

330 331

Plates and Bowls

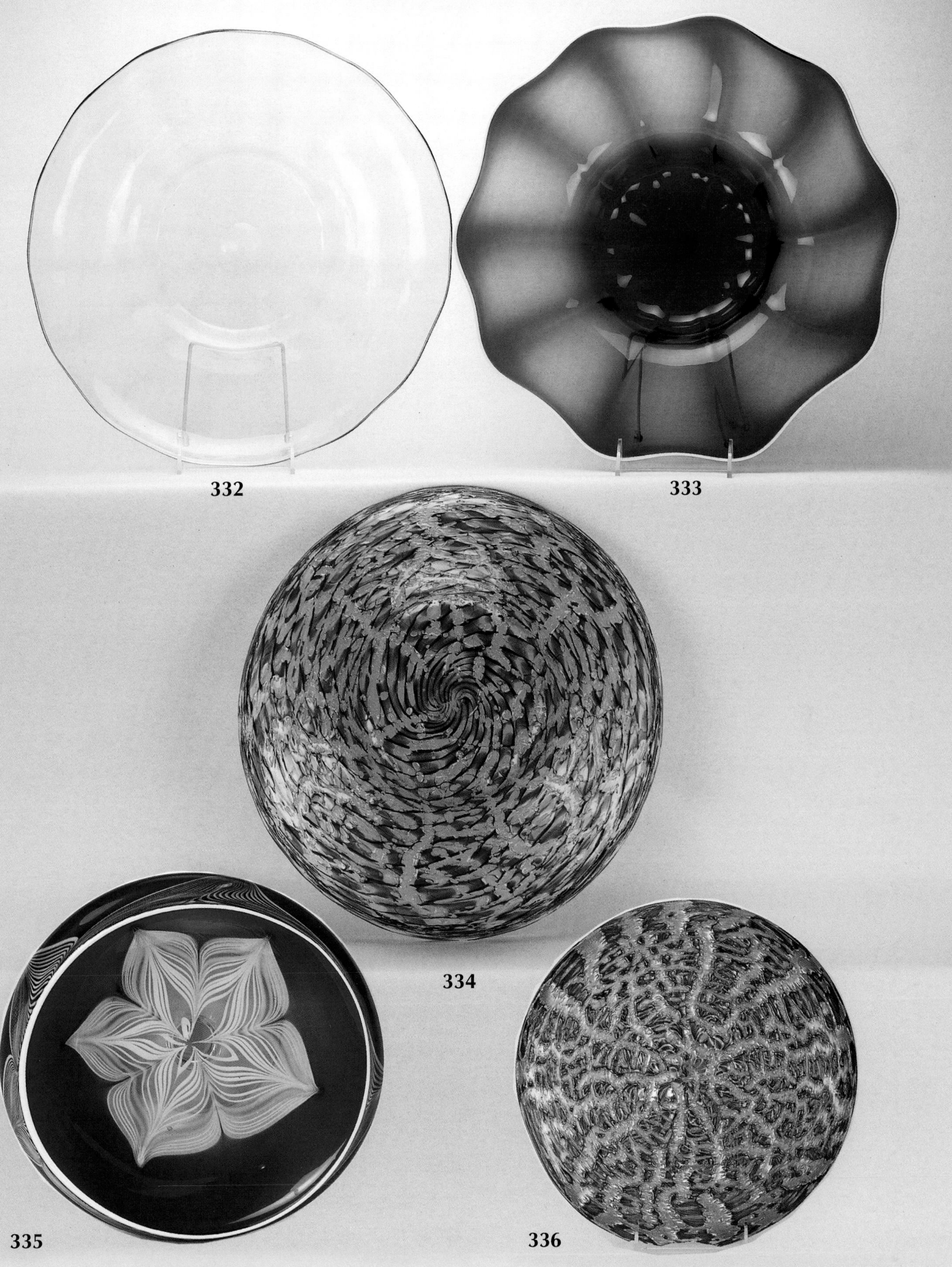
332

333

334

335

336

Cut Glass

337

338

Amethyst Ribbed Optic

339

340

341

Blue Lustre

Pulled Feather

342

343

344

Cased Cut Glass

345 346 347 348

349 350 351

352 353 354 355

356

357

Ruby Cased Cut Glass

358

359

360

Yellow Lustre

361

362

363

364

Cut Glass

365

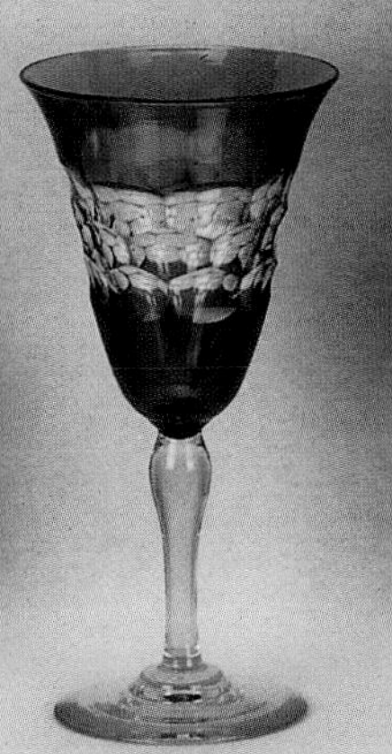
366

367

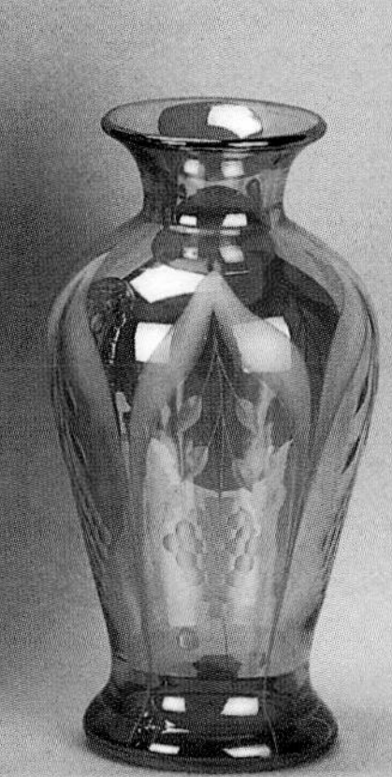
368

369

370

369

371 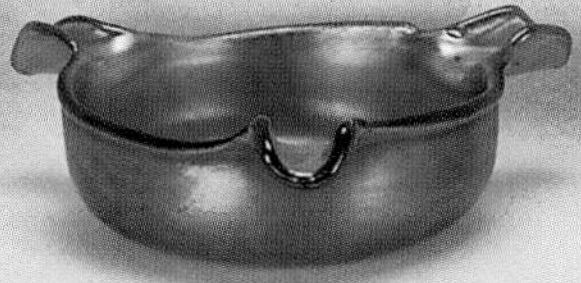 372 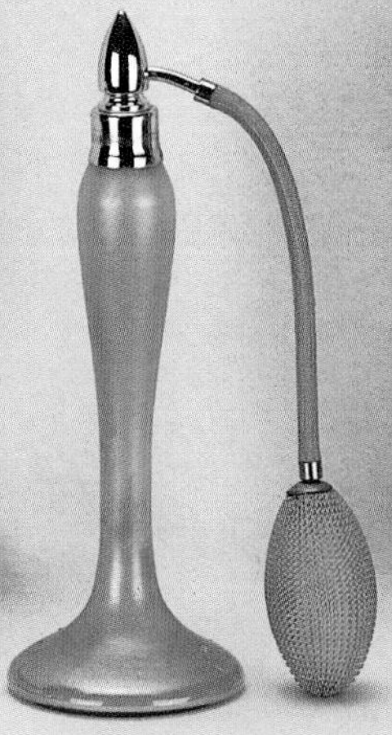 373  374

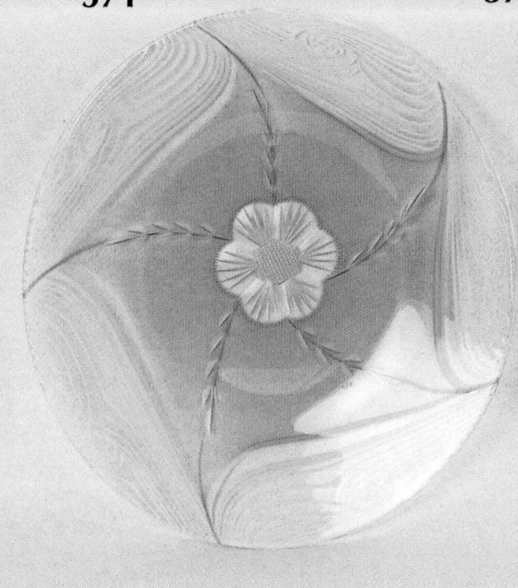

375 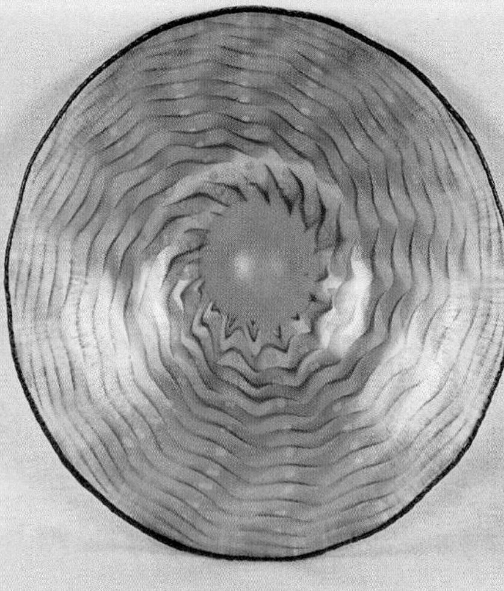 376  377

Venetian Lace

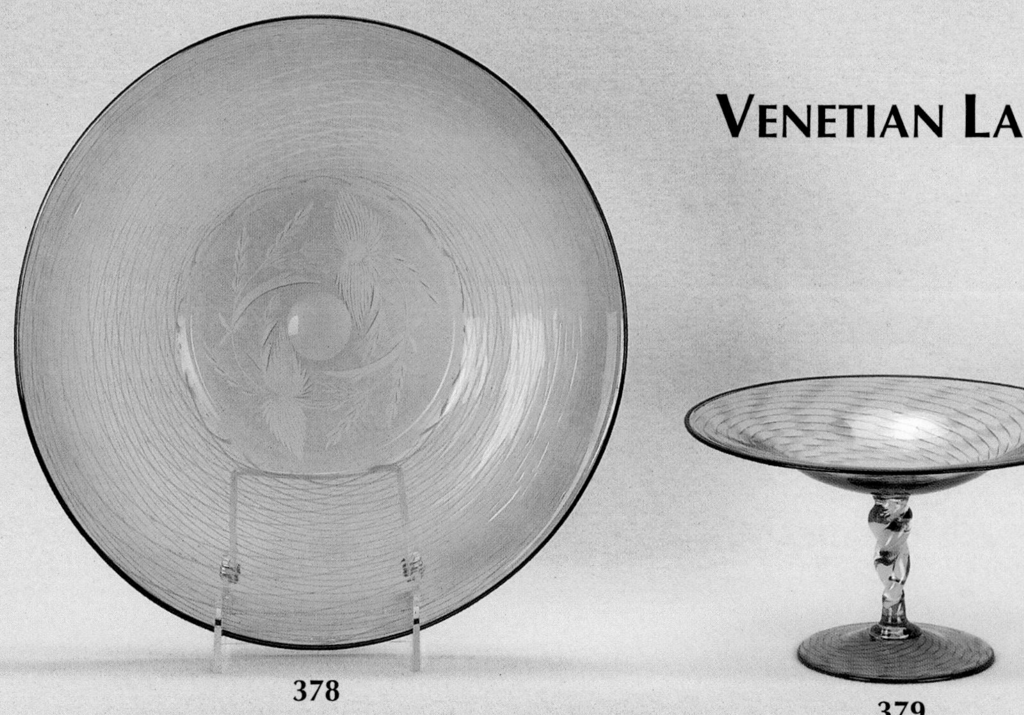

378 379

380

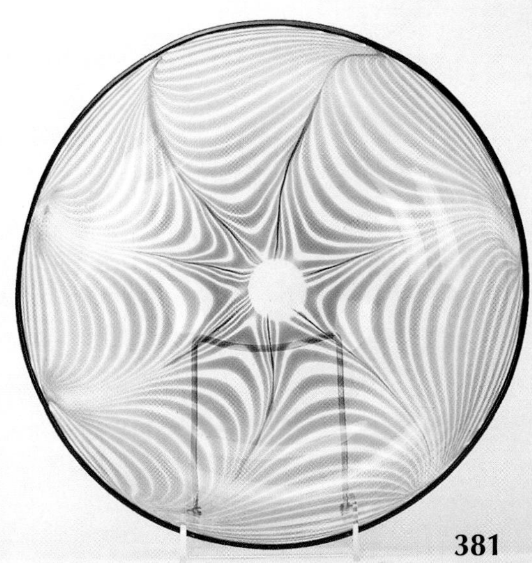
381

Pulled Feather

382

383

384

Cut

Moorish Crackle

385

386

387

389

388

390

391 392 393

Cut Decanters

394 395 396

Candle Holders

397 398 399

STEMWARE AND DINNERWARE

422

Ruby Footed Canteen Vases

Pulled Feather

423

Yellow Lustre

Amethyst Optic Ribbed

424

425

Lady Gay Rose

Cut

426

427

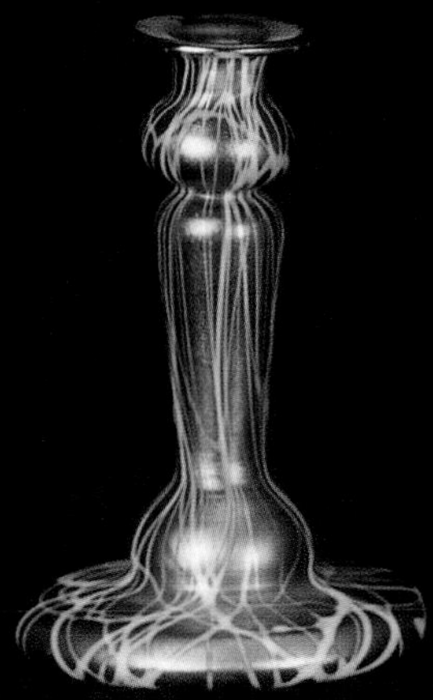

428

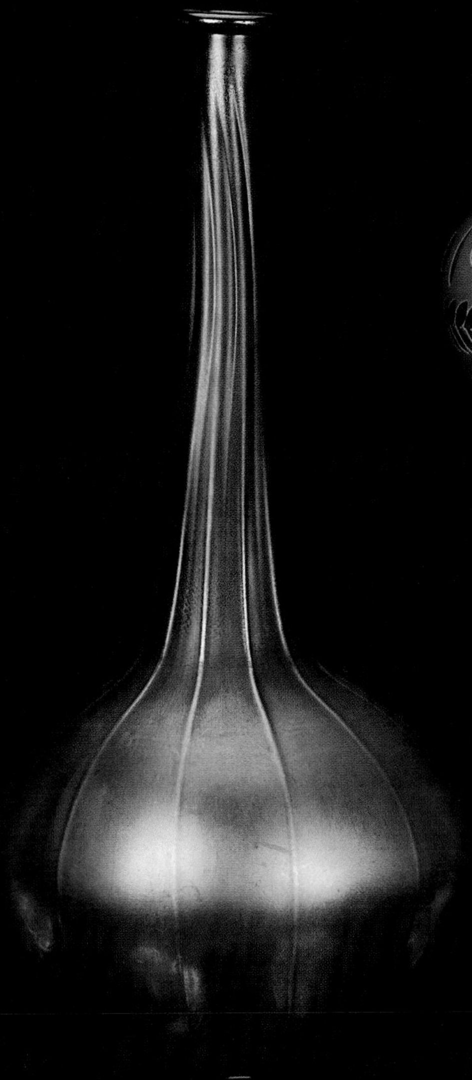

429

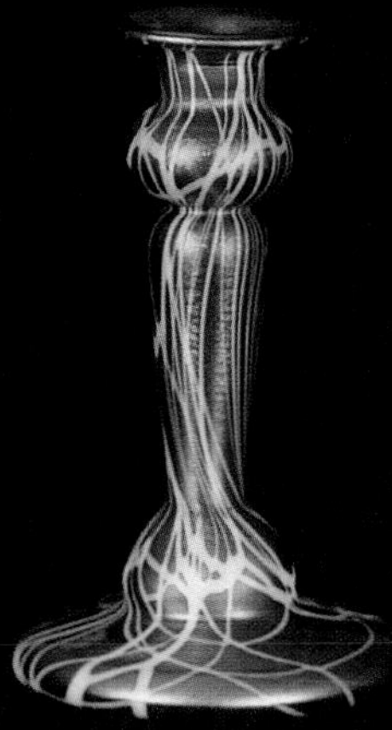

428

Blue Lustre

431

King Tut

430

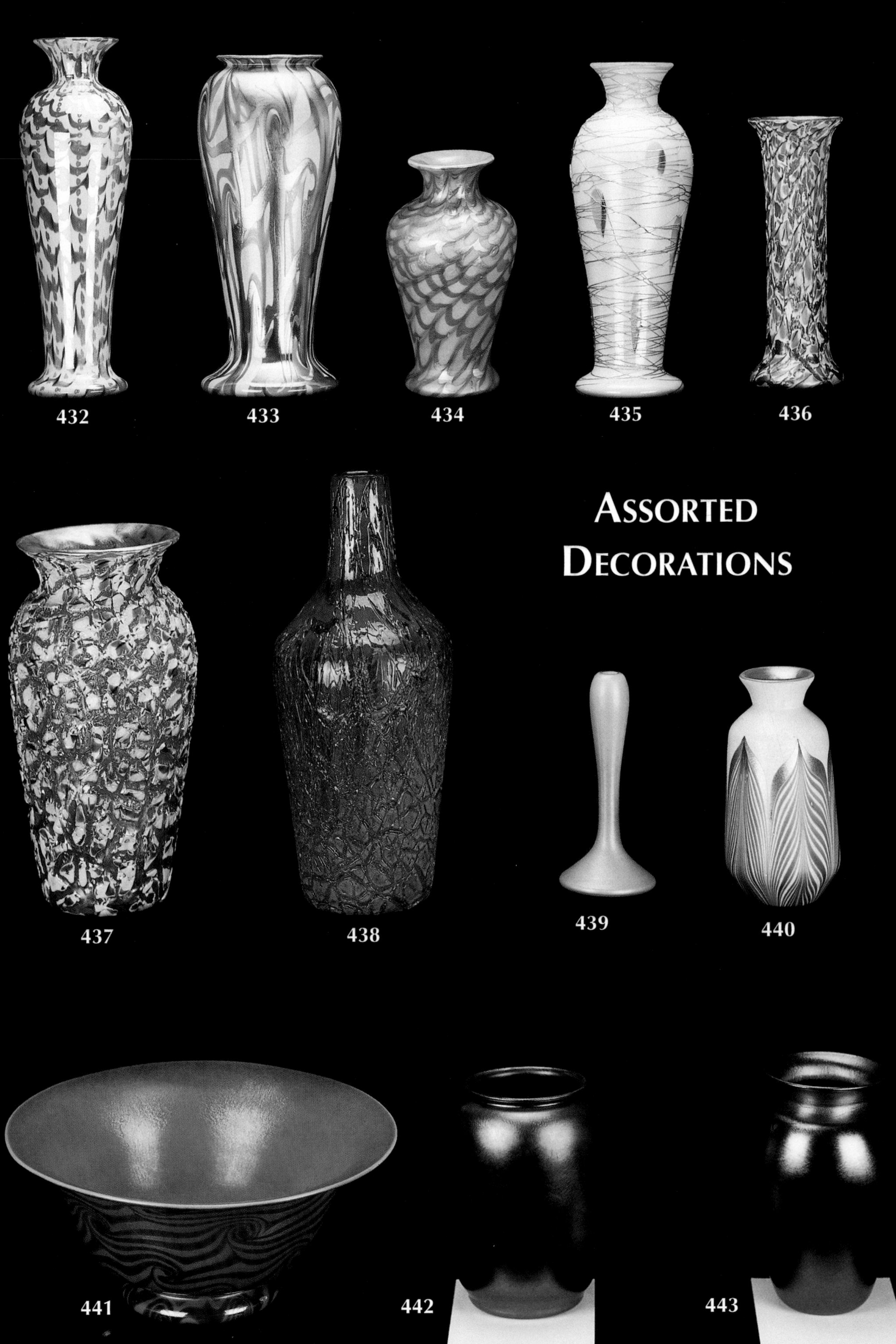
432 433 434 435 436

Assorted Decorations

437 438 439 440

441 442 443

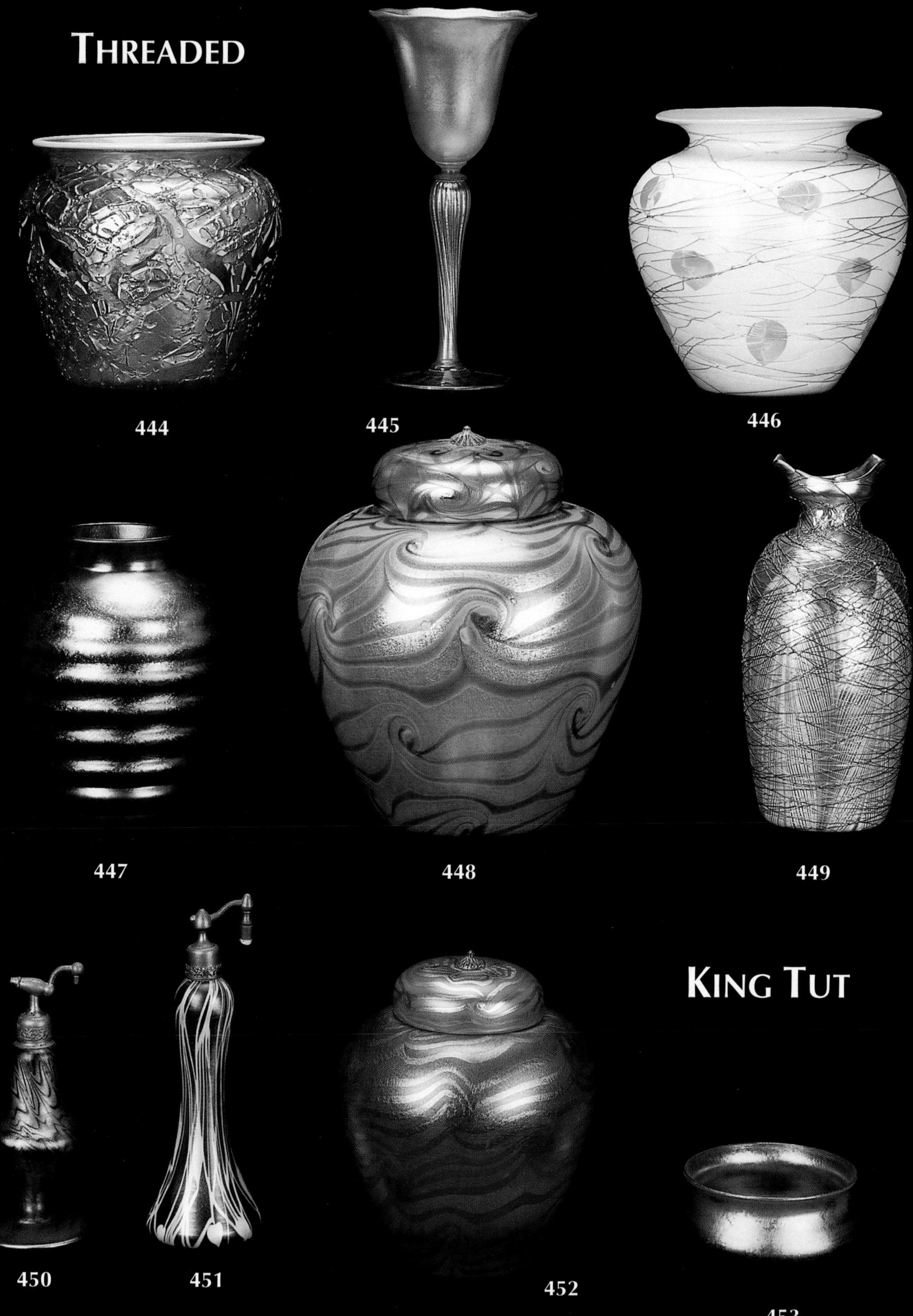

THREADED

444 445 446

447 448 449

KING TUT

450 451 452 453

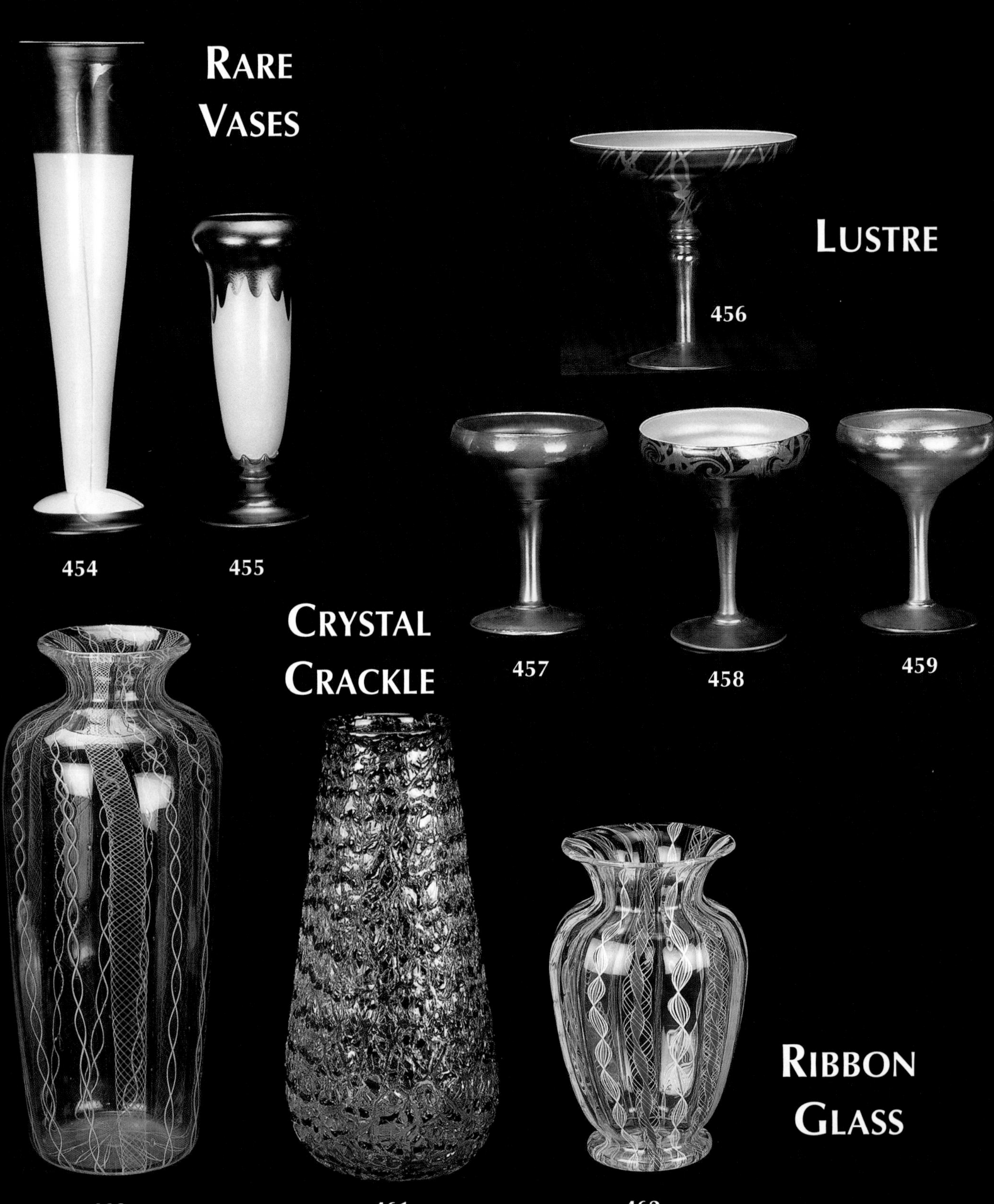
RARE VASES
LUSTRE
456
454
455
CRYSTAL CRACKLE
457
458
459
RIBBON GLASS
460
461
462

Rose Cut Sherbets

463

Heart and Vine

Blue Lustre

Pulled Feather

464

465

466

Acid Cutback

467

468

469
470
471
472
473
474
475
476
477
478
479
480
481

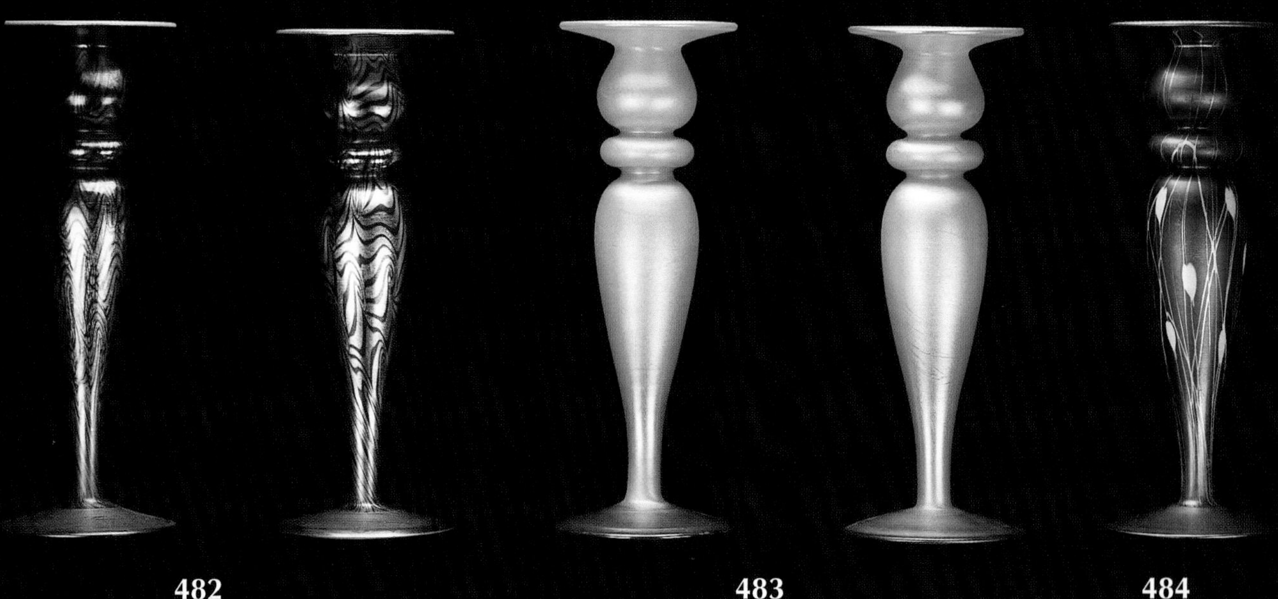

482 483 484

Candle Holders

485

486 487

Crackle Torchiere Floor Lamps

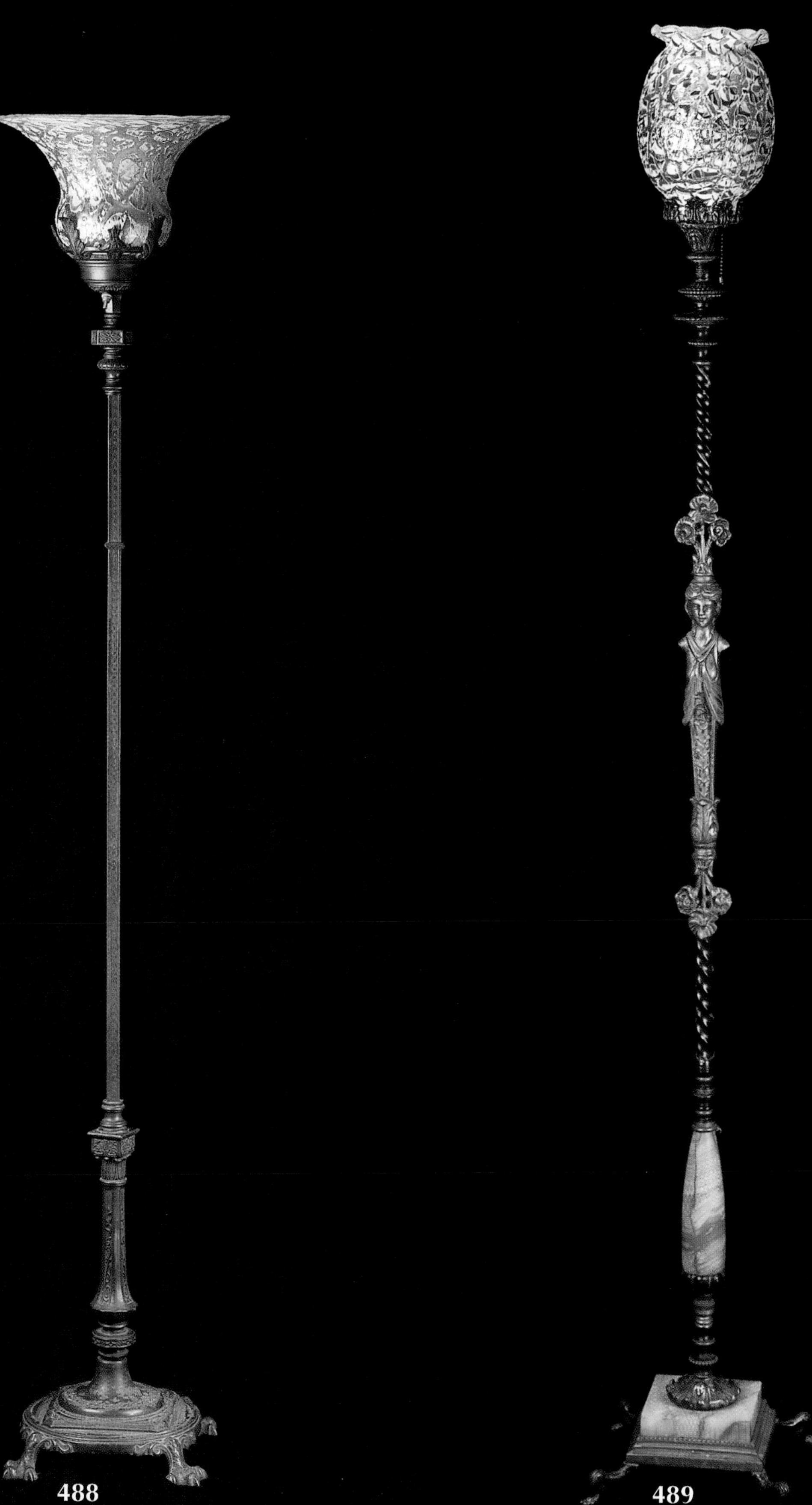

488

489

Spider Webbed Lamps

490

491

492

TABLE LAMPS

493

494

495

496

497

498

499

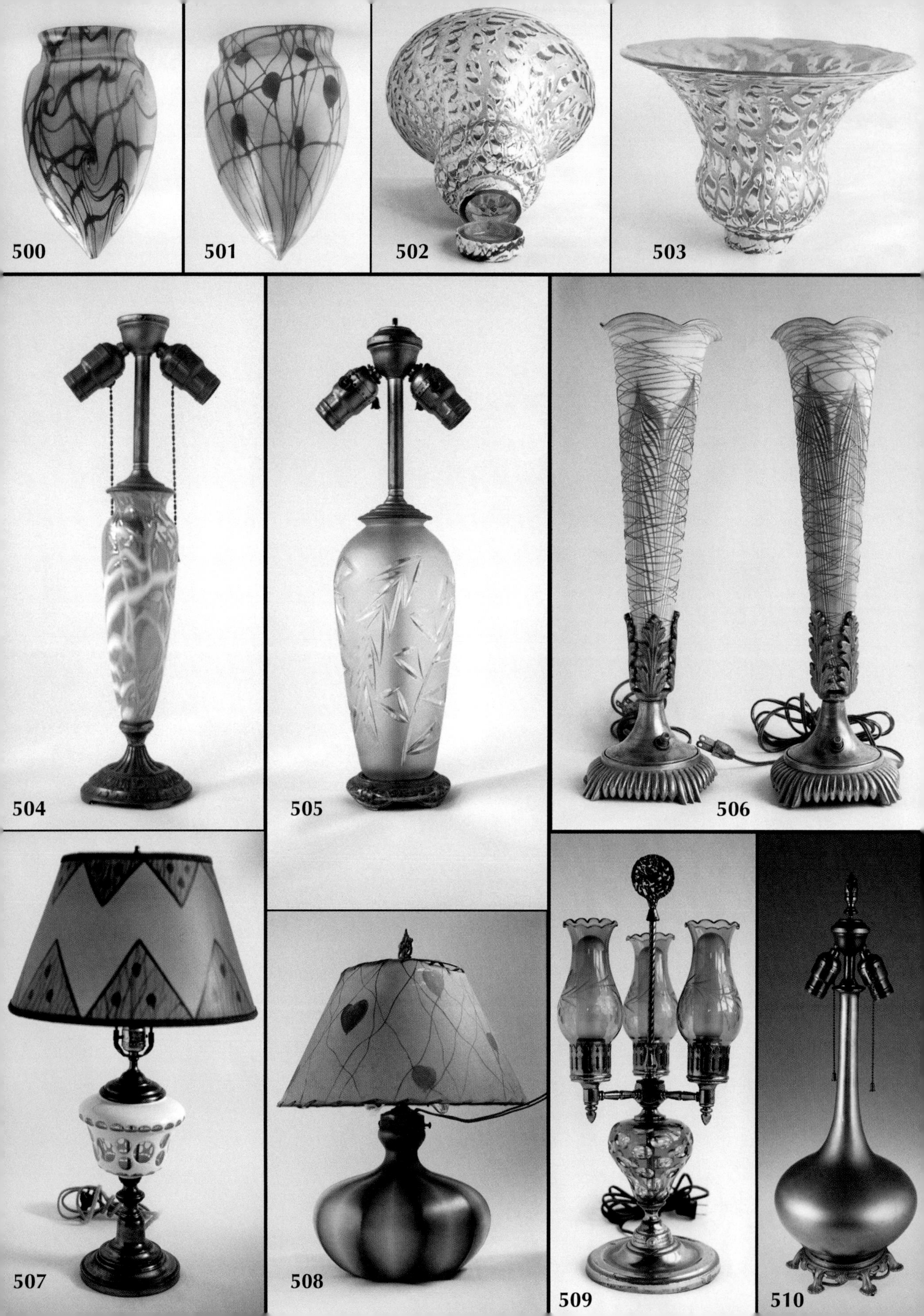
500
501
502
503
504
505
506
507
508
509
510

511

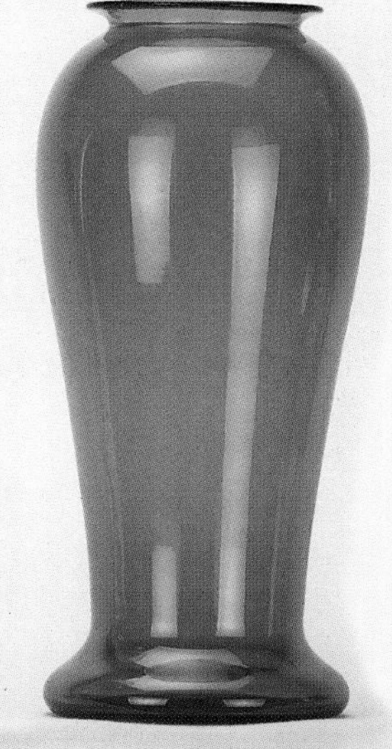

512

Vases

Cut and Banded Lamps

516

Bubble Vases

513

514

Pulled Feather

515

KIMBLE CLUTHRA GLASS

517

518

519

520

521

522

523

Descriptions to Color Pages

Descriptions are provided for each piece shown in the color section of this book (pages 33-112).

COVER:

Vase, opal with blue Pulled Feather decoration. Banded in gold with applied spider webbing and gold lustre interior. Height 9".

PAGE 33:

1. Vase, opal with blue and gold Heart & Vine decoration with gold lustre spider webbing. Height 13".

PAGE 34:

Glass courtesy of the Somershein Collection.

2. Vase, opal with blue and gold Heart decoration and applied gold spider webbing. Height 10".
3. Vase, opal with blue and gold Heart decoration and applied gold spider webbing. Height 12".
4. Covered jar in opal, with blue and gold Heart decoration and applied gold spider webbing. Height 9".
5. Vase, opal with blue and gold Heart decoration and applied gold spider webbing. Height 10".
6. Vase, opal with blue and gold Heart decoration and applied gold spider webbing. Height 5".

PAGE 35:

7. Vase, gold lustre with blue Heart & Vine decoration. Height 6 1/2".
8. Vase, silver blue lustre with opal Heart & Vine decoration. Height 9 1/2".
9. Vase, gold lustre with green Heart & Vine decoration. Height 6".
10. Vase, cased green over opal, with applied opal Heart & Vine decoration. Height 10"
11. Vase, golden yellow lustre with opal Heart & Vine decoration, pinched bottom and squared top. Height 12".

PAGE 36:

Glass courtesy of the Cunningham Johnson Collection.

12. Vase, silver blue lustre with opal Heart & Vine decoration, and applied lustre foot. Height 12".
13. Vase, silver blue lustre with opal Heart & Vine decoration, and applied lustre foot. Height 9".
14. Vase, blue lustre with opal Heart & Vine decoration. Height 7".
15. Vase, dark blue to silver blue lustre with opal Heart & Vine decoration. Height 10".
16. Vase, dark blue with silver blue lustre Coil decoration. Height 9 1/2".
17. Vase, dark blue lustre with opal Heart & Vine decoration. Height 6".
18. Vase, silver blue lustre with opal King Tut decoration. Height 6 1/2".

PAGE 37:

19. Vase, dark blue with silver blue lustre Heart & Vine decoration. Height 10 1/2".
20. Vase, golden orange lustre with applied blue Heart & Vine decoration. Height 6 1/2".
21. Vase, blue lustre with opal Heart & Vine decoration and lustre applied foot. Height 12".
22. Vase, dark blue with silver blue Heart & Vine decoration. Height 8 1/2".
23. Vase, golden orange lustre, with applied green Heart & Vine decoration, and applied lustre foot. Height 8".
24. Covered jar, golden orange lustre with applied green heart and vine decoration. Height 9".
25. Vase, golden orange with applied green Heart & Vine decoration. Height 7 1/2".
26. Bowl, opal with gold and blue Heart & Vine decoration, gold lustre interior. Height 4 1/2", diameter 10".
27. Puff or powder box, dark blue with silver blue Heart & Vine decoration. Height 3 1/2", width 4 1/2".

PAGE 38:

28. Stick vase, golden orange with blue Coil decoration. Height 13".
29. Vase, golden orange with blue King Tut decoration. Height 11 1/2".
30. Covered jar in golden orange with blue Coil decoration. Height 7".
31. Wall sconce in golden orange with blue Coil decoration, and applied ambergris knob on bottom. Height 10".
32. Rose bowl vase, golden orange with blue Heart & Vine decoration, applied and lustre foot. Height 5".
33. Vase, golden orange with blue Heart & Vine decoration. Height 10".
34. Vase, golden orange with blue Heart & Vine decoration. Height 8".

PAGE 39:

35. Vase, silver blue lustre with opal Heart & Vine decoration. Height 10".

36. Vase, silver blue lustre with opal Heart & Vine decoration. Height 10½".

37. Vase, silver blue lustre with opal Heart & Vine decoration. Height 7".

38. Vase, dark blue lustre with opal Heart & Vine decoration. Height 6".

39. Covered jar with dark blue lustre and opal Heart & Vine decoration. Height, 7".

40. Vase, silver blue lustre with opal Heart & Vine decoration. Height 4".

PAGE 40:

Glass courtesy of the Scialdone Collection.

41. Rose bowl vase, golden orange with golden yellow highlights and applied gold lustre foot. Height 5".

42. Rose Bowl vase, deep blue lustre with silver blue Heart & Vine decoration and applied gold lustre foot. Height 5".

43. Rose bowl vase, silver blue lustre with opal Coil decoration and applied lustre foot. Height 5".

44. Rose bowl vase, green with gold King Tut decoration and applied lustre foot. Height 5".

45. Rose bowl vase, golden orange with opal Pulled Feather decoration, banded in blue and applied gold webbing, and applied lustre foot. Height 5".

46. Rose bowl vase, yellow lustre with floral and vine cutting and applied foot. Height 5".

47. Rose bowl vase, dark blue with silver lustre Heart & Vine decoration and applied lustre foot. Height 5".

PAGE 41:

48. Vase, opal with blue Pulled Feather banded in gold and applied gold threading decoration. Height 9".

49. Vase, opal with blue Pulled Feather banded in gold, and applied gold threading decoration. Height 6½".

50. Trumpet vase, opal with blue Pulled Feather banded in gold decoration, with an applied lustre foot. Height 10".

51. Vase, opal with blue Pulled Feather, banded in gold and applied gold threading. Height 8".

52. Vase, opal with blue Pulled Feather, banded in gold and applied gold threading. Height 7½".

53. Vase, opal with golden orange Pulled Feather, banded in blue and applied lustre foot. Quezal look alludes to early production. Height 7".

54. Vase, opal with golden orange Pulled Feather, banded in blue. Quezal look alludes to early production. Height 6".

PAGE 42:

55. Vase, golden orange lustre with opal and gold Pulled Feather banded in blue and applied gold Coil decoration. Height 10".

56. Vase, blue lustre with opal Pulled Feather and applied gold lustre Coil decoration. Height 8½".

57. Vase, blue silhouetted Pulled Feather on opal. Height 11".

58. Vase, blue silhouetted Pulled Feather on opal. Height 6".

PAGE 43:

59. Silver blue lustre vase, with applied spider webbing. Height 6".

60. Opal vase, with applied blue Pulled Feather, topped with a gold band and applied gold spider webbing. Height 9".

61. Dark blue lustre vase, with applied gold spider webbing. Height 7".

62. Candy jar, gold lustre with applied gold spider webbing and applied lustre foot and finial. Height 10".

63. Covered jar, marigold lustre with applied gold spider webbing. Height 9".

64. Lamp blank, opal with green and gold Heart decoration and applied gold spider webbing. Height 7½".

PAGE 44:

65. Vase, gold lustre with applied opal Coil pattern. Height 6".

66. Vase, opal with applied blue Coil decoration Height 10½".

67. Vase, gold lustre with applied blue Coil decoration. Height 10".

68. Vase, opal with marigold and blue hearts, and spider webbing decoration. Height 11½".

69. Vase, blue lustre with spider webbing decoration. Height 8".

70. Vase, marigold lustre, with opal and marigold Pulled Feather banded in blue decoration, and gold spider webbing. Height 8½".

PAGE 45:

71. Vase, opal with gold Coil decoration. Height 8½".

72. Vase, golden orange with applied blue Coil decoration. Height 10".

73. Vase, opal with applied gold Coil decoration. Height 13".

74. Vase, silver blue with applied opal Coil decoration and applied lustred foot. Height 12".

75. Vase, gold lustre with applied opal Coil decoration, and applied lustred foot. Height $8^1/_2$".

PAGE 46:

76. Vase, opal with blue and gold King Tut decoration. Height 10".

77. Vase, opal with marigold Heart and gold Vine decoration. Height 13".

78. Vase, opal with green and gold Coil decoration. Height 10".

79. Vase, opal with marigold Coil decoration and applied lustre foot. Height $9^1/_2$".

80. Vase, gold lustre with opal King Tut decoration. Height $9^1/_2$".

81. Candlestick in blue and white over ambergris. Moorish Crackle and lustred. Height $4^1/_2$".

82. Vase, opal with blue Coil decoration. Height 6".

83. Vase, opal with applied gold lustre vertical ribs and gold lustre coil trim around opening. Height $9^1/_2$".

PAGE 47:

84. Vase, blue and white crackle. Pulled Feather over an ambergris base and lustred, with an applied marigold foot with opal Pulled Feather banded in blue decoration. Height 11".

PAGE 48:

Glass courtesy of the Izzo Collection.

85. Cameo vase, in three-layer cased glass, blue over opal over ambergris with acid cutting in a floral design. Height 7"

PAGE 49:

Glass courtesy of the Somershein Collection.

86. Vase, cameo acid cut, triple cased, opal over green over crystal, in a floral motif. Height 11".

PAGE 50:

Glass courtesy of the Scialdone Collection.

87. Vase, pink Lady Gay Rose with gold King Tut decoration. Height 10".

88. Puff or powder box in light pink Lady Gay Rose with gold King Tut decoration, with gold lustre foot. Star cutting on top. Height 3", width $4^3/_4$".

89. Vase, light pink Lady Gay Rose with gold King Tut decoration. Height $6^1/_2$".

90. Vase, raspberry Lady Gay Rose with red and gold wavy decoration. Height 8".

91. Vase, deep pink Lady Gay Rose with gold King Tut decoration. Height $12^1/_4$".

92. Vase, hard ribbed, cased opal over pink. Height 7".

PAGE 51:

93. Vase, cased in green over opal with applied gold King Tut decoration and applied lustre foot. Height $8^1/_2$".

94. Vase, pink Lady Gay Rose with applied gold King Tut decoration. Height $13^1/_2$".

95. Vase, apple green cased with applied gold King Tut decoration. Height $8^1/_2$".

96. Vase, cased in apple green with gold King Tut decoration. Height $8^1/_2$".

97. Vase, pink Lady Gay Rose with applied gold King Tut decoration. Height 9".

98. Stick vase, green with applied gold King Tut decoration. Height $12^3/_4$".

99. Vase, light green with applied gold King Tut decoration. Height 7".

100. Vase, light pink Lady Gay Rose with applied gold King Tut decoration. Height 4".

101. Vase, dark green with applied gold King Tut decoration. Height $8^1/_2$".

PAGE 52:

Glass courtesy of the Izzo Collection.

102. Vase, Lady Gay Rose with gold King Tut decoration. Height $9^1/_2$".

103. Vase, apple green with gold King Tut decoration. Height $10^1/_2$".

104. Stick vase, gold lustre with opal King Tut decoration. Height 16".

105. Covered jar, apple green with gold King Tut decoration. Height 7".

106. Vase, silver blue with gold King Tut decoration. Height $10^1/_2$".

PAGE 53:

107. Vase, green with gold King Tut decoration. Height 12".

108. Vase, light pink Lady Gay Rose with gold King Tut decoration. Height $6^1/_2$".

109. Vase, Green with gold King Tut decoration. Height 14".

110. Jar, Lady Gay Rose with gold King Tut decoration, no top. Height 6".

111. Vase, light green with gold King Tut decoration. Height $10^1/_2$".

PAGE 54:

112. Vase, golden orange lustre with green King Tut decoration. Height 8".

113. Vase, apple green with gold King Tut decoration and lustre interior. Height 8 1/2".

114. Vase, light pink Lady Gay Rose with gold King Tut decoration. Height 7".

115. Trumpet vase, golden yellow lustre with blue King Tut decoration, lustre applied foot. Height 14 1/2".

116. Bowl, golden yellow lustre with applied blue King Tut decoration, and applied lustre foot. Height 4", width 6".

PAGE 55:

117. Vase, blue and gold King Tut decoration on an opal base. Height 10".

118. Vase, red Lady Gay Rose with applied foot, all with gold King Tut decoration. Height 11".

119. Vase, golden yellow with blue King Tut decoration. Height 7".

120. Vase, apple green footed with gold King Tut decoration, lustred foot and gold lustre interior. Height 10".

121. Vase, opal with gold King Tut decoration. Height 10".

122. Vase, golden yellow lustre with opal King Tut decoration. Height 7".

123. Vase, opal with blue and gold King Tut decoration and gold lustre interior. Height 6 1/2".

124. Vase, deep pink Lady Gay Rose with gold King Tut decoration. Height 9".

125. Vase, silver blue lustre with opal King Tut decoration, blue lustre interior. Height 7".

126. Vase, pink Lady Gay Rose with gold King Tut decoration, gold lustre interior. Height 6 1/2".

127. Vase, apple green with gold King Tut decoration. Height 6".

PAGE 56:

Glass courtesy of the Teal/Freeman Collection.
(Glass only measurement)

128. Perfume, light pink Lady Gay Rose with gold King Tut decoration. Height 6 1/2".

129. Perfume, dark blue with silver blue King Tut decoration. Height 6 1/2".

130. Perfume, golden yellow lustre. Height 6 1/2".

131. Perfume, deep pink Lady Gay Rose, with gold King Tut decoration. Height 6 1/2".

132. Perfume, opal with gold wavy decoration. Height 6 1/2".

PAGE 57:

Glass courtesy of the Author's Collection.

133. Car vase, light green with applied gold King Tut decoration and gold lustre interior. Height 8".

134. Car vase, dark pink Lady Gay Rose with applied gold Coil decoration, and opal bottom cut (six-sided) to a point. Height 8 1/2".

PAGE 58:

135. Vase, opal with blue and marigold Coil decoration. Height 10".

136. Vase, opal with blue and gold King Tut decoration. Height 10".

137. Vase, golden orange with fine blue wavy decoration at top half and wider blue wavy decoration at bottom half and applied gold webbing. Height 9".

138. Vase, opal with gold King Tut decoration. Height 10".

139. Vase, opal with blue and gold King Tut decoration. Height 9 1/2".

PAGE 59:

Glass courtesy of the Author's Collection.

140. Deep pink Lady Gay Rose vase with triple Pulled Feather decoration all in gold and all outlined in opal, with gold lustre interior. Height 9".

PAGE 60:

Glass courtesy of the Strovel Collection.

141. Vase, green hard ribbed with gold lustre interior. Height 8".

142. Beehive vase, red Lady Gay Rose with optic ribbing. Height 10".

143. Stick vase, green optic ribbed. Height 18".

144. Vase, deep pink Lady Gay Rose with optic ribbing. Height 12".

145. Vase, orange red, hard ribbed. Height 7".

146. Jar, reddish, hard ribbed without top. Height 10".

PAGE 61:

147. Opal vase with applied vertical ribs in gold lustre and applied silver blue lustre top trimmed in white and decorated with white and dark blue criss-crossing bands. Silver blue lustre applied ring around collar. Height 10".

PAGE 62:

148. Vase, grotesque style crackle, cased crystal over opal over red, and hard ribbed. Rolled over top exposing reddish interior. Height 13".

PAGE 63:
Glass courtesy of the Somershein Collection.
149. Vase, dark blue lustre Moorish Crackle. Height 9".
150. Lava vase, green and gold lustre Egyptian Crackle, random gold threading with deep pink interior (experimental). Height 9".
151. Lava vase, red Egyptian Crackle over opal with lustre. Height 8".

PAGE 64:
Glass courtesy of the Izzo Collection.
152. Covered jar, red and opal Moorish Crackle on ambergris and lustred. Height 8".
153. Vase, golden yellow lustre Moorish Crackle with hard ribbing. Height 12".
154. Vase, red crystal crackle, bottle ball vase with lustre. Height 10½".
155. Lamp shade, blue and white Mutual Crackle with lustre. Height 8".
156. Vase, blue and white Mutual Crackle with lustre. Height 9".
157. Covered jar, red and opal Moorish Crackle on ambergris and lustre. Height 8".

PAGE 65:
158. Vase, Moorish Crackle ball bottle vase, blue and white crackle over ambergris body and lustred. Height 10".
159. Vase, Moorish Crackle ball bottle vase, green and white crackle over ambergris body and lustred. Height 10".
160. Vase, Moorish Crackle ball bottle vase, blue and white crackle over ambergris body and lustred. Height 6".
161. Vase, Moorish Crackle vase blue and white over crystal and lustred. Height 10".
162. Vase, Moorish Crackle, green and white over ambergris base and lustred. Height 9½".

PAGE 66:
163. Vase, blue crystal crackle, hard ribbed with lustre. Height 10".
164. Pitcher, red crystal crackle with applied handle. Height 8½".
165. Vase, green crystal crackle with lustre. Height 10½".
166. Vase, red hard ribbed Moorish Crackle with lustre. Height 7½".
167. Vase, red crystal crackle with lustre. Height 9½".
168. Vase, orange red crystal crackle with lustre. Height 8".
169. Vase, red ribbed crackle over crystal, with lustre. Height 6".
170. Bowl in blue crystal crackle. Height 3½", width 8".
171. Pitcher in red top and blue bottom with opal Pulled Feathers in center and applied red handle (experimental). Height 10".

PAGE 67:
172. Blue crystal crackle. Height 8".
173. Vase, amethyst crystal crackle (experimental). Height 14½".
174. Bowl, Venetian Lace with applied foot. Height 4½", width 15½".

PAGE 68:
Glass courtesy of the Scialdone Collection.
175. Bottle ball vase, Moorish Crackle green over ambergris with blue lustre highlights. Height 8".
176. Vase, blue lustre crackle with opal and ambergris Lava decoration. Height 7".
177. Grotesque crackle vase with vertical rows of dark blue over crystal and lustred. Height 13".

PAGE 69:
Glass courtesy of the Author's Collection.
178. Covered jar, golden orange lustre with applied gold spider webbing. Height 9".
179. Covered jar, silver blue lustre. Height 9".
180. Covered jar, red Lady Gay Rose hard ribbed. Height 9".
181. Covered jar, silver blue lustre with applied opal Heart & Vine. Height 7".
182. Covered jar, green and white Moorish Crackle on ambergris with lustre. Height 9".
183. Covered Jar, green with applied gold King Tut pattern. Height 7".
184. Covered Jar, cased red cut to clear. Height 7".
185. Jar, blue and white crackle with lustre, no lid. Height 6".

PAGE 70:
186. Vase, golden yellow lustre. Height 9½".
187. Vase, golden yellow lustre. Height 14".
188. Vase, dark blue to silver blue lustre. Height 12".
189. Vase, silver blue lustre with fluted top and gold lustre applied foot. Height 9½".
190. Vase, golden orange lustre. Height 12"
191. Vase, red over ambergris with lustre, and applied lustre foot. Height 8".
192. Vase, blue lustre w/gold highlights. Height 10".
193. Vase, blue lustre with applied lustre foot. Height 8½".

194. Vase, golden yellow lustre. Height 8$^1/_2$".

PAGE 71:

195. Vase, silver blue lustre. Height 11".
196. Vase, gold lustre with applied lustre foot. Height 14$^1/_2$".
197. Covered jar, silver blue lustre. Height 9"
198. One of a pair of beehive vases, golden yellow lustre. Height 8".
199. Vase, silver blue lustre. Height 6".
200. One of a pair of beehive vases, golden yellow lustre. Height 8".

PAGE 72:

201. Vase, gold lustre with hard ribbing. Height 12$^1/_2$".
202. Syrup dispenser in golden yellow. Height 10$^1/_2$".
203. Vase, golden orange. Height 11$^1/_2$".
204. Vase, cased opal over green. Height 8".
205. Vase, cased opal over pink with gold lustre foot. Height 12".
206. Vase, golden yellow lustre. Height 8".

PAGE 73:

Glass courtesy of the Matalucci Collection.

207. Covered jar in silver blue lustre with gold lustre finial. Height 11".
208. Vase, baluster form in golden orange with blue King Tut decoration, gold lustre applied handles and foot. Height 12".
209. Vase, silver blue lustre with opal Heart & Vine decoration. Height 10".
210. Vase, golden orange with opal and gold Pulled Feather, banded in blue decoration and all over gold threading. Height 10".
211. Vase, golden orange with green King Tut decoration. Height 9".
212. Vase, silver blue lustre. Height 10".
213. Nappy in gold lustre. Height 3", width 4$^1/_2$".
214. Compote in custard color, ambergris over opal with blue trim on rim and applied yellow lustre foot. Height 3$^1/_2$", width 9"
215. Almond dish in gold lustre with fluted top. Height 2", width 5$^1/_2$".

PAGE 74:

216. Vase, opal with gold all-over spattered decoration, fluted top and lustre applied foot. Height 14".

PAGE 75:

Glass courtesy of the Author's Collection.

217. Vase, acid cut back, gold lustre cut away exposing an ambergris base and leaving a gold lustre floral and flame motif. Height 12".

PAGE 76:

218. Vase, red overlay to clear with opal and red Peacock Feather decoration. Height 10".
219. Vase, green overlay to clear with opal and green Peacock Feather decoration, applied foot. Height 12".
220. Vase, red overlay to clear with opal and red peacock feather decoration. Height 12".
221. Serving plate, red overlay to clear with opal and red Peacock Feather decoration. Diameter 14$^1/_2$".
222. Flower Spill, crystal with blue and opal Peacock Feather design. Height 8".
223. Bowl, Blue overlay to clear with blue and opal Peacock Feather with applied silver lustre foot. Height 3$^1/_2$", width 13".

PAGE 77:

Glass courtesy of the Matalucci Collection.

224. Goblet in red over crystal with opal and red Peacock Feather, yellow lustre stem and foot. Height 6$^1/_2$".
225. Cocktail in red over crystal with opal and red Peacock Feather and red stem and foot. Height 4$^1/_2$".
226. Goblet in ruby optic ribbed with Spanish yellow stem and ruby foot. Height 8$^1/_2$".
227. Glass in ruby optic ribbed. Height 6$^1/_2$".
228. Champagne in ruby flashed with opal rim, Spanish yellow stem and ruby foot. Height 6".
229. Champagne ruby flashed with Spanish yellow stem and ruby foot. Height 6".
230. Pair candlesticks, ruby with Spanish yellow holder and stem, with ruby foot. Height 6".
231. Compote, ruby optic ribbed with Spanish yellow stem, ruby foot. Height 4", width7$^1/_2$".
232. Lemonade glass in ruby optic rib. Height 5$^1/_2$".
233. Finger bowl in ruby optic rib. Height 2", width 4$^1/_2$".
234. Salad plate, ruby, with opal and ruby Peacock Feather decoration. Diameter 8".
235. Creamer, ruby flashed, with opal and ruby Peacock Feather decoration and crystal applied handle and foot. Height 3$^1/_2$".
236. Bullion in ruby with applied Spanish yellow handles and ruby foot. Height 2$^1/_2$", width 6".
237. Cup in ruby flashed with opal and red Peacock Feather, no handle. Height 3".

PAGE 78:

238. Vase, blue overlay to clear with opal and blue

Peacock Feather decoration, with applied foot. Height 8".

239. Vase, red overlay to clear with opal and red Peacock Feather decoration, with applied foot. Height 12".

240. Iced tea glass, green over yellow lustre with opal and green Peacock Feather and applied lustre foot. Height 6".

241. Flower spill, crystal with opal and red Pulled Feather decoration. Height 8".

242. Vase, blue overlay to clear with opal and blue Peacock Feather decoration. Height 8".

243. Bowl, red overlay to clear with opal and red Peacock Feather decoration, geometric and feather cutting and applied light ambergris foot. Height 5 1/2", width 10".

244. Bowl, red overlay to clear with opal and red Peacock Feather decoration. Height 3", width 12 1/2".

245. Compote, green overlay to clear with opal and white Peacock Feather decoration, and crystal stem and foot. Height 6 1/2", width 8".

246. Iced tea glass, blue overlay to crystal with blue and opal Peacock Feather decoration, with feather cutting and applied yellow lustre foot, Height 6".

247. Compote, red overlay to crystal with opal and red Peacock Feather decoration, and crystal stem and foot, and feather cutting. Height 6 1/2", width 8".

PAGE 79:

248. Champagne, red with Spanish yellow stem and red foot. Height 6".

249. Goblet, blue with Spanish yellow stem and blue foot. Height 8 1/2".

250. Goblet, clear crystal. Height 8 1/2".

251. Goblet, red with Spanish yellow stem and red foot. Height 8 1/2".

252. Goblet, ice blue crystal. Height 9".

253. Goblet, amethyst. Height 8".

254. Goblet, green over crystal with geometric cutting. Height 6".

255. Lemonade glass, red optic ribbed. Height 5 1/2".

256. Glass, blue over crystal with geometric cutting. Height 5".

257. Claret, gold lustre. Height 5 1/2".

258. Cocktail whimsy, ambergris with fluted top and white applied coil on bowl and foot. Height 4 1/2".

259. Glass, green over crystal with geometric cutting. Height 4 1/2".

260. Sherry, blue over crystal with blue and opal Peacock Feather decoration and Spanish yellow foot and feather cutting. Height 3 1/2".

261. Sherbet, gold lustre with blue Coil decoration. Height 3 1/2".

262. Claret in gold lustre. Height 4 1/2".

263. Cocktail in blue over crystal with blue and opal Peacock Feather decoration, crystal stem and foot. Height 5".

264. Sugar bowl in yellow lustre with applied handles and floral cutting. Height 4".

265. Creamer in yellow lustre with applied handle and floral cutting. Height 4 1/2".

266. Cocktail in red with white trim and light ambergris stem and foot. Height 5".

267. Sherbet in yellow lustre. Height 3 1/2".

PAGE 80:

268. Bowl in yellow lustre with opal Pulled Feather, banded in blue and applied foot in the same decoration. Height 9", width 10".

269. Bowl, blue over crystal with triple Pulled Feather—pink surrounded by opal, rose and vine cutting, applied crystal foot. Height 5" , width 10".

270. Vase, blue over crystal with opal and blue Peacock Feather, applied foot in the same decoration. Height 10".

271. Trumpet Vase, blue over crystal with opal and blue Peacock Feather with applied foot in the same decoration and double ambergris ring at the foot. Height 14".

272. Bowl in Venetian Lace, ambergris with opal Pulled Feather banded in blue center and circular opal threads around rim, trimmed in blue. Height 3", width 15".

PAGE 81:

Glass courtesy of the Strovel Collection.

273. Bowl, red over crystal with opal Peacock Feather decoration and fine cross hatching cut center. Height 4", width 10 1/2".

274. Trumpet Vase, blue over crystal with opal and blue Peacock Feather decoration and with applied Pulled Feather decorated foot. Height 13 1/2".

275. Vase, green over crystal with opal and blue Peacock Feather decoration. Height 12".

276. Vase, blue over crystal with opal and blue Peacock Feather decoration and floral and vine cutting. Height 9".

277. Bowl, yellow lustre with opal Peacock Feather banded in blue decoration. Height 4",width 10 1/2".

278. Bowl, blue over crystal with opal and blue Peacock Feather decoration. Height 4", width $10^1/_2$".

279. Bouillon cup in red over crystal with opal Peacock Feather decoration, and applied yellow lustre handles and cutting around top. Height 2", width 6".

280. Flower spill in green over crystal with opal and green Peacock Feather decoration. Height $5^1/_2$".

281. Compote in red over crystal with opal Peacock Feather decoration and crystal stem and foot. Height $4^1/_2$", width 6".

PAGE 82:

282. Vase, blue over crystal with opal and blue Peacock Feather decoration. Height $12^1/_2$".

283. Bowl in red over crystal with opal and red Peacock Feather decoration and applied ambergris foot. Height 4", width 11".

284. Decanter in blue over ambergris with opal and blue Peacock Feather decoration, with matching stopper and applied lustre foot. Height 14".

285. and
286. Console set, bowl and pair of candlesticks in green over crystal with opal and green Peacock Feather decoration, applied ambergris foot on candlesticks. Bowl $2^1/_2$" x 14", candlesticks $3^1/_2$" x 4".

287. Puff box in blue over crystal with opal and blue Peacock Feather decoration, and cross-hatch cut top. Height 3", width $4^1/_2$".

288. Bowl in blue over crystal with opal and pink Peacock Feather decoration in center and opal feathering all around, opal trim on rim and applied ambergris foot. Height 4", width 11".

289. Cup and saucer in blue over crystal with opal and blue Peacock Feather decoration, with applied crystal handle on cup and cut center on saucer. Cup height 3", saucer diameter $4^1/_2$".

PAGE 83:

290. Vase, silver lustre with opal Heart & Vine decoration. Height 12".

291. Plate in green over crystal with opal and green Peacock Feather decoration, and all over lustre. Diameter 15".

292. Covered jar in red over crystal with opal and red Peacock Feather decoration. Height 9".

293. Plate in yellow lustre outside, center in opal with blue Pulled Feather, banded in yellow lustre decoration. Diameter 11".

294. Vase, cased blue cut to clear in geometric and vine cutting. Height 10".

PAGE 84:

295. Bread and butter plate in green over crystal, optic ribbed with cut center. Diameter 6".

296. Lay plate in green over crystal, optic ribbed with cut center. Diameter 11".

297. Salad plate in green over crystal with opal and green Peacock Feather and cut center. Diameter 8".

298. Salad plate in blue over crystal with blue pulled center surrounded with opal pulls. Diameter $7^1/_2$".

299. Salad plate in blue over crystal with blue flanked by white triple Pulled Feather. Diameter 8".

300. Salad plate in blue over crystal with opal and blue Peacock Feather decoration. Diameter 8".

301. Salad plate in laced ribbon on crystal with white criss-crossing lines in a fan shape effect. Diameter 8".

302. Salad plate in yellow lustre with cutting around perimeter. Diameter 8".

PAGE 85:

303. Vase, green over crystal with opal and green Peacock Feather. Height 7".

304. Bowl in green over crystal with opal and green Peacock Feather. Height 4", width $9^1/_2$".

305. Compote in green over crystal with opal and green Peacock Feather, and light ambergris stem and foot. Height $6^1/_2$", width $8^1/_2$".

306. Salad plate in yellow lustre. Diameter 8".

307. Lemonade in ambergris with optic rib and green trim. Height $5^1/_2$".

308. Iced tea in ambergris with green trim. Height 6".

309. Finger bowl in green with opal trim. Height $2^1/_2$", width $4^1/_2$".

310. Finger bowl and under plate in ambergris with green trim. Bowl $2^1/_2$" x 5", plate $6^1/_2$".

311. Salad plate in yellow lustre with optic ribbed and green trim and scalloped edge. Diameter $8^1/_2$".

PAGE 86:

312. Vase, amethyst optic ribbed with applied foot. Height 8".

313. Vase, deep amethyst optic ribbed with applied foot. Height l6".

314. Vase, light amethyst optic ribbed. Height 6".

315. Compote, amethyst optic ribbed. Height $6^1/_2$", width $5^1/_2$".

316. Finger bowl and saucer, amethyst optic ribbed Bowl 3" x 4", saucer 1" x 6".
317. Champagne glass, amethyst optic ribbed Height 6".

PAGE 87:
318. Lay plate in blue optic rib, scalloped edge. Diameter 11½"".
319. Salad plate in blue optic rib, scalloped edge. Diameter 8½".
320. Iced tea in blue optic rib. Height 6".
321. Goblet in blue optic rib with yellow lustre stem and blue foot. Height 8½".
322. Finger bowl and under plate in blue with scalloped edge. Bowl 2½" x 5", plate 6".
323. Finger bowl and under plate in blue optic rib with scalloped edge. Bowl 2½" x 5", plate 6".

PAGE 88:
324. Salad plate in blue over crystal with Peacock Feather decoration. Diameter 8".
325. Salad plate in yellow lustre with geometric feather cutting. Diameter 8½".
326. Salad plate in red over crystal with Peacock Feather decoration. Diameter 7½".
327. Salad plate in green optic rib with scalloped edge. Diameter 8".
328. Salad plate in amethyst optic rib with scalloped edge. Diameter 8".
329. Salad plate in blue with scalloped edge. Diameter 8".
330. Salad plate in ice blue. Diameter 7".
331. Salad plate in gold lustre. Diameter 7".

PAGE 89:
332. Ice blue bowl. Height 2½", width 14".
333. Bowl in blue optic rib with scalloped edge and white trim. Height 3", width 14½".
334. Bowl in blue crystal crackle. Height 3" x 13"
335. Bowl in blue over crystal with opal and pink Peacock Feather decoration in center and opal feathering all around, opal trim on rim and applied ambergris foot. Height 4", width 11".
336. Underplate in green over ambergris crackle. Diameter 11".

PAGE 90:
Glass courtesy of the Cunningham Johnson Collection.
337. Vase, blue over crystal with star burst cutting. Height 8½".
338. Vase, blue over crystal with star burst cutting, applied foot. Height 10".
339. Vase, amethyst optic rib. Height 10".
340. Candy jar in amethyst optic rib. Height 8".
341. Goblet in green with applied white coil on bowl and foot crystal stem and green foot. Height 6½".
342. Puff or powder box in silver blue lustre over blue base with cutting around base and lid and star cutting in center of lid. Height 3½", width 3".
343. Bowl in yellow lustre, footed with white trim around top edge, blue and white criss-crossing bands all around. Height 4½", width 10½".
344. Candlesticks in red with flared top with opal and red Peacock Feather. Height 3½", width 4½".

PAGE 91:
Glass courtesy of the Matalucci Collection.
345. Vase, red over crystal with geometric cutting. Height 8".
346. Trumpet vase, blue over crystal, geometric cutting with applied foot and double crystal ring around stem. Height 14".
347. Vase, green over crystal with floral and feather cutting. Height 8".
348. Vase, red over crystal with geometric cutting. Height 8".
349. Vase, yellow lustre with green applied banding and floral cutting. Height 7".
350. Cake tier in red over crystal with floral and geometric cutting. Height 12", diameter 10" and 8".
351. Cocktail blue over crystal with opal and blue Peacock Feather and feather cutting, and yellow lustre stem foot. Height 4½".
352. Goblet in red over crystal, cut with an applied crystal stem and foot. Height 7".
353. Bouillon in yellow lustre with floral cutting and applied handles. Height 2", width 6".
354. Glass in green over crystal with geometric cutting. Height 5".
355. Glass in red over crystal with geometric cutting. Height 5".

PAGE 92:
356. Vase, red cut to clear cased with geometric cutting. Height 10".
357. Vase, red cut to clear cased with geometric cutting. Height 10".
358. Vase, red cut to clear cased with floral cutting. Height 10".
359. Vase, red cut to clear cased with geometric cutting. Height 8".
360. Covered jar, red cut to clear cased with geometric cutting. Height 7".

PAGE 93:

361. Vase, yellow lustre with cross hatch cutting. Height 7".

362. Flower spill, red over crystal with floral and geometric cutting. Height 6".

363. Decanter, yellow lustre with floral and vine cutting. Height $14^1/_2$".

364. Vase, yellow lustre with blue band decoration, and cut with floral pattern. Height $7^1/_2$".

365. Rose bowl vase, silver lustre with geometric cutting and applied foot. Height 5".

366. Goblet, green cut to clear with crystal stem. Height 7"

367. Vase, red over crystal with geometric cutting. Height 10"

368. Vase, yellow lustre with opal band decoration and grape and vine cutting. Height $6^1/_2$"

369. Pair candlesticks, yellow lustre with leaf and flower cutting. Height $3^1/_2$", width $3^1/_2$".

370. Goblet, blue over crystal w/geometric zipper cutting and crystal stem and foot. Height 7".

PAGE 94:

371. Match holder whimsy, in blue crystal crackle. Made from a candlestick. Height 4".

372. Ashtray in golden yellow lustre. Height $1^1/_2$" x 4".

373. Gold perfume. Height $6^1/_2$".

374. Gold perfume with blue King Tut decoration. Height 7".

375. Salad plate, pink center surrounded by opal pulled threads with floral and vine cutting. Diameter $7^1/_2$".

376. Plate, in wavy green decoration over light ambergris. Diameter $7^1/_2$".

377. Bowl, crystal lustre w/pink King Tut decoration and pink trim along edge. Height 2", width $4^1/_2$".

378. Plate in Venetian Lace with opal threading on yellow lustre, trimmed in green along edge and floral cutting in center. Diameter 11".

379. Compote in yellow lustre with green threading, green trim and twisted stem. Height 4", width $7^1/_2$".

PAGE 95:

380. Bowl in red over ambergris with Pulled Feather banded in blue decoration (experimental). Height 3", width 12".

381. Bowl in crystal with green pulled decoration. Height 3", width 11".

382. Salad plate in red over crystal optic rib with cut center. Diameter 8".

383. Bowl in yellow lustre with opal blue band decoration and geometric feather cutting in bottom and around circumference. Height 4", width $8^1/_2$".

384. Salad plate in green over crystal with geometric cutting. Diameter 8".

385. Vase, yellow lustre with floral and vine cutting all around. Height 9".

386. Vase, blue over crystal with circle cutting. Height 4".

387. Bubble vase, yellow lustre with optic rib and vertical rows of bubbles. Height $6^1/_2$".

388. Whimsy in green and white Moorish Crackle. Made from the bottom cutting of a torchiere shade to create opening. Diameter 3".

389. Whimsy in red and white Moorish Crackle. Made from the bottom cutting of a torchiere shade to create opening. Diameter 3".

390. Whimsy in red and white Moorish Crackle with cutting. Made from the bottom cutting of a torchiere shade to create opening. May have been used as an ashtray. Diameter 3".

PAGE 96:

391. Decanter in blue cut to crystal with cut stopper and matching cut shot glass. Height 12".

392. Decanter in green cut to crystal with cut stopper. Height 12".

393. Decanter in blue cut to crystal with double row of cutting on neck. Height 12".

394. Pair of candlesticks with flared top in blue with Peacock Feather decoration and ambergris foot. Height $3^1/_2$", width $4^1/_2$".

395. Candlesticks in green with flared top. Height $3^1/_2$", width $4^1/_2$".

396. Candlesticks in green with opal ring decoration in center. Height $3^1/_2$", width $4^1/_2$".

397. Amethyst candlestick in optic rib flared top. Height $3^1/_2$", width $4^1/_2$".

398. Candlestick in blue with white trim decoration, with blue foot and light ambergris holder and stem. Height 5".

399. Candlestick in yellow lustre with flared top. Height $3^1/_2$", width $4^1/_2$".

PAGE 97:

Glass courtesy of the Strovel Collection.

400. Yellow lustre sherbet trimmed in green. Height 5".

401. Champagne, Spanish yellow trimmed in green. Height 7".

402. Iced tea glass, Spanish yellow trimmed in green. Height 6".

403. Goblet, yellow lustre trimmed in green. Height $8^1/_2$".

404. Iced tea glass in red optic ribbed. Height 6".
405. Goblet, blue optic ribbed with Spanish yellow stem and blue foot. Height 8$^{1}/_{2}$".
406. Goblet, green over crystal with opal Peacock Feather and crystal stem and foot. Height 6$^{1}/_{2}$".
407. Yellow lustre goblet, with opal Peacock Feather, banded in blue and white trim around top edge. Height 7".
408. Parfait, red over crystal with red and opal Peacock Feather, crystal foot and feather cutting. Height 5$^{1}/_{2}$".
409. Sherbet, Spanish yellow with white Peacock Feather banded in blue, with white trim along top edge. Height 4".
410. Champagne, amethyst optic ribbed. Height 4".
411. Champagne, ruby red with Spanish yellow stem and red foot. Height 5$^{1}/_{2}$".
412. Goblet, red over crystal with opal Peacock Feather crystal stem and foot. Height 6".
413. Cocktail, blue over crystal with opal and blue Peacock Feather, crystal stem and foot. Height 5".
414. Sherbet, green over crystal with opal Peacock Feather and crystal stem and foot. Height 4$^{1}/_{2}$".
415. Sherbet, red over crystal with opal Peacock Feather. Height 3$^{1}/_{2}$".
416. Finger bowl, red with white trim. Height 2$^{1}/_{2}$", width 4$^{1}/_{2}$".
417. Finger bowl and plate, Spanish yellow trimmed in green. Height 2$^{1}/_{2}$" , width 5"; plate 6".
418. Finger bowl and plate in amethyst. Height 2$^{1}/_{2}$", width 4$^{1}/_{2}$"; plate 6".
419. Goblet, blue over crystal with geometric zipper cutting, crystal stem. Height 7".
420. Water glass, red trimmed in white with crystal foot. Height 6".
421. Goblet, green over crystal with geometric cutting and crystal stem and foot. Height 7".

PAGE 98:

422. Vases, red banjo shape body with applied crimped ambergris decoration along sides, and silver lustre applied foot. Height 14".
423. Vase, cased red over ambergris with amethyst lustre Pulled Feather decoration, banded in opal and all over lustre. Height 9$^{1}/_{2}$".
424. Bubble vase, ribbed yellow lustre, with vertical rows of bubbles. Height 6".
425. Vase, amethyst optic ribbed. Height 6".

PAGE 99:

426. Vase, red Lady Gay Rose, hard ribbed. Height 8".
427. Vase, triple cased green over opal over transparent blue, with geometric cut design. Height 7".
428. Pair candlesticks in blue lustre with opal vine decoration. Height 7$^{1}/_{2}$".
429. Stick vase, blue lustre with hard ribbing. Height 19".
430. Covered jar in blue lustre with opal King Tut decoration. Height 7".
431. Candlestick in apple green with gold King Tut decoration, flared gold top and lustre foot. Height 3$^{1}/_{2}$", width 4$^{1}/_{2}$".

PAGE 100:

432. Vase, opal with gold wavy and zipper decoration. Height 10".
433. Vase, opal with green and gold Coil pattern. Height 9$^{1}/_{2}$".
434. Vase, pink Lady Gay Rose with gold wavy decoration. Height 6$^{1}/_{2}$".
435. Vase, opal with blue and gold hearts and gold lustre spider webbing. Height 9$^{1}/_{2}$".
436. Vase, Moorish Crackle in green and opal over ambergris base. Height 8".
437. Vase, in green and white Moorish Crackle. Height 10".
438. Bottle vase, gold lustre Moorish Crackle (experimental). Height 11$^{1}/_{2}$".
439. Perfume, golden yellow lustre. Height 6".
440. Vase, opal with blue Pulled Feather, banded in gold. Height 6".
441. Bowl in golden orange lustre with blue King Tut decoration and lustred interior. Height 4", width 9$^{1}/_{2}$".
442. Vase, blue lustre. Height 6$^{1}/_{2}$".
443. Vase, blue lustre. Height 6$^{1}/_{2}$".

PAGE 101:

444. Vase, gold lustre crackle with green bands. Height 6".
445. Goblet, gold lustre. Height 9".
446. Vase, opal with green and gold Heart and gold webbing decoration. Height 9".
447. Vase, silver blue lustre beehive shape. Height 6$^{1}/_{2}$".
448. Covered jar, golden orange with green King Tut decoration on bottom and blue Coil decoration on lid (marriage). Height 9".
449. Vase, gold lustre with opal Pulled Feather banded in green, gold webbing. Height 8$^{1}/_{2}$".
450. Perfume, dark blue with silver blue wavy decoration, and lustre applied foot. Height 4$^{1}/_{2}$".
451. Perfume, silver blue with opal Heart & Vine decoration. Height 6".

452. Covered jar, deep pink Lady Gay Rose with gold King Tut decoration. Height 6$^1/_2$".
453. Bowl, gold lustre. Height 2", width 4".

PAGE 102:
454. Vase, opal with dark blue applied at top portion and around outside of foot. Silver blue floral decoration in top dark blue portion with trailing vine of silver blue to ambergris and back to silver blue as it reaches bottom edge of foot. Height 13$^1/_2$".
455. Vase, opal with blue lustre top that's done in dripping manner and applied gold lustre foot. Height 8".
456. Compote, dark blue with silver blue Heart & Vine decoration, gold lustre stem and foot. Gold lustre interior. Height 6$^1/_2$".
457. Small claret, lustre. Height 5$^1/_2$".
458. Small claret, golden yellow lustre. Height 5$^1/_2$".
459. Small claret, dark blue with silver blue Coil decoration, gold lustre stem and foot. Height 5$^1/_2$".
460. Vase, ribbon glass, clear with vertical bands of yellow and white criss-crossing. Height 16".
461. Vase, red crystal crackle with lustre. Height 12".
462. Vase, ribbon glass in vertical rows of red, white and yellow ribbon. Height 8".

PAGE 103:
463. Sherbets, set of six, ruby with opal and ruby Peacock Feather and crystal stem and foot. Cut with rose decoration all around. Height 4$^1/_2$", width 3$^3/_4$".
464. Sweat pea vase, marigold with blue Heart & Vine decoration, with applied lustre foot. Height 6".
465. Goblet, opal with gold Pulled Feather banded in blue, with gold lustre applied foot and stem. Quezal look suggests early Durand. Height 8".
466. Covered bon bon, silver blue lustre with opal Coil decoration, applied gold lustre foot and finial. Height 6", width 4$^1/_2$".

PAGE 104:
Glass courtesy of the Cunningham Johnson Collection.
467. Vase, gold lustre acid cut back with Thistle pattern. Height 10".
468. Vase, gold lustre, acid cut back with daffodil and butterfly pattern. Height 14".

PAGE 105:
469. Vase, blue lustre with opal Heart & Vine decoration. Height 10".
470. Covered jar, golden yellow lustre. Height 7".
471. Rose bowl vase, golden orange with green Coil decoration and lustred foot. Height 5".
472. Bowl, red overlay cut to clear with geometric and leaf cutting. Height 3$^1/_2$", width 8".
473. Shallow bowl, blue overlay cut to clear with geometric and brilliant period type cut center. Height 2", diameter 10".
474. Serving plate, green overlay cut to clear with opal and green Peacock Feather decoration, geometric and vine cutting with cross-hatched cut center. Diameter 13$^1/_2$".
475. and
476. Vases, pair of golden orange with blue King Tut decoration. Height 9$^1/_2$".
477. Vase, green over crystal with opal and green Peacock Feather decoration. Height 8".
478. Vase, golden orange lustre with blue Heart & Vine decoration. Height 5".
479. Vase, red over crystal with opal and red Pulled Feather decoration. Height 12".
480. Vase, pink Lady Gay Rose with gold Pulled Feather banded in opal decoration. Height 8".
481. Vase, deep pink Lady Gay Rose with optic ribbing. Height 19".

PAGE 106:
482. Baluster candlesticks, dark blue with silvery blue King Tut decoration and gold lustre foot. Height 10".
483. Baluster candlesticks, golden orange with gold lustre foot. Height 10".
484. Baluster candlestick, blue lustre with white Heart & Vine decoration and gold lustre foot. Height 10".
485. Candlesticks with flared top in red Lady Gay Rose with King Tut decoration, marigold top and lustred foot. Height 3", width 4".
486. Candlesticks with flared top in silver blue lustre with lustre foot. Height 3$^1/_2$", width 4$^1/_2$".
487. Candlesticks with flared top in yellow to orange gold with lustre foot. Height 3$^1/_2$", width 4$^1/_2$".

PAGE 107:
(*NOTE: Lamps are measured in glass height only.*)
488. Floor lamp, red and white over ambergris Moorish Crackle shade with lustre, on metal floor base. Shade height 8", width 10".
489. Floor lamp with a blue and white Moorish Crackle over ambergris shade in a bulbous form with fluted top. Shade height 8".

PAGE 108:

(*NOTE: Lamps are measured in glass height only.*)

490. Lamp, gold lustre with opal Pulled Feather banded in blue with gold spider webbing decoration. Height 8".

491. Lamp, opal with blue and marigold hearts and gold spider webbing decoration also matching painted parchment shade. Height 7$^{1}/_{2}$".

492. Lamp, golden orange lustre with gold spider webbing. Height 10".

PAGE 109:

493. Crystal stick vase with cut stem and applied foot. Height 10".

494. Lamp, green and opal Moorish Crackle over ambergris base, lustred, light in base. Height 9".

495. Lamp, crystal bubble ball with metal base. Lit from base. Height 5", width 6$^{1}/_{2}$".

496. Table torchiere lamp in opal with green Pulled Feather, banded in gold with gold spider web decoration and white metal base. Height 13".

497. Decorated Lamp in green with white hearts and gold spider webbing. Height 8".

498. Floral cut lamp in blue over crystal with opal and blue Peacock Feather decoration. Height 9".

499. Lamp in opal, hard ribbed. Height 7$^{1}/_{2}$".

PAGE 110:

500. Wall pocket in golden yellow with blue Coil decoration. Height 9".

501. Wall pocket in golden yellow with blue Heart & Vine decoration. Height 8$^{1}/_{2}$".

502. Shade for torchiere lamp in red and opal Moorish Crackle over ambergris and lustred. Bottom of shade cut off to create opening. These items were used most commonly for ashtrays. Height 1", width 3".

503. Shade for torchiere lamp in red and opal Moorish Crackle over ambergris and lustred. Height 8", width 10".

504. Lamp in Egyptian Crackle, green and gold over opal. Height 8".

505. Lamp in rose frosted with geometric cutting. Commercial glass. Height 10".

506. Table torchiere lamps in bluish-grey Pulled Feather banded in gold, with spider webbing on cast bronze bases. Height 12".

507. Lamp in cased glass opal cut to ambergris with painted parchment shade. Height 4", width 5".

508. Lamp in green optic ribbed with painted parchment shade. Height 8".

509. Colonel lamp in green center glass cut to clear with three green shades with grape and vine cutting on a brass base. Height 3$^{3}/_{4}$", width 3$^{3}/_{4}$"; shades 6$^{1}/_{2}$".

510. Lamp, golden yellow lustre. Height 12".

PAGE 111:

511. Vase, yellow lustre. Height 10".

512. Vase, red over crystal. Height 9$^{1}/_{2}$".

513. Bubble vase, blue over ambergris, hard ribbed with rows of vertical bubbles. Height 8".

514. Bubble vase, crystal rose bowl with vertical rows of bubbles. Height 4".

515. Whimsy in red over crystal with opal Peacock Feather and white trim and white applied ring in center. Possibly used as a candleholder. Height 5$^{1}/_{2}$".

516. Pair of lamps, in yellow lustre with blue and white banding and cut with floral motif, with white metal base and bakelite inserts. Height 9".

PAGE 112:

Examples of Kimble Cluthra Glass.

517. Vase. Height 10".

518. Vase. Height 12".

519. Vase. Height 14".

520. Vase. Height 17$^{1}/_{2}$".

521. Vase. Height 10".

522. Vase. Height 6".

523. Vase. Height 15".

Lamps

Originally Durand fancy lamp production was produced by the L & S Lamp and Shade Company. This small company was established by Martin Bach Jr. and Ernest Dorrell and operated from Dorrell's home in Alloway, New Jersey. They bought Durand's imperfect or rejected vases to make into lamps. Dorrell added a nice touch to these lamps by painting parchment shades to match or coordinate with the art glass. This combination of art glass body and painted shade made for a highly marketable product. Bach and Dorell were very successful and eventually formed a partnership with Emil S. Larsen, a New York City distributor for Durand art glass. Only by coincidence an almost identical name as the gaffer of the fancy shop. He became their sales agent and displayed these lamps in a New York City showroom. The L & S Company began placing such large orders for rejects that it captured the attention of Durand himself. He soon realized that he should enter the lamp business as well. About 1928, Durand began producing lamps. The L & S Company went out of business, but Dorrell continued supplying Durand with his painted shades and Bach continued to run the fancy shop.

The foreman of this newly formed lamp shop was a man named Everingham. Durand's lamp shop proved to be a successful department. Instead of using only rejected art glass, they began making decorated and undecorated glass that would be used for lamps. Now they also needed to design mountings and fixtures that were more suited to their new lamp production. Table and floor model wrought-iron stands were made to hold crackle-glass shades. Ornate brass mountings were made as elegant table lamps with beautifully decorated pieces of art glass. Moorish crackled ball bottles and covered jars were made to house a light from within the base, giving off a soft mellow glow. Cast metal bases to house a light on which a bubble ball sat were sold as decorative night-lights. Some lamps took on a rustic look, others a look of elegance, and some had a more commercially produced look.

Most of the art glass made could be ordered as a lamp with the exception of articles with an applied foot, which were probably too difficult to drill for mounting. The art-glass lamps used the same numbering and lettering system as the art glass. In this way a representative could order lamps in the same manner. A different numbering system was used for the more commercial lamps. One catalog advertised: "We specialize in exclusive shapes for lamp manufacturers, making the shapes from their sketches and for further information about these items, write direct to lamp department." Durand lamps, whether executed by the L & S Company or the Durand Lamp Shop, were as diverse as the art glass made by Durand. On the following pages you see how varied, how interesting, and how beautiful these objects are.

A Charming Selection of Lamps

is presented to you with the knowledge that they are of the very finest type. While the majority are replicas of Old Colonial pieces, they at the same time have that smartness and feeling that make them desirable merchandise.

SEVERAL TYPES OF GLASS

are used in the manufacture of the items shown in this folder. The most prominent are Iridescent and Cased Glass.

CASED GLASS

is the finest achievement of the glassmaker's art. It consists of casings or layers of various colors of glass, one above the other. As an example of double casing, a sapphire layer may be entirely imposed over crystal, and then in regular design the sapphire cut away till the crystal is reached, thus giving a double tone effect. It may be had in Crystal with Ruby, Emerald, Topaz or Sapphire, with or without an extra casing of Opal on the outside.

IRIDESCENT GLASS

is one of the highest grades of glass made and retains its iridescent effect forever. Hand wrought.

OPTIC GLASS

is obtainable either clear or frosted, in Amethyst, Crystal, Rose, Green or Amber.

THE SHADES

are all hand decorated, while many of them have gold applique, and all are designed to match or harmonize with the particular colors of glass ordered.

No. 214-406 — Cased Glass Lamp with marble and antique brass base 5" square, and large cased glass ~~font 9" in diameter, 22" high~~ overall. 16" Drum Shade.

Prices:
- With shade .... ~~$30.75~~ 22.50
- Without shade .... ~~$24.75~~ 17.50

No. 213-437—Colonial Lamp with attractive bronze casting and marble base and cased glass font. Antique brass finish. 22" high overall. 16" Empire Shade.

Prices:
- With shade .... ~~$23.75~~ 18.90
- Without shade .... ~~$18.75~~ 14.50

No. 211-409—Colonial Lamp of triple cased glass with square base of marble and finished attractively in antique brass. 22½" high with finial. 14" Empire Shade.

Prices:
- With shade .... ~~$21.50~~ 17.90
- Without shade .... ~~$16.75~~ 13.50

No. 28-421 — Three light Colonial Lamp with hand cut cased glass font and shades to match. Attractively finished in Roman Gold, Antique Brass or Pewter. 18" high overall.

Price .... ~~$10.00~~ 10.35

No. 24-418—Colonial Lamp with sand blasted cut glass font and shades. Bronze, Pewter or Antique Brass finish base and trimmings. Saucer shape base. 18" high overall.

Price .... ~~$6.85~~ 6.75
with shades

No. 206-432 — Colonial Lamp with cut cased Opal glass font and shade. Marble base 3½" square. Antique Brass, Bronze or Pewter finishes. 15" high overall.

Price .... ~~$10.00~~ 8.50

No. 32-433—Boudoir Lamp with clear optic glass twist font. Pewter or Ivory and Gold finishes. 18½" ~~high, 8" Empire Shade.~~

Prices:
- With shade .... ~~$3.50~~ 2.55
- Without shade .... ~~$1.90~~ 1.75

No. 402—Boudoir Lamp of all glass base and stem which may be had in Green, Crystal and Rose. The stem and foot are hand cut, and the wiring goes through the stem, a new feature hiding the cord. 15" high overall. 8" Empire shade to match.

Prices:
- With shade .... ~~$39.00 doz.~~ 29.40
- Without shade .... $19.80 doz.

No. 142—A very graceful tall table Torchiere of hand-made glass in Peacock design, without Gold webbing. The base is Antique Gold finish. 16½" high.

Price .... ~~$7.50~~ 7.00

No. 204-423 — Colonial Lamp with double or triple case glass font. 18" high overall. 10" Empire Shade. (Particularly good in Pewter with Blue and Crystal cased glass font). Also furnished in Antique Brass or Bronze finishes.

Prices:
- With shade .... ~~$8.25~~ 6.80
- Without shade .... ~~$6.00~~

No. 205-429 — Colonial Lamp with cased cut glass font. 14" high overall. 8" Empire shade.

Prices:
- With shade .... ~~$6.75~~ 6.80
- Without shade $5.00

No. 209-425 — Colonial Lamp with cased glass font and marble base 3½" square. Antique Brass, Bronze or Pewter finishes. 17" high, 10" Empire shade.

Prices:
- With shade .... ~~$9.50~~ 7.00
- Without shade .... ~~$6.75~~ 6.00

No. 36-500—Colonial Lamp simulating the old wick lamps. It has a saucer shaped base and handle of ~~either Bronze or Pewter finish, and~~ a font of cased glass. Hand engraved shade to match. 15½" high overall.

Price $10.00

No. 45-407 — Colonial Lamp with round cylindrical font of frosted glass cut in grape design. Saucer shaped base. Dim-a-Light with three degrees of light. Chimney of frosted crystal cut design. 18½" high overall. 14" Drum shade.

Price:
- With shade .... ~~$13.50~~ 12.5

No. 2028—Iridescent glass vase lamp mounted on metal base. In assorted colors and decorations of glass. 24¼" high overall. 16" lined silk shade to match.

Price .... $6.25 each
complete with shade.

No. 441 — Solid Bubble Ball Lamp with decorative Gold or Silver plated finish base. Light is inserted in base which reflects through the bubble ball and casts a soft glow. Base is 5½" long by 3½" wide.

Price .... ~~$7.50~~ 500

~~**No. 203** — Hollow Bubble Ball Lamp~~ on plated Roman Gold or Silver square base, which is modernistic in design. Base is 3½" square. Bubble ball can be had in Amber, Green, Rose or Crystal. Light comes up from the base which holds a small bulb.

Price .... ~~$8.50~~ 3.25

No. 46-505—Desk Lamp with Iridescent glass shade in Green with Gold frill design. Base and stem are of Bronze plated metal. 15" high overall.

Price $10.00 9.75

PRICES QUOTED ARE PER EACH NET

All prices quoted are without bulbs, unless otherwise specified. Special bulbs for all colonial lamps can be furnished at $.50 each net.

All merchandise is shipped F. O. B. Vineland, N. J. Prices subject to change without notice. No packing charges. No goods may be returned without notice and permission to do so. In case of breakage in transit notify your carrier. All merchandise is inspected and carefully packed before leaving plant.

204-423
205-429
209-425
36-500
45-407
2028
441
503
46-505

214-406
213-437
211-409
28 - 421
24 - 418
206-432
32 - 433
402
142

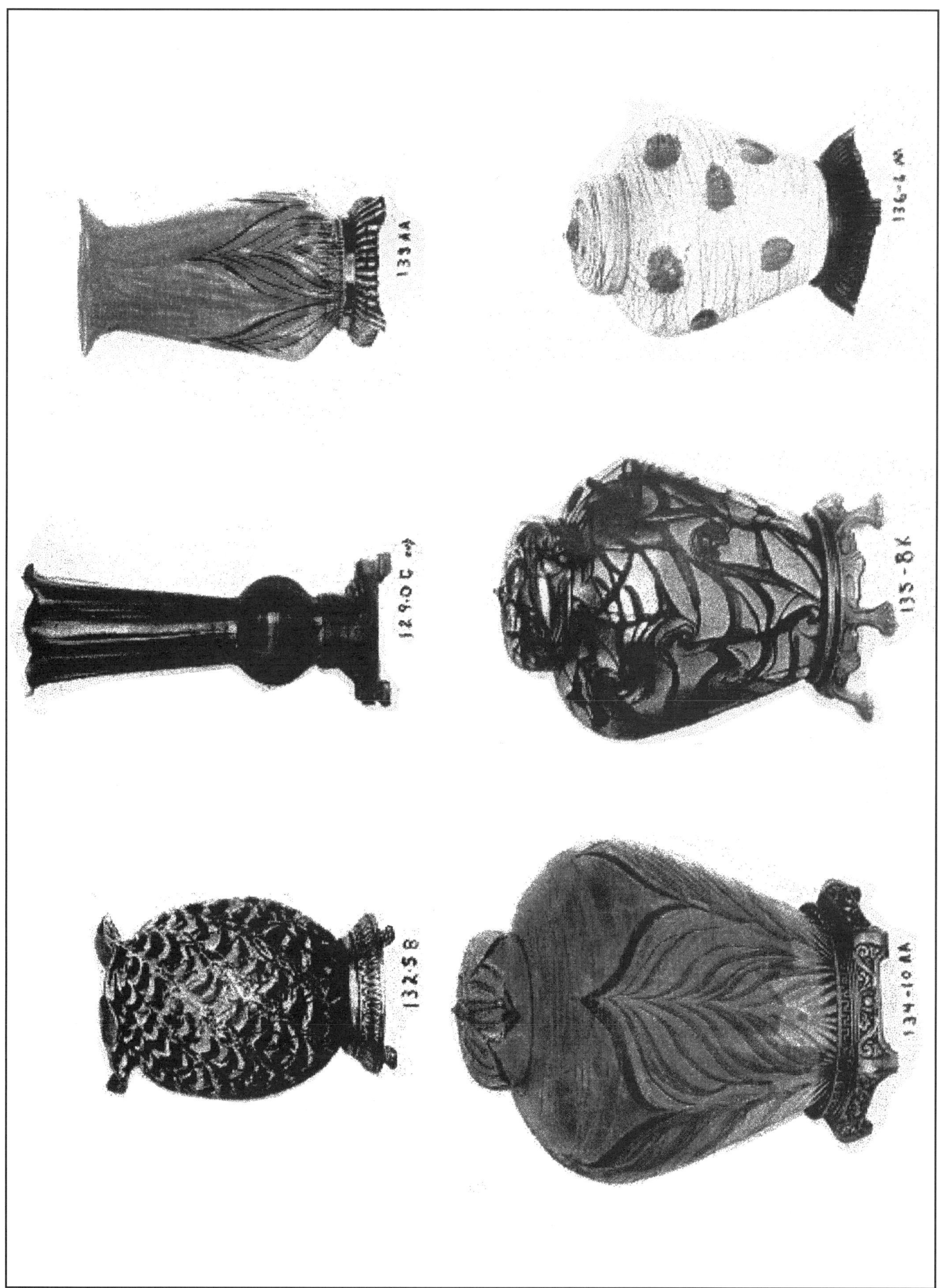
133AA
135-BK
134-10AA

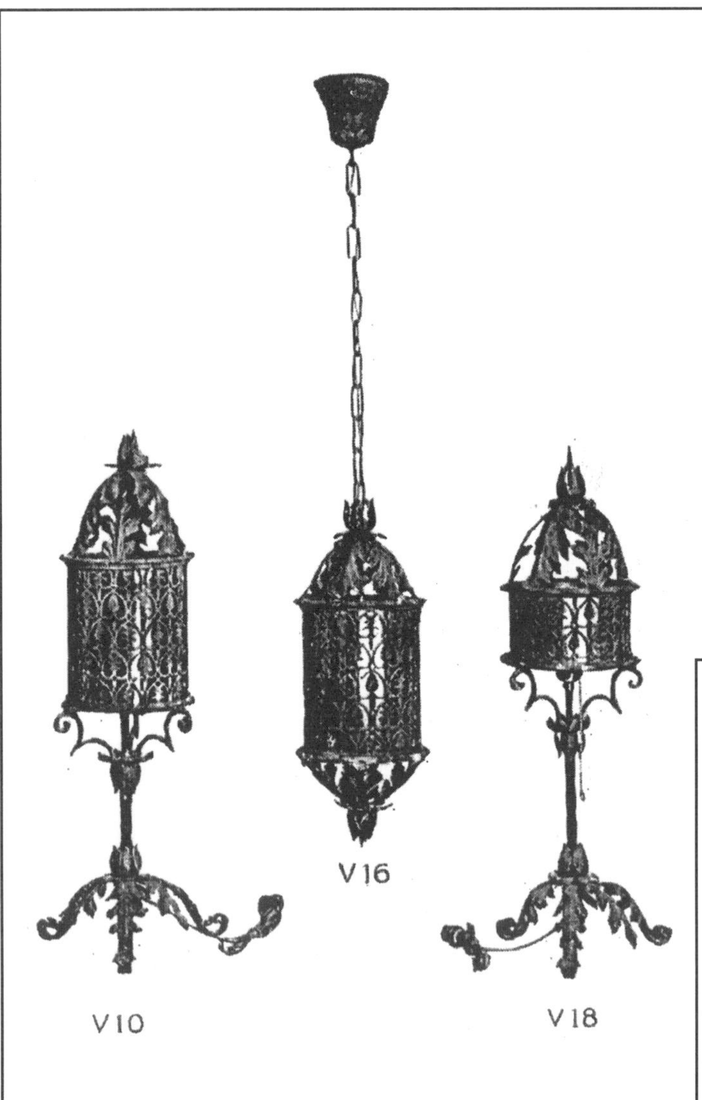

Left: Wrought iron table and hanging lamps. These lamps were sold with a golden yellow lustre semi-transparent glass insert.

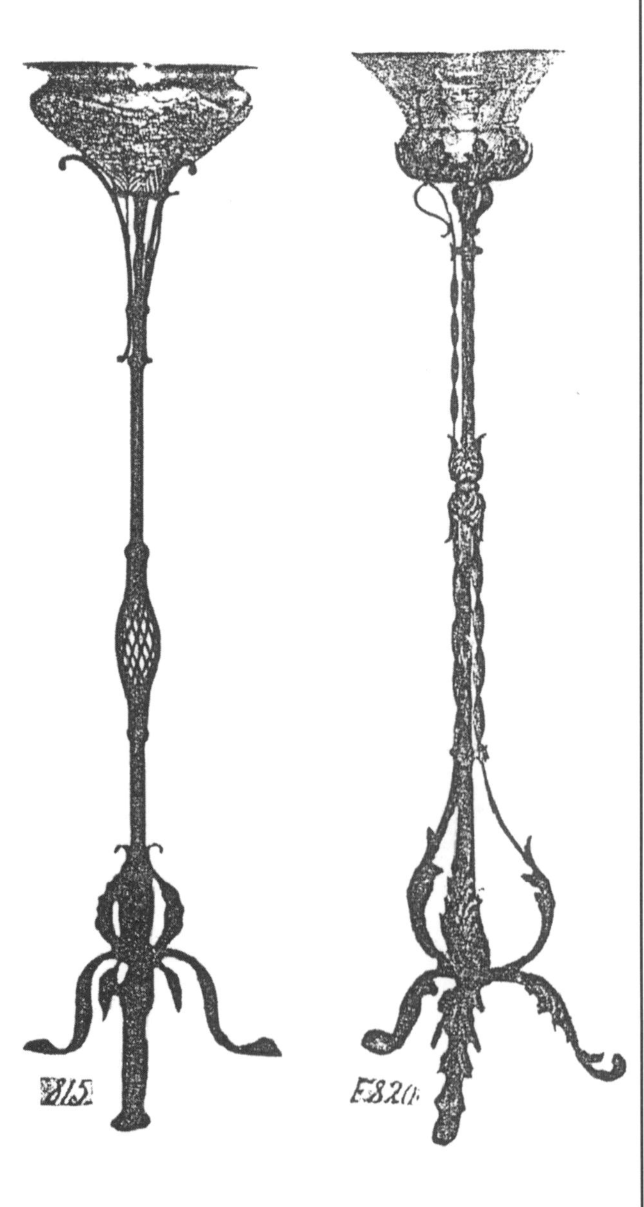

Right: Wrought iron torchiere floor lamps were offered with a semi-transparent Moorish Crackle shade.

1716

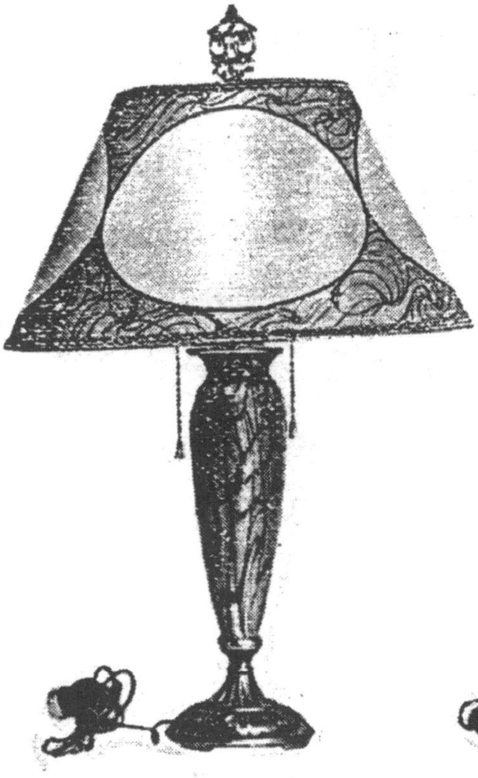

2028

2029

10" BALL BOTTLE

R1

CYLINDER

Wrought iron table lamps. The left lamp has a Pulled Feather shade decoration and the shade on the right lamp is Moorish Crackle.

Charming

Colonial Lamps

OF HAND MADE GLASS

by

DURAND ART GLASS

Art Division of the

VINELAND FLINT GLASS WORKS

V. DURAND, *Prop.*

Vineland, N. J.

SHOW ROOMS

NEW YORK

Emil S. Larsen & Co., Inc.
225 Fifth Ave., New York

WEST COAST

Roy C. Yourstone
839 E 31st St.
Los Angeles, Calif.

NEW ENGLAND

Robt. W. Corey
2 & 9 Parker House
Boston, Mass.

SOUTHERN

C. L. Wilcken
700 Harwood Ave.
Orlando, Florida

Illustrations shown on pages 135 through 138 are taken from a brochure for the Art Division of the Vineland Flint Glass Works advertising colonial lamps.

No. 5/150—Unusual reproduction of Colonial lamp with crystal font, shade and chimney, sand-blasted, hand made glass, with cut design. The prisms are either hand cut or plain. Metal is brass plated with silver or gold finishes. Heighth 23″. Price $36.00.

No. 4/149—Attractive Colonial table lamp with Blue font, crystal sand-blasted hand made shade with attractive cut design. The Colonial prisms come either with hand cut design or plain. Metal of brass, plated with silver or gold finishes. Heighth 21½″. Price $40.00.

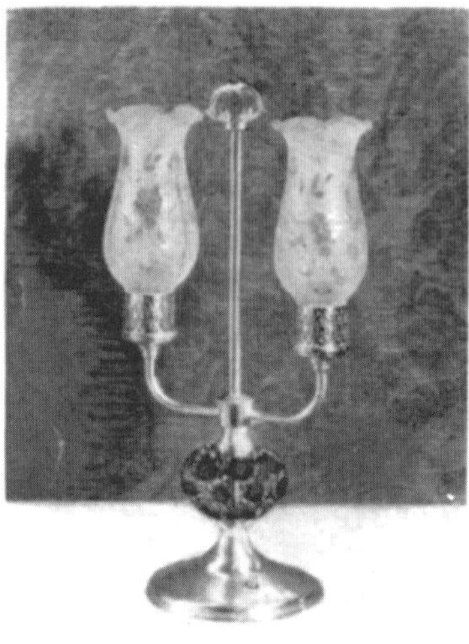

No. 9/154—Colonial lamp with two shades of hand made crystal sand-blasted glass with beautiful cut design. Font is of cased hand cut glass in Ruby, Green or Blue. Colored shades may be had to match font or crystal font to match shades. Metal of brass, plated in silver or gold finishes. 16″ high. Price $20.00.

No. 11/156—Three light Colonial lamp with shades and font of hand made frosted, sand-blasted glass with cut design. Metal of brass, plated in silver or gold finishes. Heighth 18″. Price $20.00.

Illustrations from a brochure for the Art Division of the Vineland Flint Glass Works advertising colonial lamps.

No. 1/158—Colonial lamp on left is made with sand-blasted and cut font. 10″ high. Price $3.90. Same with clear glass font. Price $3.50.

No. 8 Special—On right is made with clear glass font. Price $2.50. 8″ high. Same with sand-blasted and cut font. Price $3.00.
Metal parts on both these lamps are of brass, plated in either pewter or English bronze finishes. Colors of glass fonts on above lamps are Amethyst, Green, Rose, Amber and Crystal.

Colonial lamps shown above are made of double or triple plated glass. White outside, predominating colors showing through cutting are either Ruby, Green, Blue or Topaz. These bases are made of cast brass and plated with either silver or gold finishes.
No. 170—Colonial lamp (left) is 11″ high. Price $9.00.
No. 171—Colonial lamp (center) with chimney. 15½″ high. Price $15.00.
No. 172—Colonial lamp (right) is 8″ high. Price $8.50.

No. 1994—Illuminated Aquarium. This unusual and attractive aquarium is made with a finely designed metal base and cover. Something entirely new and novel with electric light bulb in the base reflecting into the glass aquarium above. This is made additionally attractive by using a triple bubble glass ornament in the center which is magnified by the light in the base, giving a fascinating glow over the entire object. Heighth 20″. Price $30.00.

Illustrations from a brochure for the Art Division of the Vineland Flint Glass Works advertising colonial lamps.

No. 2/147—Colonial lamp of hand made glass and with hand cut design on a sand-blasted font and globe. Metal of brass, plated in pewter or English bronze finish. 15½" high. Price $7.50.

No. 6/151—Quaint Colonial lamp with sand-blasted and cut chimney and font of glass with beautiful cut design on both. Metal of brass, plated in pewter or English bronze finishes. 13½" high. Price $7.00.

No. 7/152—Hand made Colonial lamp with sand-blasted glass base, chimney and shade. Beautiful cut design on all three pieces. Bowl and base are in one piece. 15½" high. Price $10.00.

No. 10/155—A charming all hand made, sand-blasted, beautifully cut glass Colonial lamp. Font and shades to match. Metal of brass, plated in silver or gold finishes. 20" high. Price $22.00.

Illustrations from a brochure for the Art Division of the Vineland Flint Glass Works advertising colonial lamps.

BUBBLE LAMPS

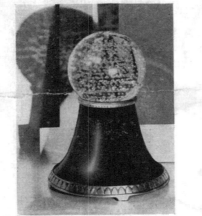

45—Mounted on a high metal pedestal. Wired for use. 6½″ high.....$8.00

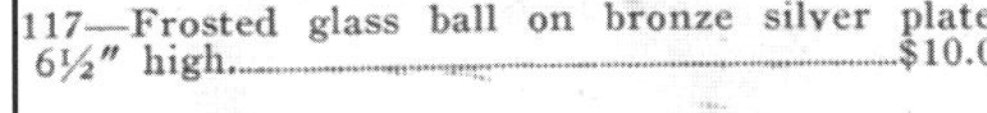

117—Frosted glass ball on bronze silver plated 6½″ high.....$10.00

No. 137—Double Bubble Crystal Ball mounted on an illuminated Black Glass base, with a Bronze, Silver or Gold plated edge at the bottom of the base. 9½″ high. $20.00

Above, No. 138—Black Base with Crystal Tear Drop Ball. 7½″ high. $20.00

Unique
LIGHTING

Presenting a beautiful collection of the finest of hand made glass with exceptional bases of the best quality of cast bronze.

by

DURAND ART GLASS

VINELAND, N. J.

New York Show Rooms
225 Fifth Avenue
EMIL S. LARSEN CO., Inc.

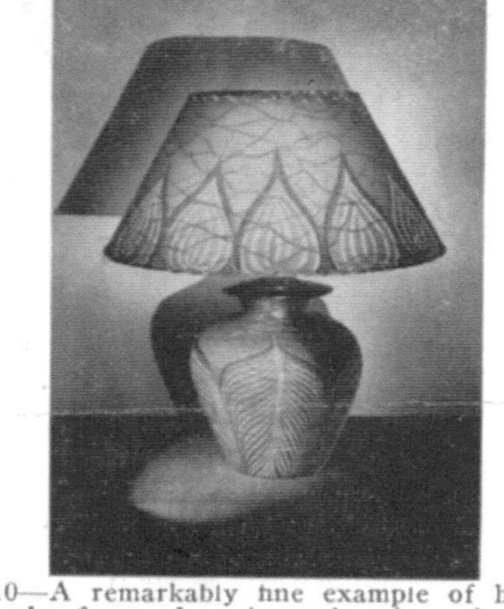

No. 1710—A remarkably fine example of hand-made glass in the form of an innerglow lamp base with a perfectly matching shade. The Peacock feather design, trimmed off with Blue, is on a Golden Yellow background, covered with Gold webbing. An exceptional value. $40.00

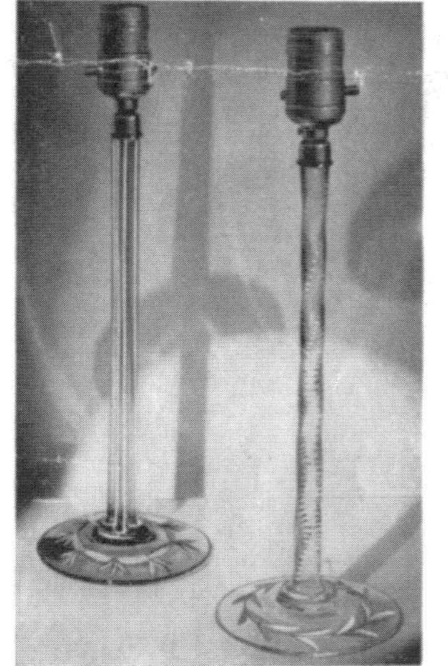

Boudoir Sticks in hand-made Rock Crystal Glass, which come in Rose, Green or Crystal. Nickeled sockets. On the left, 5 point fluted with cutting on foot, 16″ high, $2.75 hollow stem, $1.98 solid stem. On the right, cutting on both twisted stem and foot. 13″ high. $1.98

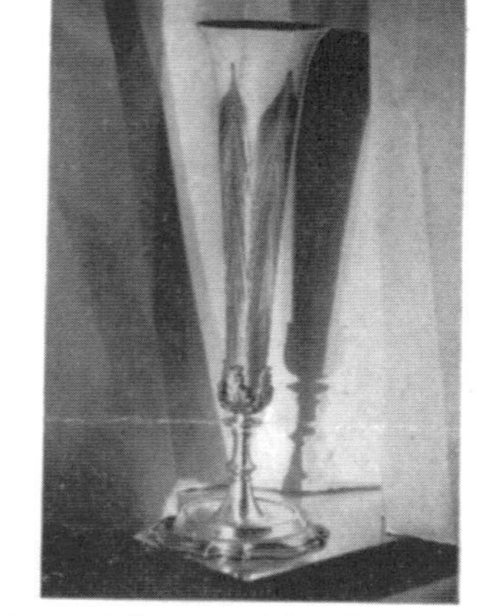

No. 142—A specially graceful tall table Torchere of hand-made glass, Peacock design, without Gold webbing. The base is solid Bronze in Silver, Gold or Bronze finishes, 16½″ high. $15.00

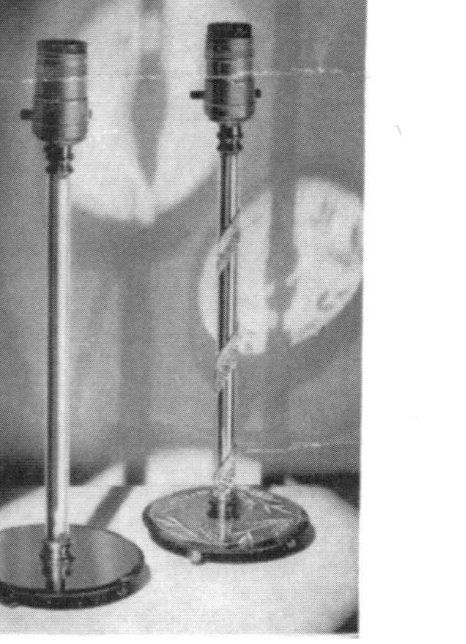

Boudoir Sticks of hand-made Mirror Glass, which rest on four dainty ball feet, with cord running from under the base. At the left, No. A in plain Mirror Glass, 15″ high, $1.85. At the right, No. E/1B with hand-cut design, 15″ high. $3.00

No. 141 — Ruby colored ribbed lustre glass lamp mounted on a particularly attractive modern base of solid Bronze in Silver, Gold, or Bronze finish. 11″ high. $15.00

No. 126—Table Torchere of hand-made glass in Green, Blue or Ruby over White with Yellow contrasting. Base is rust finish. 17″ high. $15.00

DURAND ART GLASS

VINELAND FLINT GLASS WORKS

5/150 A-107 A-112 A-115 A-109 A-110 4" CYLINDER

11/156 10/155 A-114 A-113 A-111 OIL FOUNT A-108

Shades

Durand produced a large variety of lampshades, and mostly to fit their own lamps. The shades on the following pages are from one of Durand's catalogs. Copied from a Quezal catalog, they were renumbered for shape by adding a zero to the existing four-digit number and relettered for decoration by using two and three letters instead of one. They appeared in the Durand catalog with the new five-digit number and new lettering code. Even though they were shown in Durand's catalog, these shades were excess inventory from the Quezal Art Glass and Decorating Co. Whether they were purchased outright by Durand or sold for Marty Bach Jr. is not known.

Unlike Quezal, Durand made few if any shades for commercial lamp manufacturers. Therefore few conventional shades with a 2¼" opening as used in wall brackets and ceiling fixtures were produced by Durand. Of those that Durand produced the classic decorative pattern is so distinctive that they could have been made only by Durand.

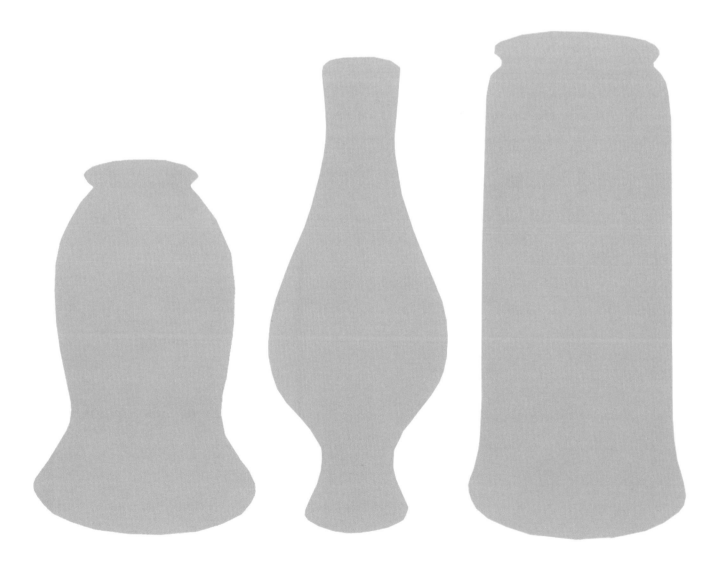

ELECTRIC DECORATIONS

Prices as shown on pages 16, 17 and 18 are for shapes only. Decorations XA, XB, XD and XEE do not take additional price. For other decorations add decoration price as listed below.

		Add to List per dozen
XP	White and Green Frill on Lustre	$5.00
XDD	Opal, Gold Leaf and Gold Lined	4.00
XY	A White Block and Dot	12.00
XA	Lustre	
XB	Opal, Gold Lined plain	
XS	T. S. G. Spider, Blue and Gold Hearts	8.00
XM	A. O. S. Lustre White leaf, Green Band	4.00
XH	Gold Leaf, Green Band, Gold Lined	4.00
XEE	Gold, Opal Lined	
XD	Opal, Gold Lined 8-16 Rib	
XG	A. O. S. Spider	12.00
XK	Ruby Leaf, Gold Band, Gold Lined	24.00

All electrics on page 16, are for decorations only, with the exception of those where numbers are specified. These can be ordered as shown or decorations can be reversed as any shape number can be reproduced in any decoration shown on page 16.

Prices shown are in dozen lots only.

We make a specialty of Lamp Bases, Fixture Breaks, Spindles, Stalactites, Bowls, Cylinders, Ball Lamp Shades, etc., made to sketch or sample in any decoration shown on page 16.

All electrics shades shown are made with 2¼" holders, unless otherwise specified.

10140
10040
10180
10210
10020
10120
10100
10030
10110
10150
10070
10200

10060
10190
10050
10090
10080
10220
10010
10170
10240
10130
10160
10230

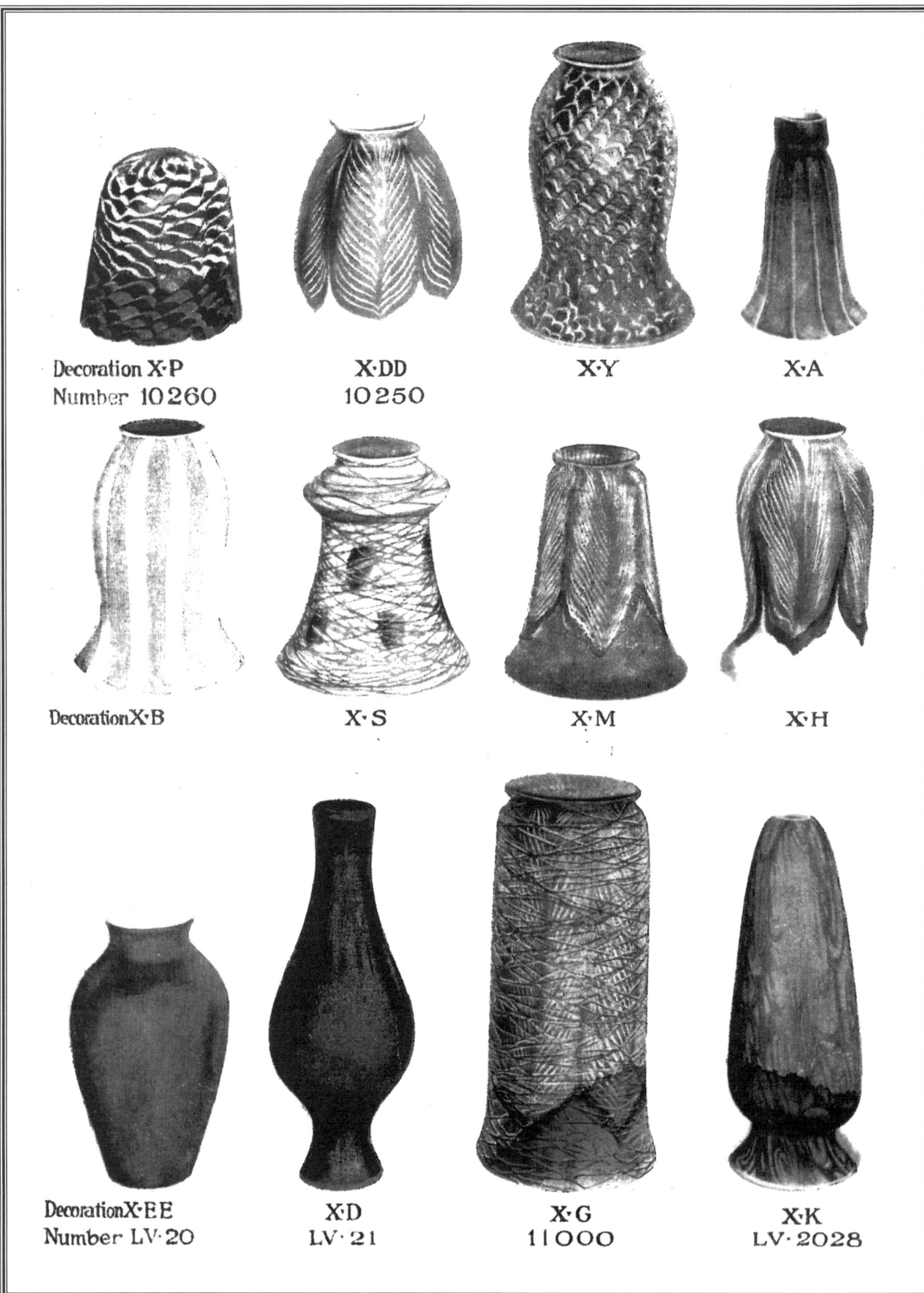
Decoration X·P
Number 10260
X·DD
10250
X·Y
X·A
Decoration X·B
X·S
X·M
X·H
Decoration X·EE
Number LV·20
X·D
LV·21
X·G
11000
X·K
LV·2028

Decoration Letters

Durand used letters as a reference to describe each type of decoration. Thus a distributor could simply note the code letter from under the picture and description in the catalog and order that decoration. Buyers could also have a particular decoration put on any shape they wanted simply by choosing the appropriate number of that shape in the catalog. This simplistic system for the buyer and the seller seemed to work quite well. These letters and numbers covered most of what Durand made in art glass.

Some decorations were never cataloged and therefore had no letter. I have used several catalogs and flyers from the Vineland Flint Glass Works to compile this letter system and quote verbatim the descriptions from those catalogs. What would seem to be inconsistencies are really just minor changes in wording in an effort to better describe the decorations each time Durand published a new catalog. I have included those somewhat duplicated descriptions in order to show the subtle changes Durand made. Two designs, Coil and King Tut, are somewhat similar. Durand often used either of these terms to describe either decoration. If you refer to the Durand terminology chapter, it clarifies these two terms.

A: Gold Lustre Body; Semi-Transparent. No design.

AA: Lustre In and Out, White Leaf, Green Band, Spider.

AA: Golden Yellow with White Feather or Peacock design with Blue Band to trim off the Blue and with a Gold Webbing.

B: Silver Blue, White Clinging Vine, White Hearts.

B: Silver Blue Body with White Hearts and Vines.

BB: Blue Lustre, Clinging Vine.

C: Golden Yellow Body with Blue Hearts and Vines.

C: Lustre In and Out, Blue Clinging Vine, Blue Hearts.

D: Silver Blue.

Decoration C R

S.G.

D: Silver Blue Body. No Design.

D-Spider: Silver Blue Body with Gold Webbing.

E: Lustre In and Out.

E: Golden Yellow. No Design.

E-Spider: Lustre In and Out, Spider Web.

E-Spider: Golden Yellow Body with Gold Webbing.

FF: Opal Spider with Blue and Gold

G: Opal, Gold Lined, Silver Lustre King Tut

H: Opal, Gold Clinging Vine, Gold Lined.

K: Lustre In and Out. Blue King Tut.

K: Golden Yellow Body with Blue Coiled Design

KK: Green Body with Gold Coiled Design.

L: Opal, Blue and Gold King Tut.

LGR: Lady Gay Rose Body with a Gold Coiled Design.

M: Opal Spider, Blue and Gold Hearts, Gold Lined.

M: Opal Spider, with Gold and Blue Hearts, with Gold Webbing.

N: Opal Gold Lined, Gold King Tut

OG Cup: Green Body with Hard Rib, Gold Lined.

OG Lined: Opal, Hard Ribbed, with Green Lining.

OR Cup: Rose Body with Hard Rib, Gold Lined.

OR Lined: Opal, Hard Ribbed, with Rose Lining.

R: Silver Blue, White King Tut.
R: Silver Blue, White Coil Design.

R: Silver Blue Body with White Coiled Design.

Special: Lustre Opal and Blue with Lustre King Tut.

SG: Gold Double Decoration, Blue Band.

SB: Blue, Green, or Ruby. This glass, when used in Torchier lamps or vases and with an inner glow light, shows a very mellow light with a blue, green or ruby design over the white and just enough of the yellow to make an attractive contrasting color. Also crackled.

Mutual: Soft Yellow Body with White and Blue, White and Green, or White and Ruby design all over. Moorish Crackled.

XJ: Opal with Blue or Green Feather or Peacock design with Gold Band to trim off the Blue and with a Gold Webbing.

Y: Lustre White King Tut.

Z: Blue with Lustre Hearts and Lustre Clinging Vine.

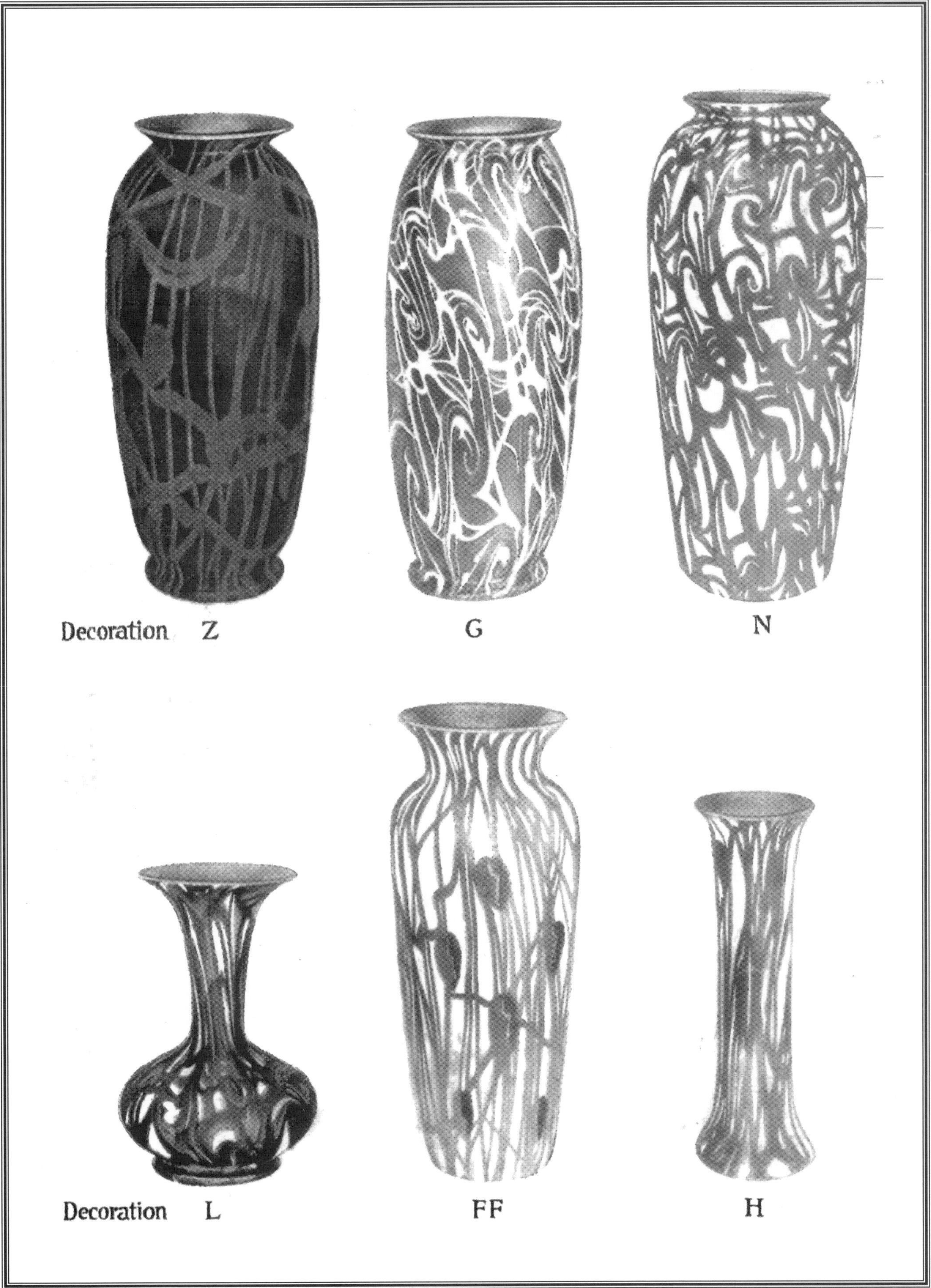
Decoration Z
G
N
Decoration L
FF
H

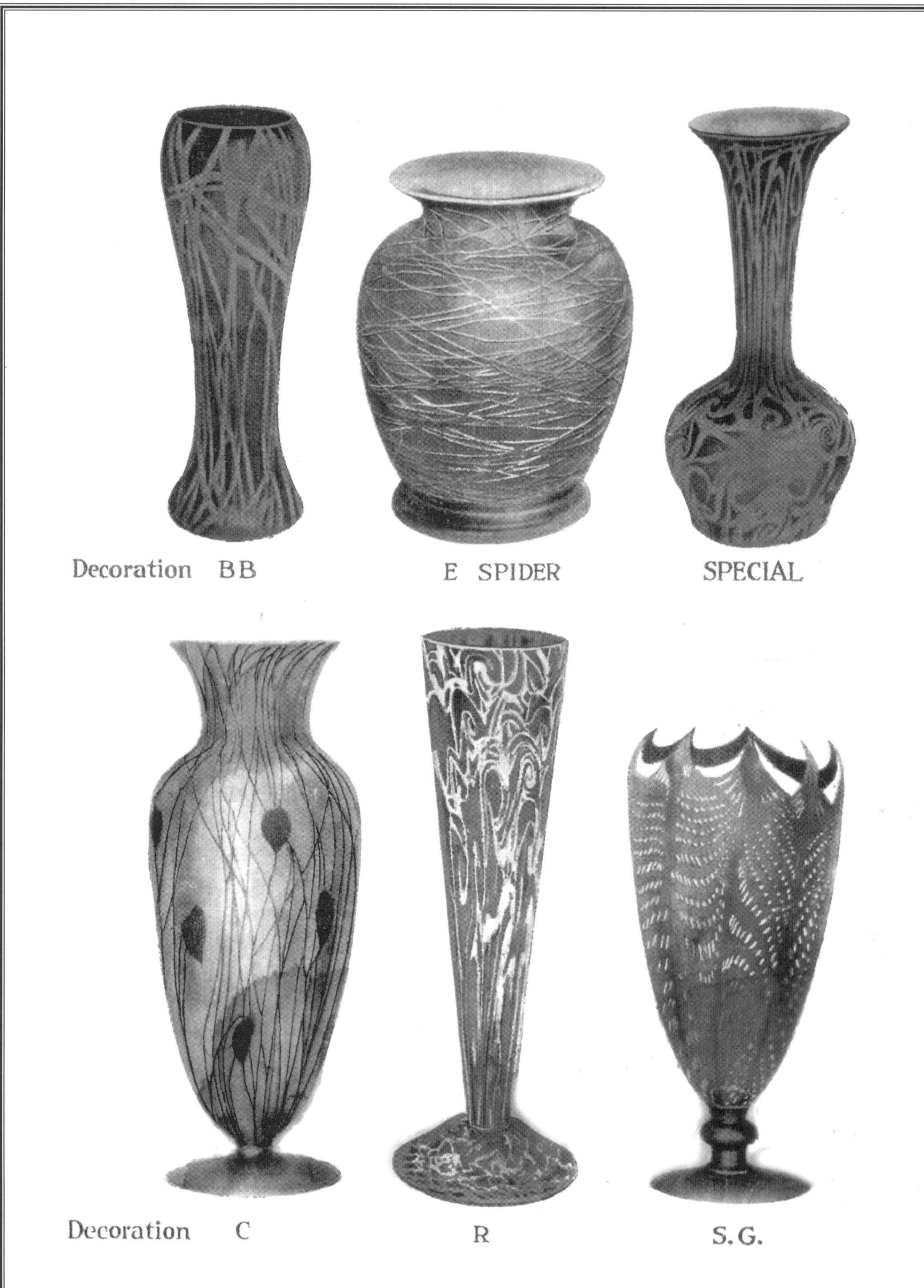

Decoration BB E SPIDER SPECIAL

Decoration C R S.G.

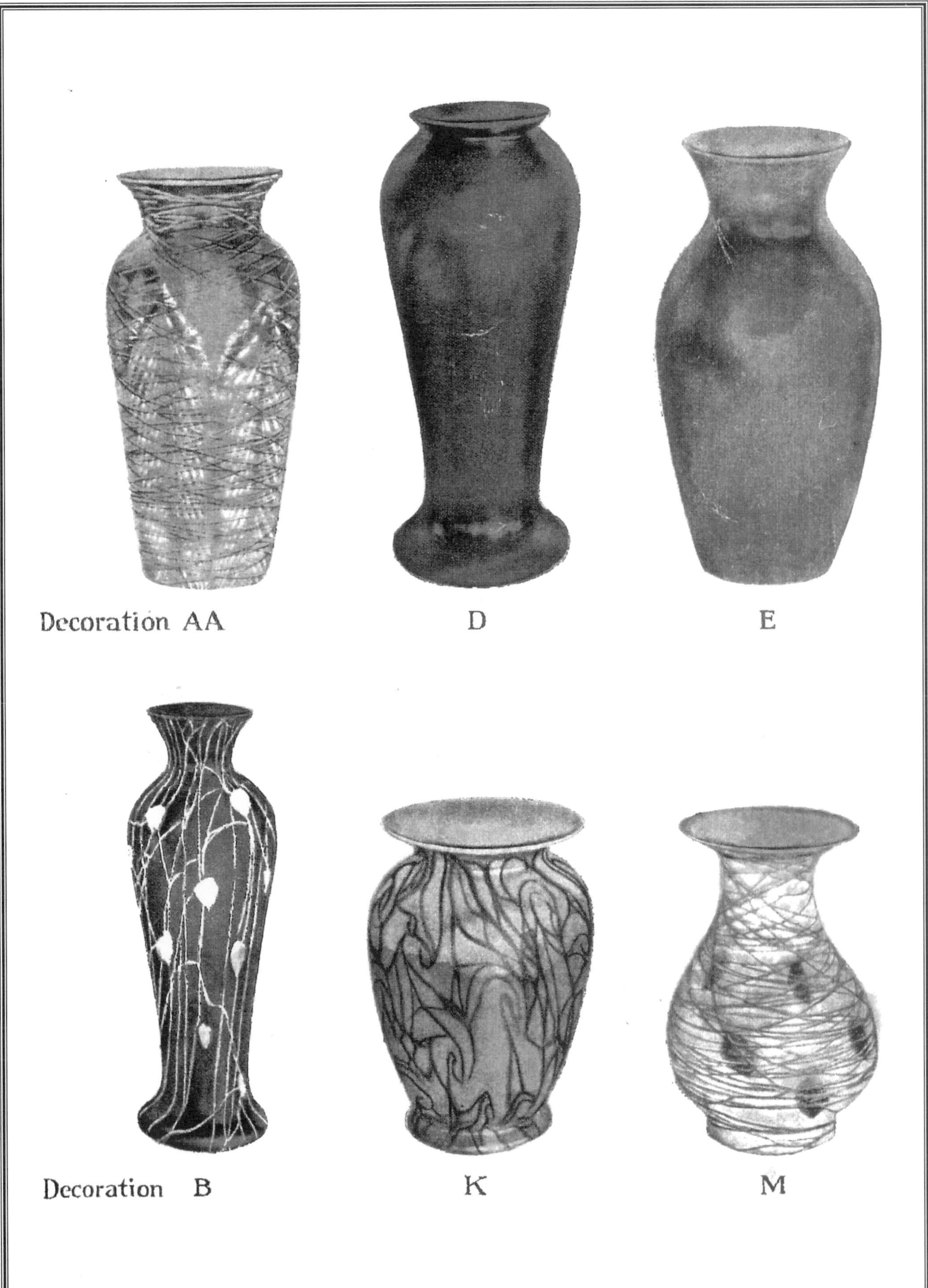

Decoration AA D E

Decoration B K M

Cuttings

Durand's grinding and polishing shop was kept busy cutting floral and geometric patterns. Cutting was done primary on cased glass, which was also called layered or flashed glass. The artisans would layer two, three or even four layers of contrasting colors of glass one over the other. Cutting away the outer layer or layers and exposing the base glass, which usually was crystal or another transparent color, created some unique effects. Ambergris glass by itself was also used for cutting.

Durand's cuttings could vary from nothing special to an involved cutting of absolute brilliance. The cuttings on the cased glass had great clarity and character. Many pieces of cut glass were exhibited at the Sesquicentennial Exposition in Philadelphia in 1926. The influence of Charles Link, a master cutter during the brilliant period, can be seen in many of these pieces.

I have compiled a listing of many of the cuttings done at Durand's shop. Although not a complete list, you can see how diverse the cuttings are. Some cuttings were offered commercially, while others were specially done. I have documented cutting numbers where I could. We can document most of the cuttings that were done by the polishing and grinding shop at the Durand factory, but Durand also offered blank cased glass for sale, so some cuttings may appear on Durand glass that were not cut by his shop. Determining that will be a judgment call and the cuttings on the following pages should help you make that call. Nonetheless, the glass is still Durand. I have included, where possible, the three digit numbers Durand used to describe their cutting patterns. I have taken these directly from signed cut glass pieces that would occasionally have the cutting numbers along with the signature. I found that cutting marks in catalogs are either nonexistent or at times contradictory. Some of these cutting patterns have names in the cut glass world, and I have no intention of trying to change that. However, these cuttings need to be organized into a simple system that every buyer and collector can use and understand. Thus I have adopted Durand's simple but adequate system of letters and numbers.

Cuttings at Durand, for the most part, can be put into three categories. The first and most prolific category is geometric cuttings and these are denoted by the letter G. The second, is floral and vine cuttings, denoted by the letters FV, and the third category is the combination of geometric and floral and& vine denoted by the letters GFV. As new cuttings arise, they can easily be added to the system. So until the day arrives when we have a complete catalog of Durand cutting patterns, I believe this system will be adequate.

Code for Cuttings: **G - Geometric** **FV - Floral and Vine** **GFV - Geometric Floral and Vine**

G1

G2 (Durand's #850)

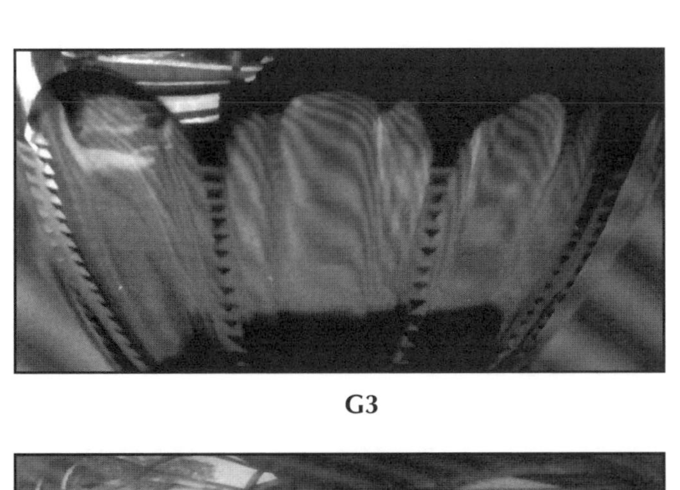

G3

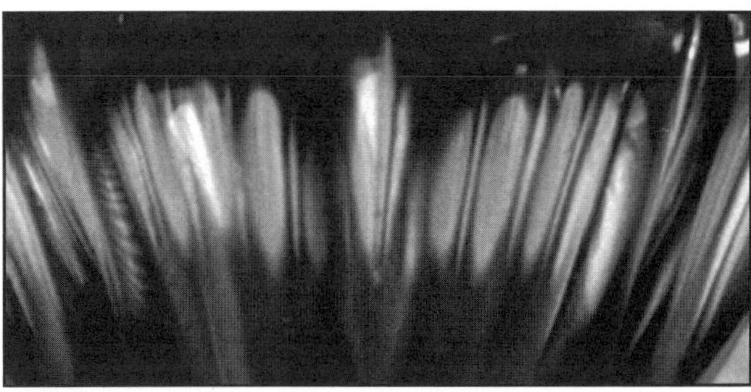

G4 (Durand's #535)

G5 (Durand's #710)

G6

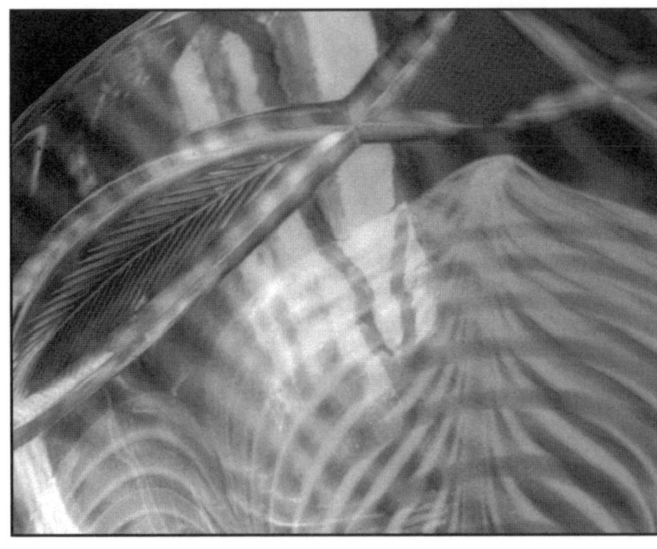

G7

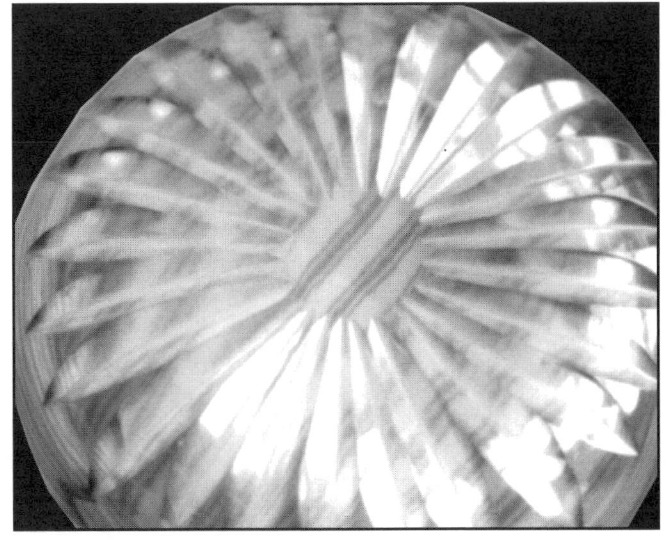

G8

G9 (Durand's #866)

G10

G11

G12

G13

G14

G15

G16

G17

G18

G19

G20

G21

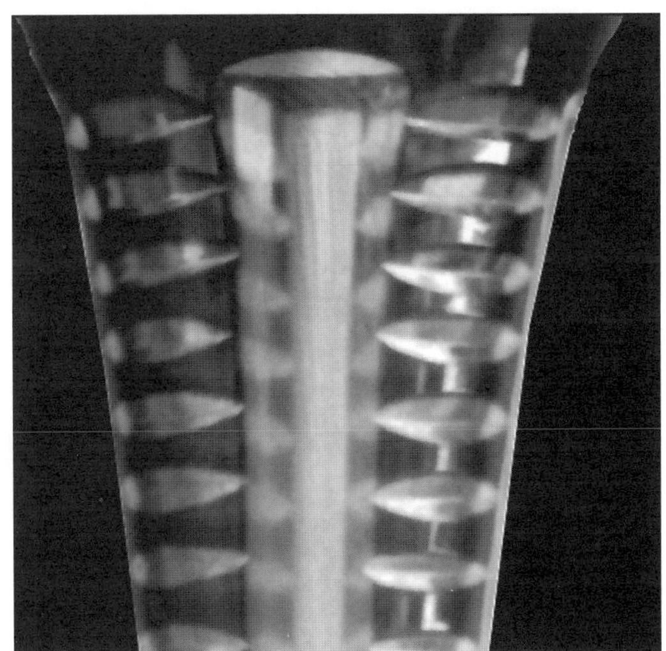

G22 (Durand's #566)

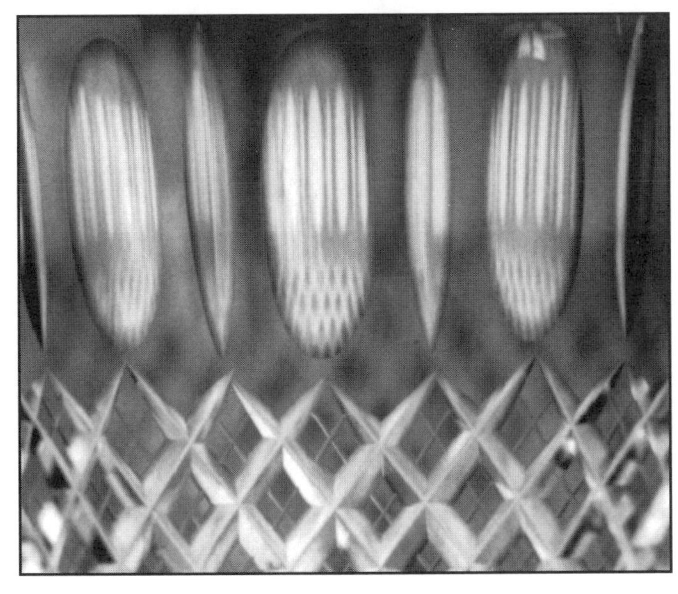

G23

G24

G25

G26 (Durand's #855)

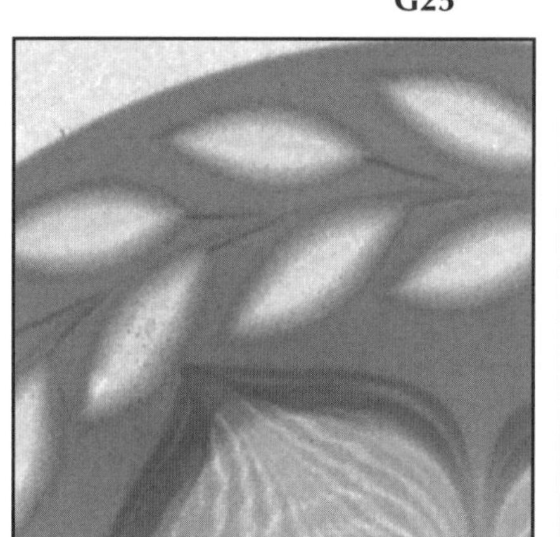

FV1

FV2

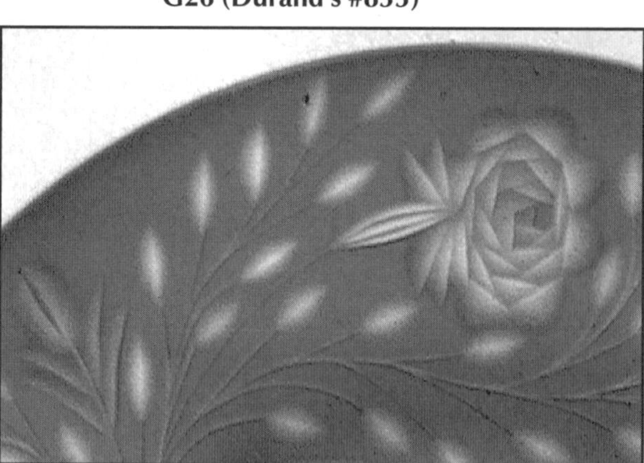

FV3

FV4

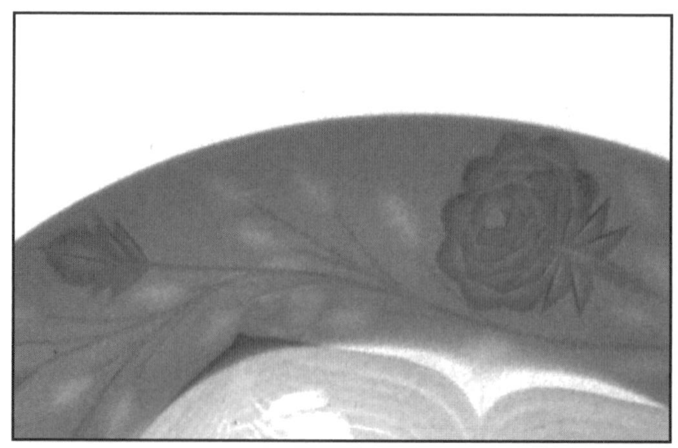

FV5

FV6

FV7

FV8

FV9

FV10

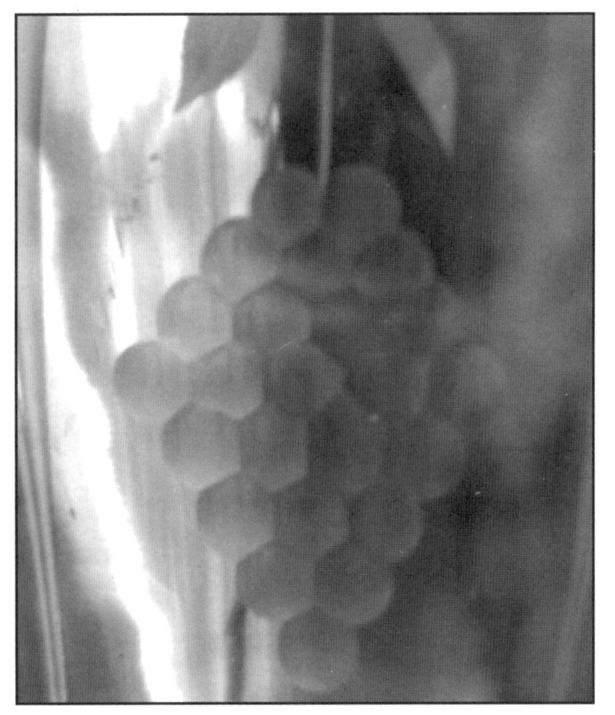

FV11

FV12

GFV1

GFV2

GFV3

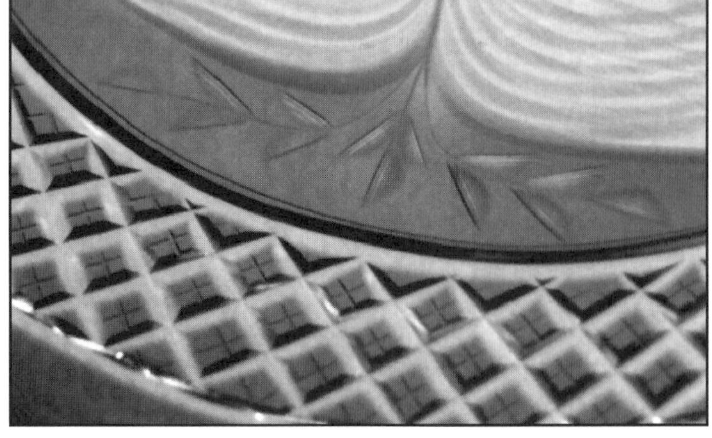

GFV4

GFV5

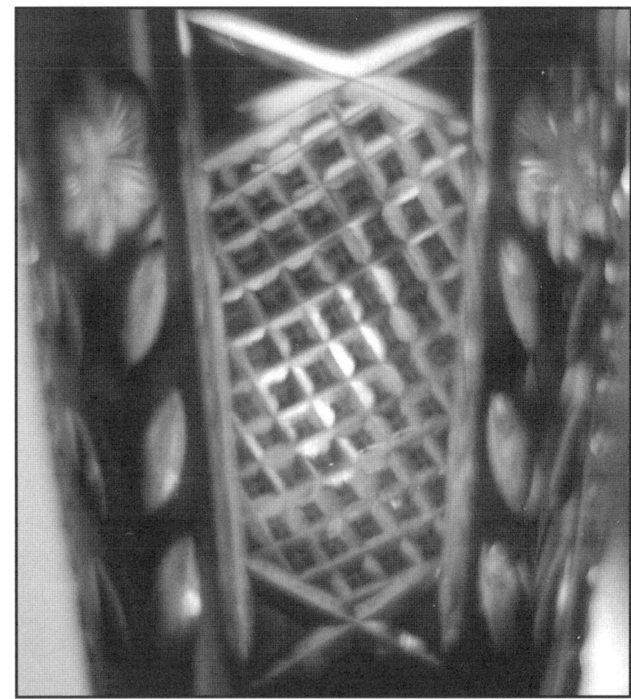

GFV6 (Durand's #705)

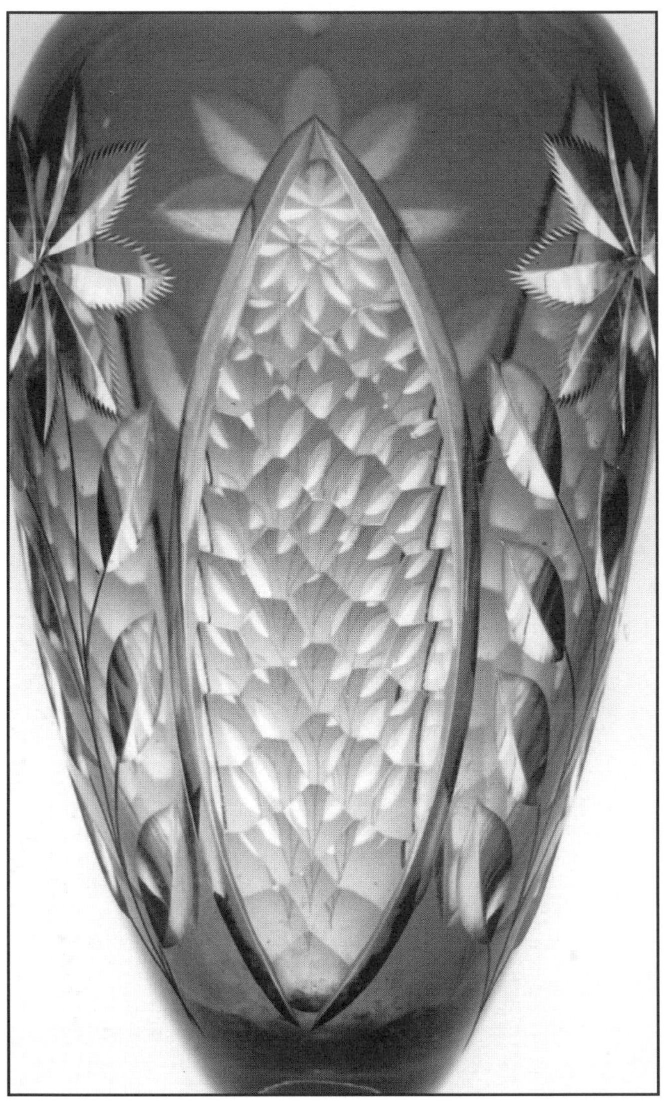

GFV7

GFV8

GFV9

Signatures

During the early years of production, Durand art glass was rarely signed. As the glass became more popular, it became apparent that a signature was needed, but even then most pieces remained unsigned. The small team of workers of the fancy shop were kept so busy making glass that signing was often overlooked. Only near the very end did signing become more commonplace.

I have compiled examples of the three basic (#1,#7,#11) signature types Durand used and I have added to that the many variations of those types. Signatures were marked in the pontil with an aluminum pencil, thus producing a silver finish. Occasionally, paper labels were found, there is no evidence as to whether they were placed on the glass by Durand or by one of the distributors. Signatures on Durand art glass are not common, but when they do appear they are bold, unique and in silver script. The signatures themselves mimic the beauty of the piece of glass itself and the pride of its maker.

Figure #1 is the name Durand in upper case script running across the top of a large V.

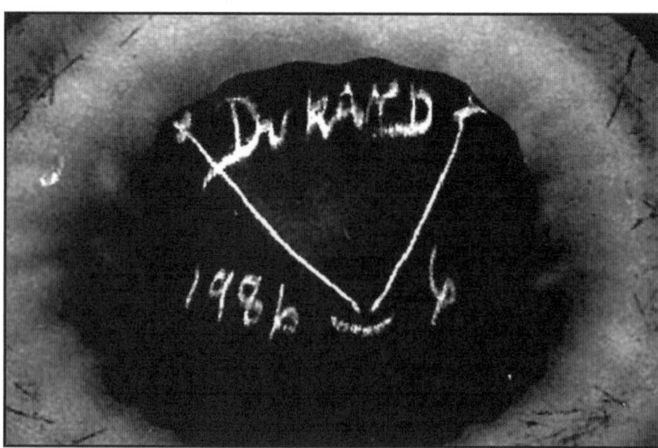

Figure #2 is the name Durand in upper case script running across the top of a large V. Catalog shape number is at the lower left of the V and height in inches at the lower right of the V.

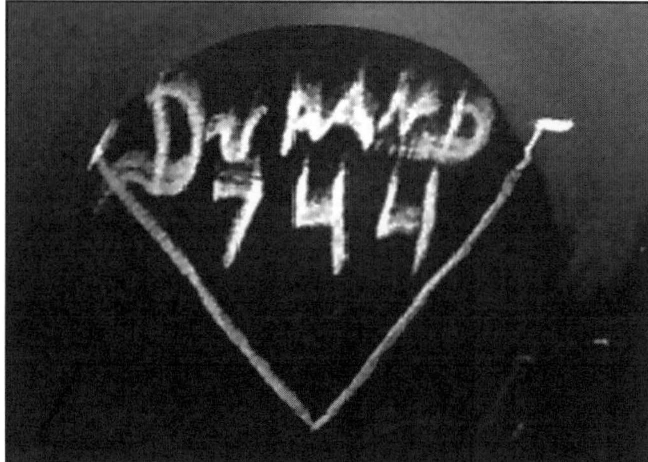

Figure #3 is the name Durand in upper case script running across the top of a large V. Catalog number is under the name Durand and within the V. In this case #744 being a number used to describe a pattern of stemware, dinnerware and accessories and not shape.

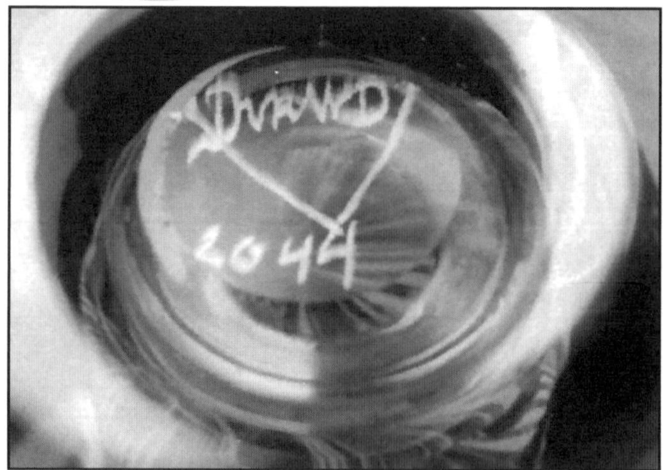

Figure #4 is the name Durand in upper case script running across the top of a large V. Catalog shape number is to the lower left of the V.

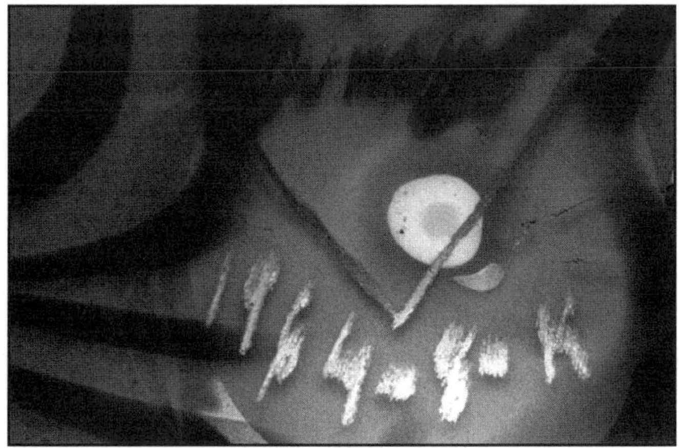

Figure #5 is the name Durand in upper case script running across the top of a large V. Catalog shape number is the lower left of the V and height in inches at the lower right of the V and an added letter following the height. This letter is from the catalog and designates the decoration used. A signature type rarely used.

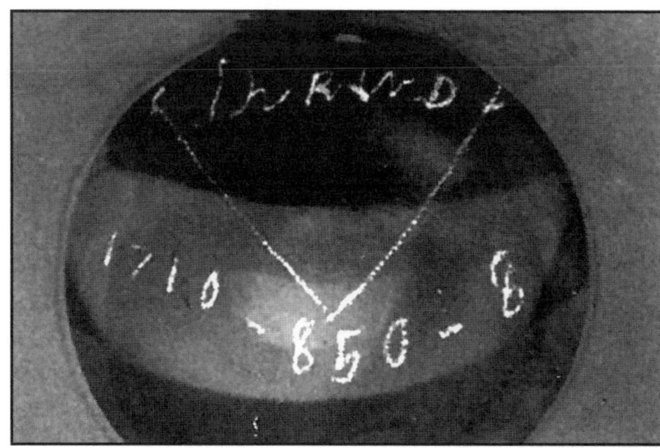

Figure #6 is the name Durand in upper case script running across the top of a large V. Catalog shape number is at the lower left of the V, followed by a 3 digit number under the point of the V designating the cutting pattern used, followed by the height in inches to the lower right of the V.

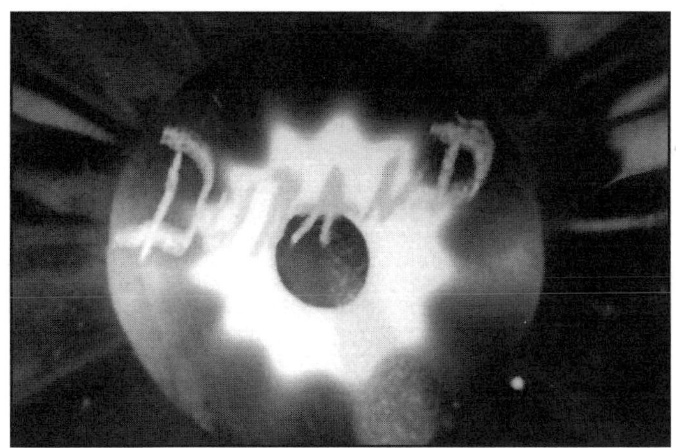

Figure #7 is the name Durand in upper case script without a V.

Figure #8 is the name Durand in upper case script without a V and with catalog shape numbers below the name.

Figure #9 is the name Durand in upper case script without a V. Catalog shape number followed by the height number in inches below the signature.

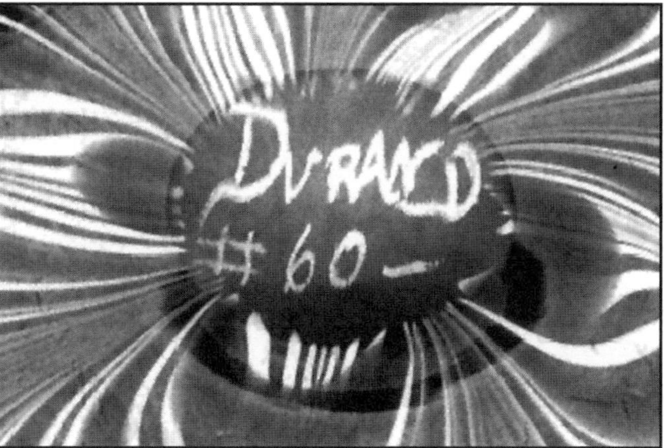

Figure #10 is the name Durand in upper case script without a V. Catalog shape number preceded by a pound sign below the signature.

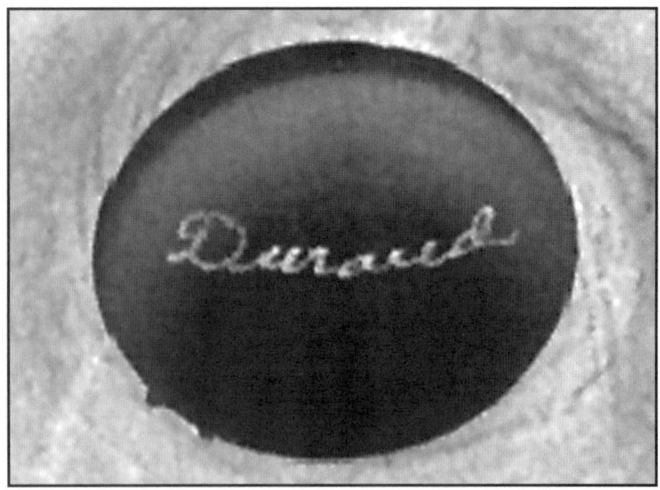

Figure #11 is the name Durand in cursive using very small penmanship.

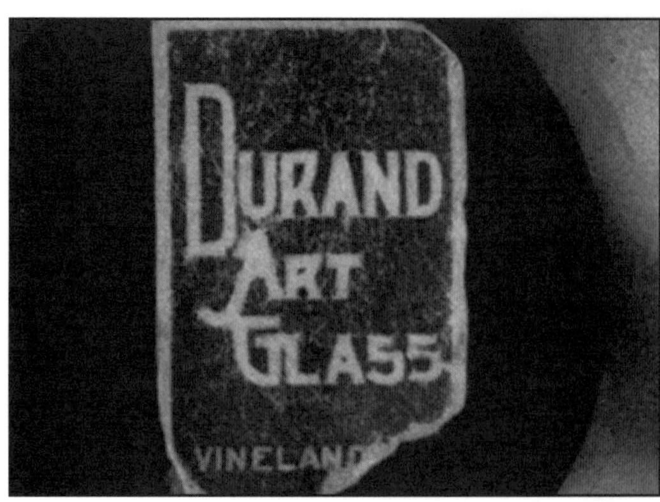

Figure #12 is a paper label with a black background and the words Durand Art Glass, Vineland, N. J. in white lettering. Also the entire label is bordered in white.

Figure #13 is a paper label with a white background and the words Durand Art Glass, Lady Gay Rose in black letters and a red border around these words. Also there is a No. line for shape and/or size to be written. This label was to be used specifically on Lady Gay Rose glass (cased red over opal), but occasionally is found on other decorated glass made by Durand.

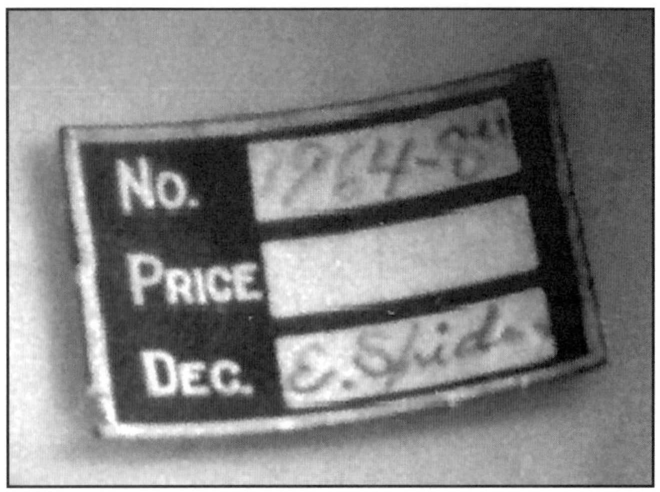

Figure #14 is a paper label with a brown background and the words No., Price, and Dec. in white, followed by a white rectangular area. This label is trimmed in white. The three white areas were for writing in the shape number, retail price, and the decoration used. I could find no evidence as to weather Durand or a distributor placed these labels on the glass.

Figure #15 is a paper label used by the Vineland Flint Glass Works to affix to molded glass made in a division other than the fancy shop. This glass was artistic in nature, usually a lustred clear glass. However it is not what we are referring to as Durand art glass. The lettering is in purple on a white background and denotes the color by name and the shape by number.

Shapes

Although shape is not an absolute identifier, in the case of Durand glass you will find it to be a great asset. I have compiled, from various catalogs and from various pieces of signed and numbered glass made by Durand, over 170 shapes with their corresponding numbers. Distributors would use their catalog to order by number the shape and by letter the decoration desired. Although most of the shapes made by Durand are included in the following pages, there are some shapes that no number could be found. Keep in mind that the Fancy Shop was experimenting on a continual basis, some shapes were not produced commercially. I'm sure however that additional numbers associated with shapes will continue to surface long after this book is put to print. Some shapes appear to be contradictory in the catalog but subtle differences can be found that can be difficult to show in silhouette.

Some of the shapes were originally Quezal Art Glass and Decorating Co. shapes taken from the catalog brought to Durand by Martin Bach Jr. Those shapes were then renumbered using the Durand numbering system. I have noted many of them by way of an asterisk, using original Quezal catalogs as a reference. It will be the glass in these shapes (although produced for a short time and therefore less common) that will sometimes be difficult to determine whether they are Durand or Quezal art glass.

Keep in mind also that some of these shapes, in particular those with applied handles, were not often made by Durand. They were more difficult to produce and therefore more costly. As Durand glass evolved, shapes that they produced took on a newer look that was theirs alone, leaving the Quezal look behind.

Numbers will sometimes appear on dinnerware and stemware. These numbers refer to a particular pattern, rather than a shape. One example is #744 which refers to Optic ribbed dinnerware. Another is #5030 which refers to peacock feather dinnerware.

Durand Shape Numbers

1700 *
1701
1703 *
1704
1705 *
1706
1707
1708
1709
1710 *
1711 *
1712
1713
1714
1716
1717
1719
1720
1721
1722 *
1723
1730 *
1731 *
1733
1734
1735
1736
1737

1800
1801
1803
1804
1805 *
1806 *
1808
1810 *
1811
1812
1815
1818
1819
1820
1821
1823
1824

1900
1901
1902
1903
1905
1907
1909
1910
1916
1917
1919
1920
1921 *
1922
1923
1924
1928
1929
1940
1941
1942
1944
1945
1946
1947
1949
1950
1952
1955
1956
1957
1958
1959
1960
1963
1964
1965
1966
1967
1968
1970
1971
1974
1977
1978
1986

1990
1991
1994
1995
1996
1997
1998

2000
2001 *
2002 *
2003
2005
2007 *
2008 *
2009 *
2010 *
2011 *
2012
2013
2014
2015
2016
2017
2018
2021
2022 *
2023
2024
2025
2026 *
2028 *
2028 1/2
2029
2030
2031
2032
2033
2035
2036
2037
2038 *
2039
2040
2044
2048

2502 *
2503 *

2601
2602
2603
2611

3000
3001

5000
5002
5005
5008
5009
5011

60/60000

20120
20121
20122
20123
20124
20133
20135
20136
20139
20150
20155
20161
20164
20167
20170
20177

Console Sets and
After Dinner Sets:
2600
2650
2500
2506
4000
** Quezal shapes used at Durand*

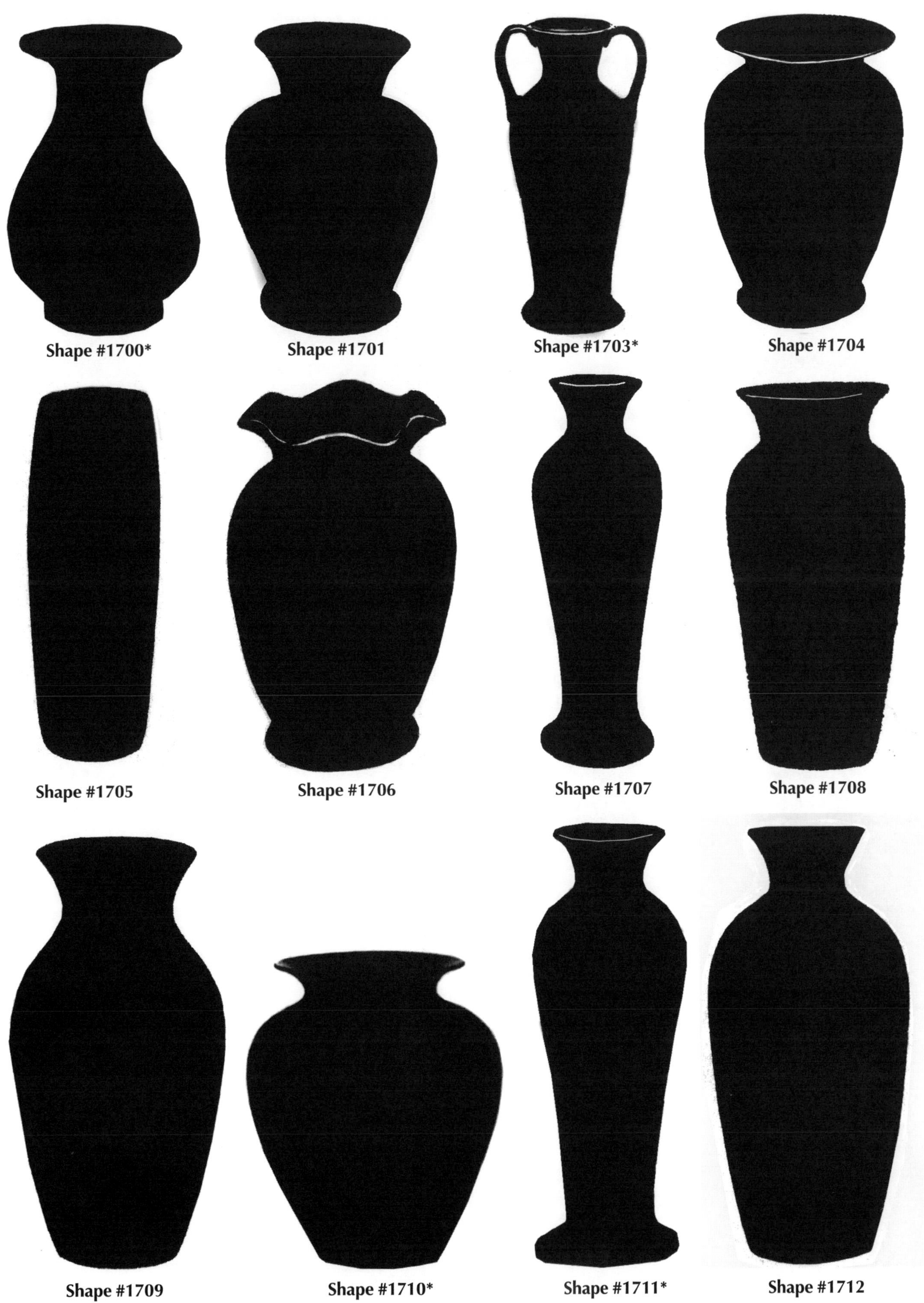
Shape #1700*
Shape #1701
Shape #1703*
Shape #1704
Shape #1705
Shape #1706
Shape #1707
Shape #1708
Shape #1709
Shape #1710*
Shape #1711*
Shape #1712

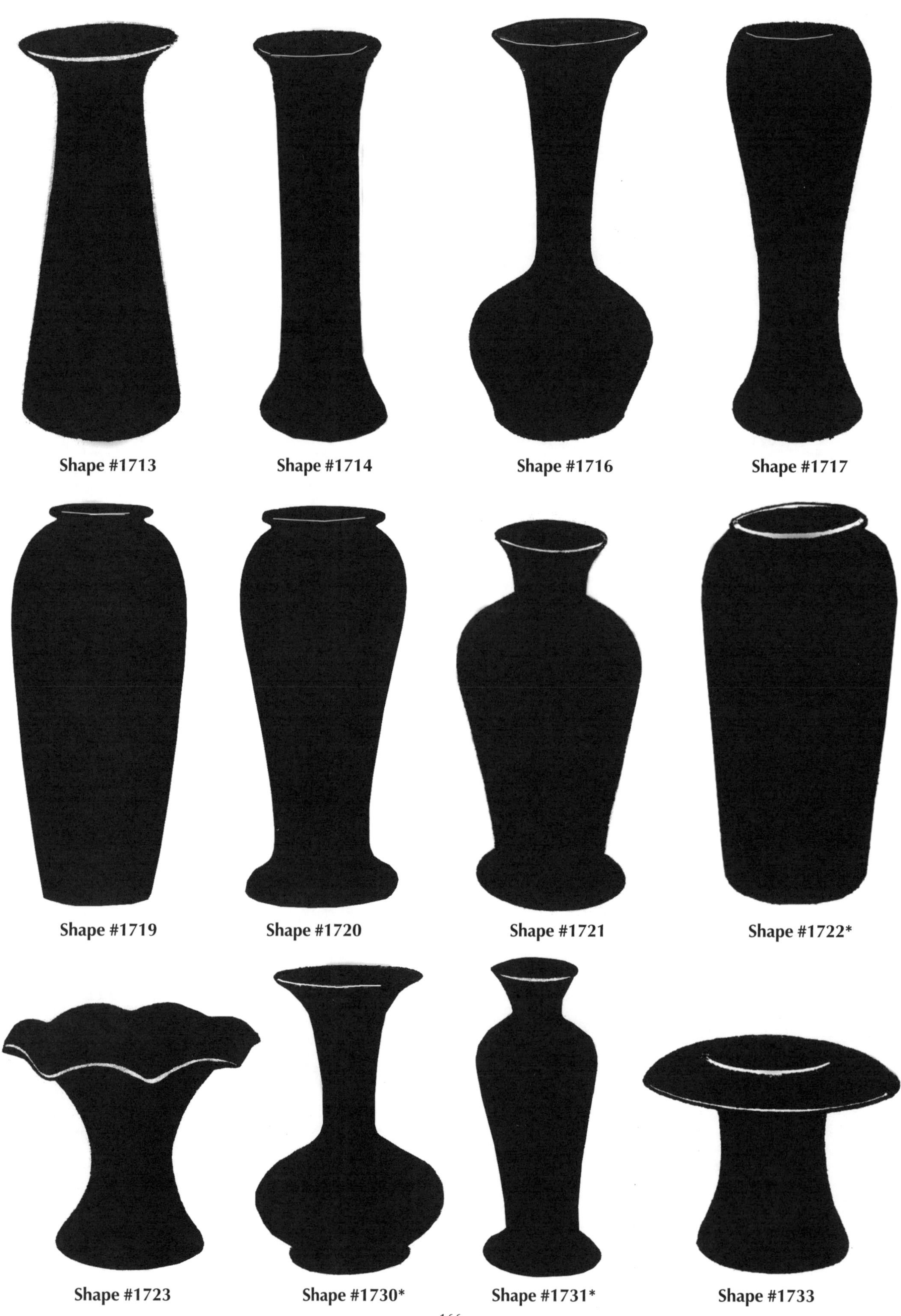
Shape #1713
Shape #1714
Shape #1716
Shape #1717
Shape #1719
Shape #1720
Shape #1721
Shape #1722*
Shape #1723
Shape #1730*
Shape #1731*
Shape #1733

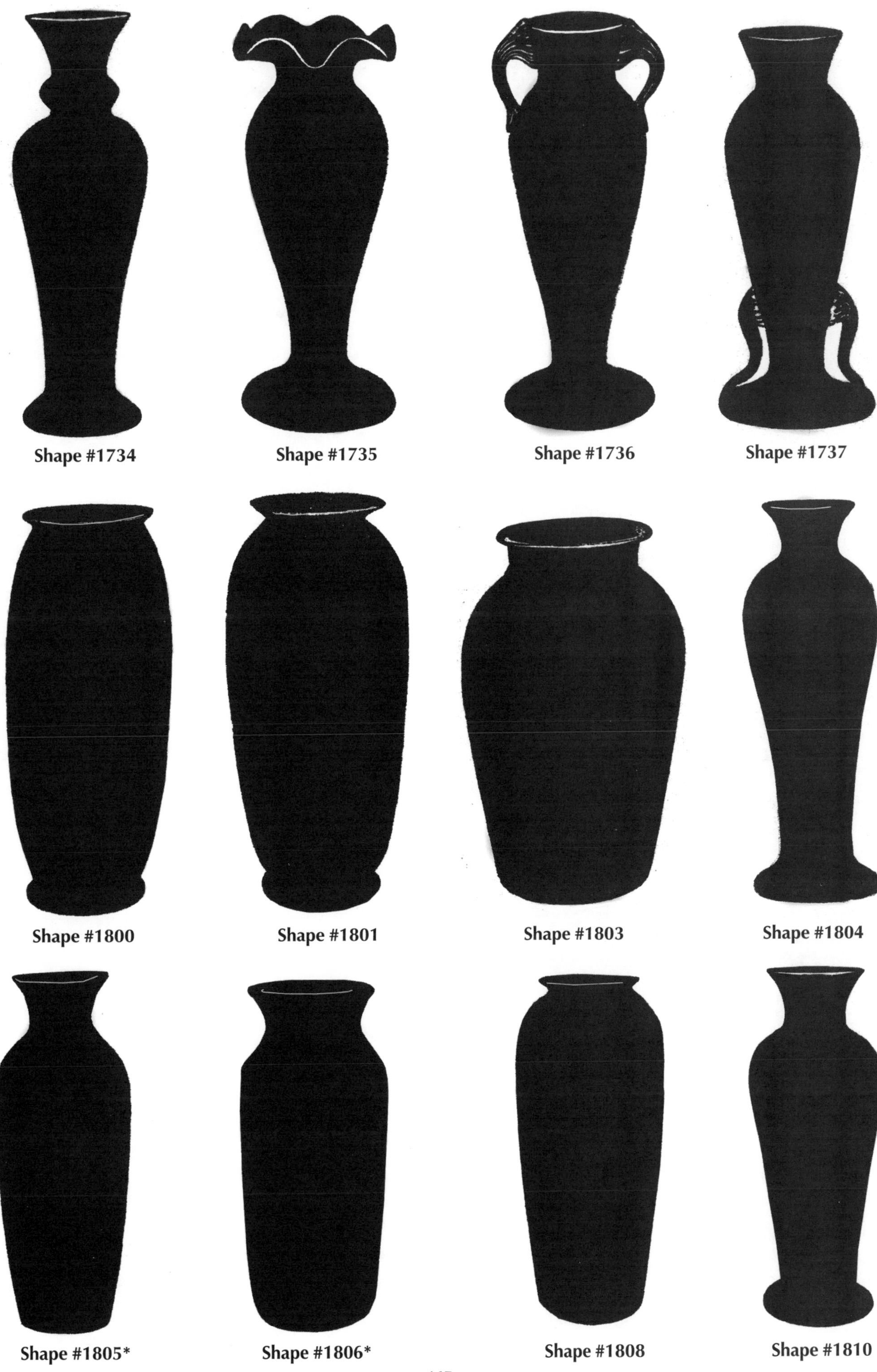
Shape #1734
Shape #1735
Shape #1736
Shape #1737
Shape #1800
Shape #1801
Shape #1803
Shape #1804
Shape #1805*
Shape #1806*
Shape #1808
Shape #1810

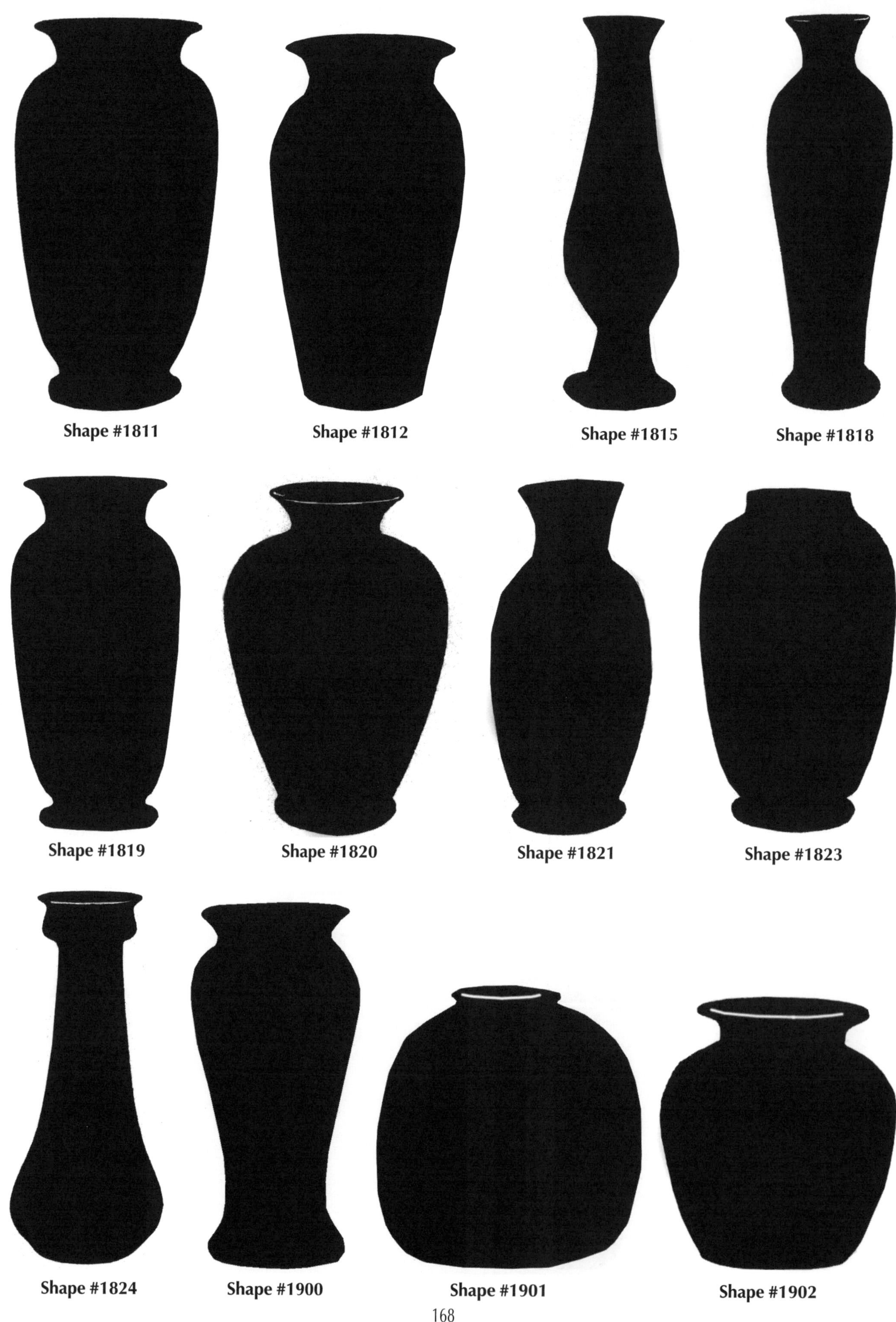
Shape #1811
Shape #1812
Shape #1815
Shape #1818
Shape #1819
Shape #1820
Shape #1821
Shape #1823
Shape #1824
Shape #1900
Shape #1901
Shape #1902

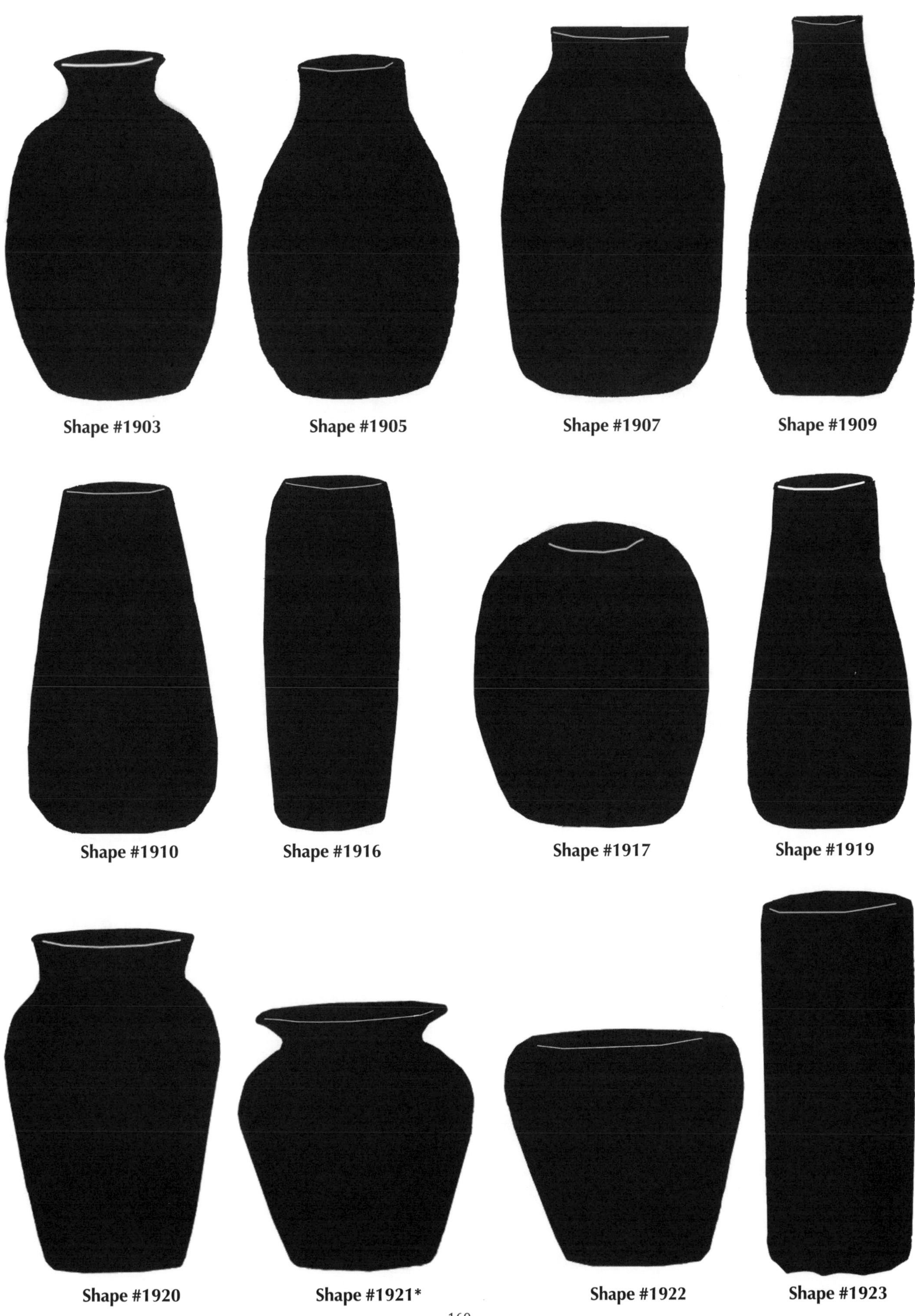

Shape #1903

Shape #1905

Shape #1907

Shape #1909

Shape #1910

Shape #1916

Shape #1917

Shape #1919

Shape #1920

Shape #1921*

Shape #1922

Shape #1923

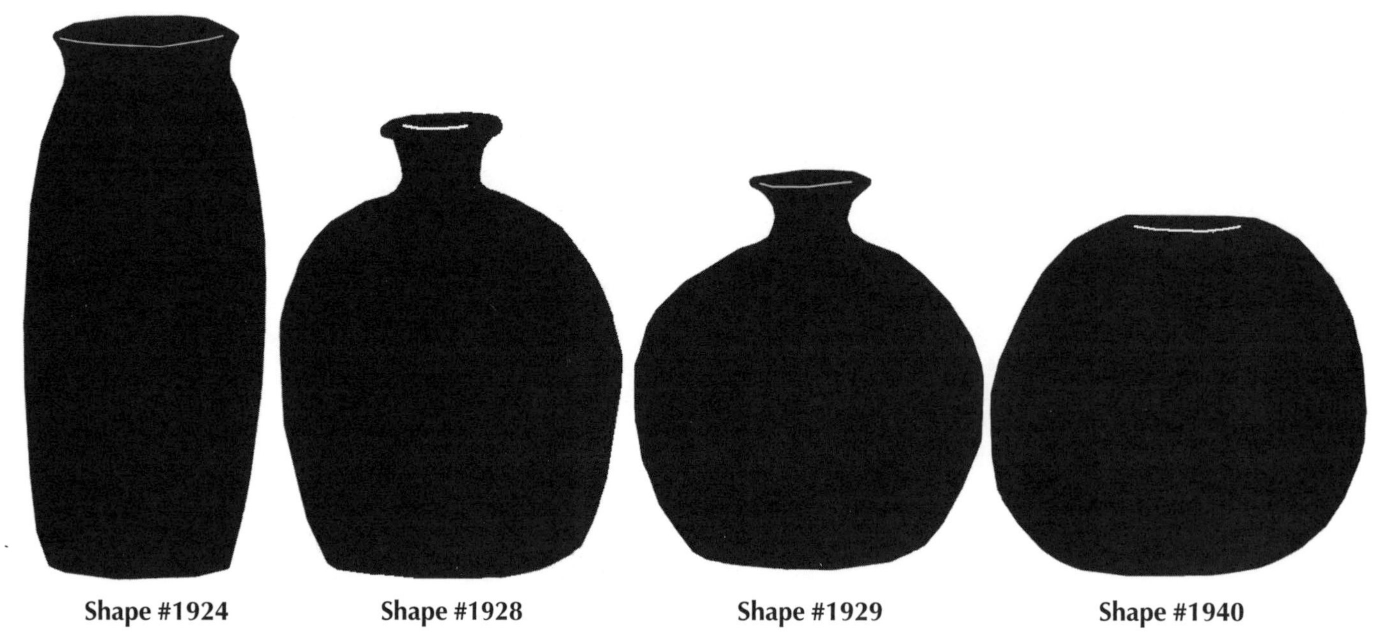

Shape #1924 Shape #1928 Shape #1929 Shape #1940

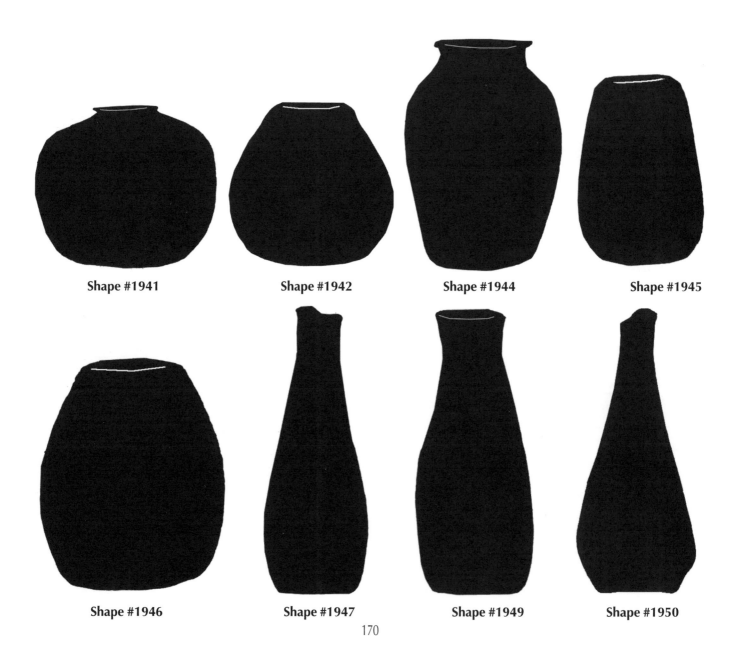

Shape #1941  Shape #1942 Shape #1944  Shape #1945

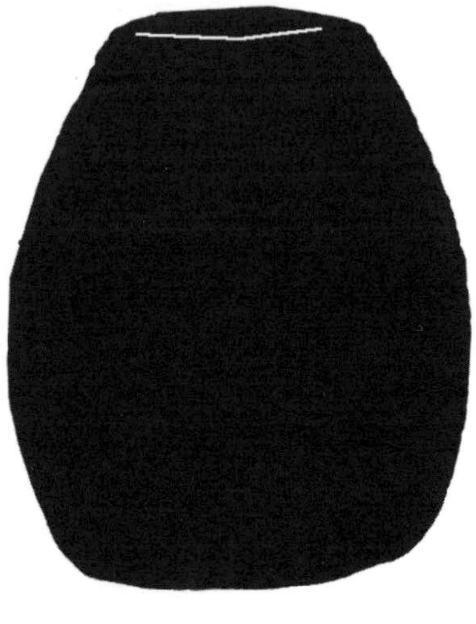

Shape #1946  Shape #1947  Shape #1949  Shape #1950

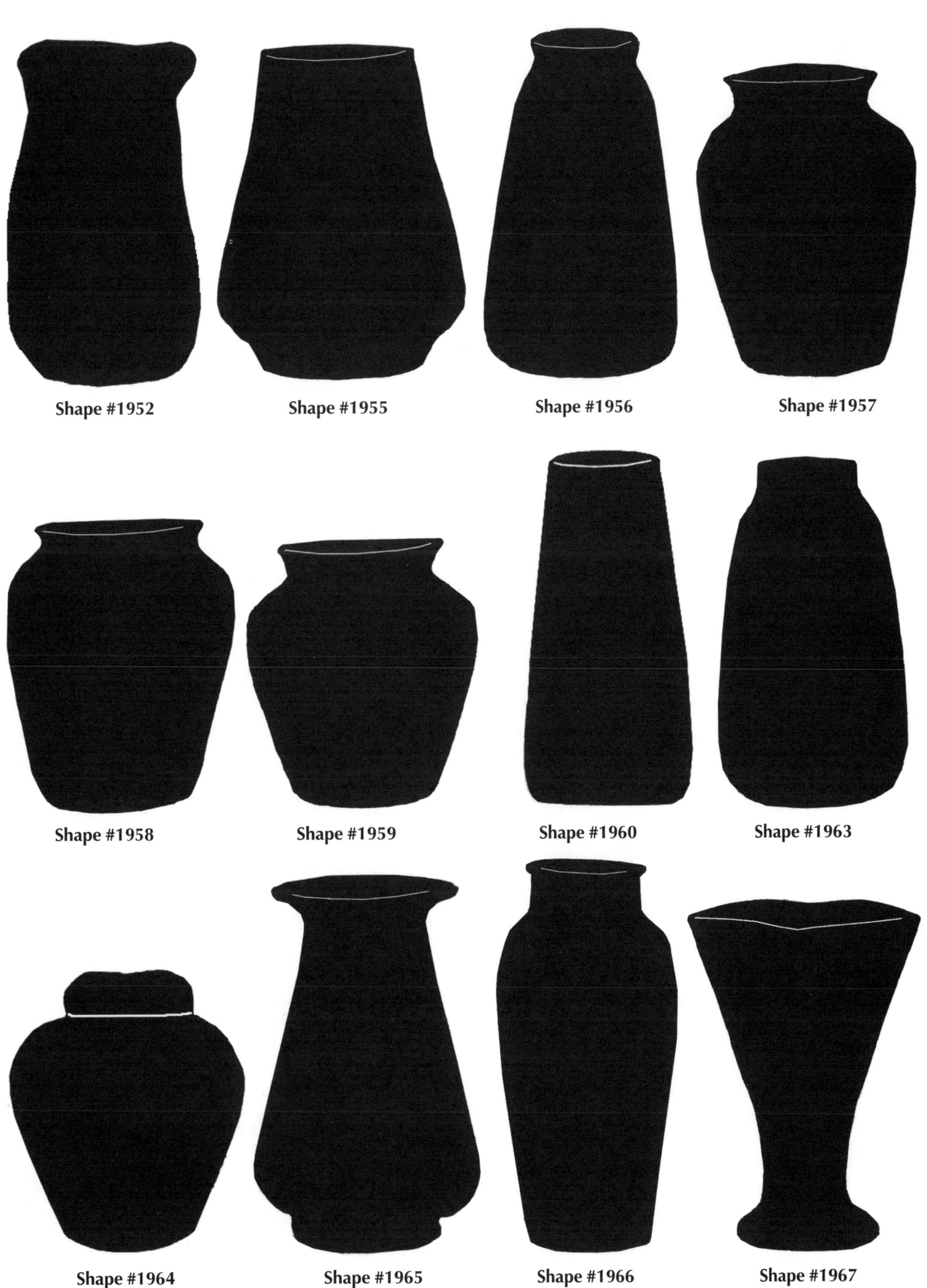

Shape #1952 Shape #1955 Shape #1956 Shape #1957

Shape #1958 Shape #1959 Shape #1960 Shape #1963

Shape #1964 Shape #1965 Shape #1966 Shape #1967

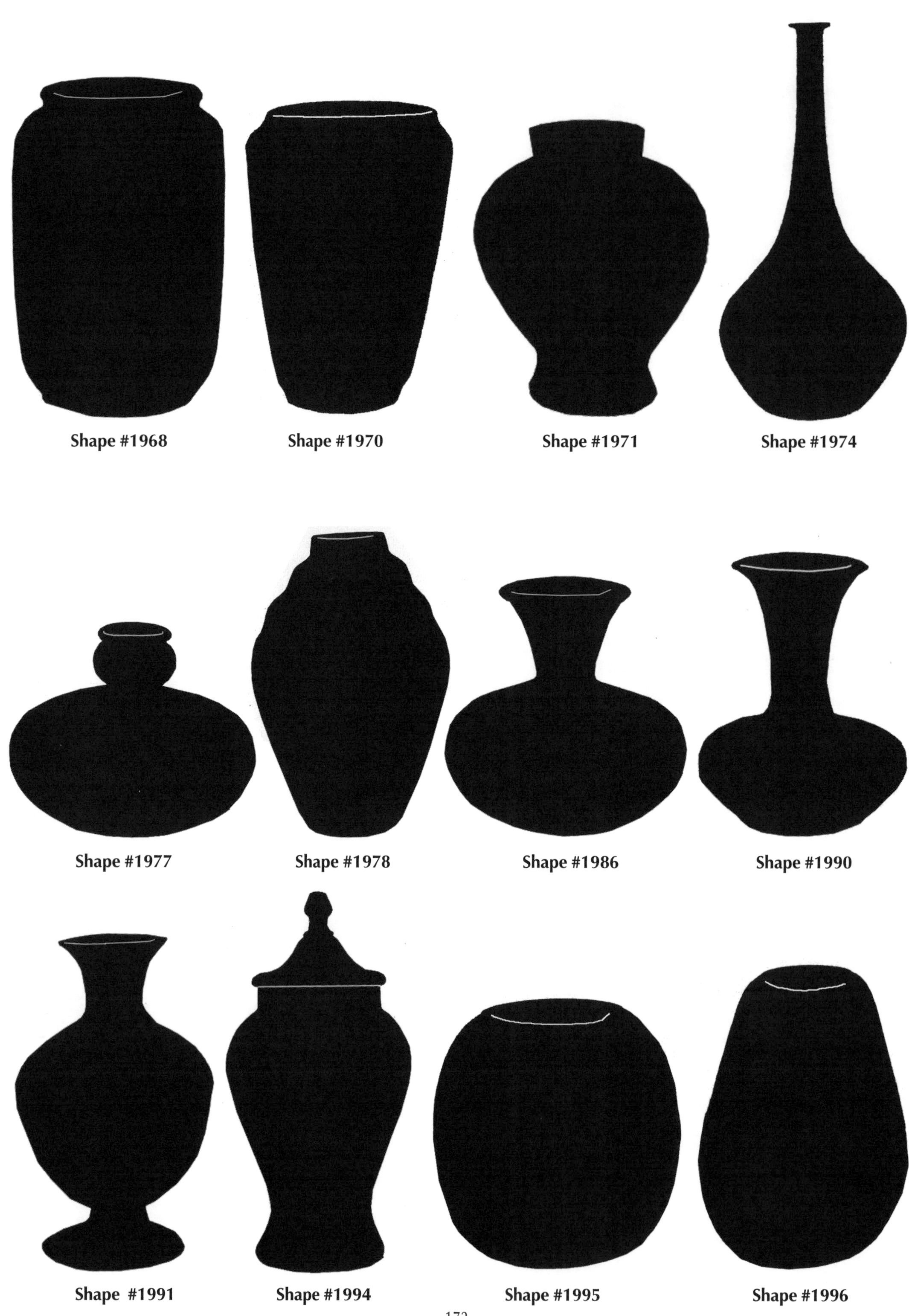

Shape #1968 Shape #1970 Shape #1971 Shape #1974

Shape #1977 Shape #1978 Shape #1986 Shape #1990

Shape #1991 Shape #1994 Shape #1995 Shape #1996

Shape #1997

Shape #1998

Shape #2000

Shape #2001*

Shape #2002*

Shape #2003

Shape #2005

Shape #2007*

Shape #2008*

Shape #2009*

Shape #2010*

Shape #2011*

Shape #2012 Shape #2013 Shape #2014 Shape #2015

Shape #2016 Shape #2017 Shape #2018 Shape #2021

Shape #2022* Shape #2023 Shape #2024 Shape #2025

Shape #2026*

Shape #2028

Shape #2028½

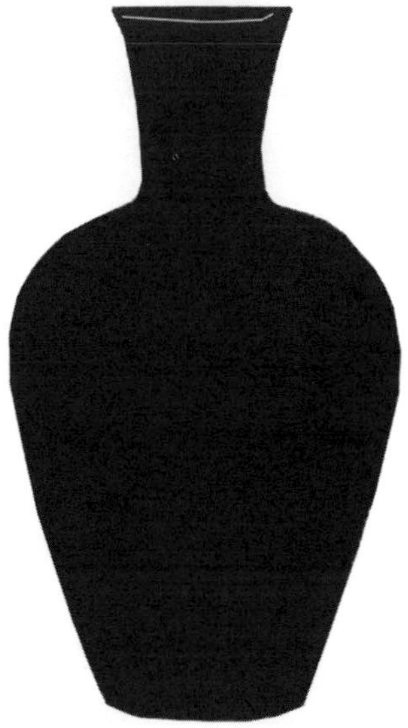

Shape #2029

Shape #2030

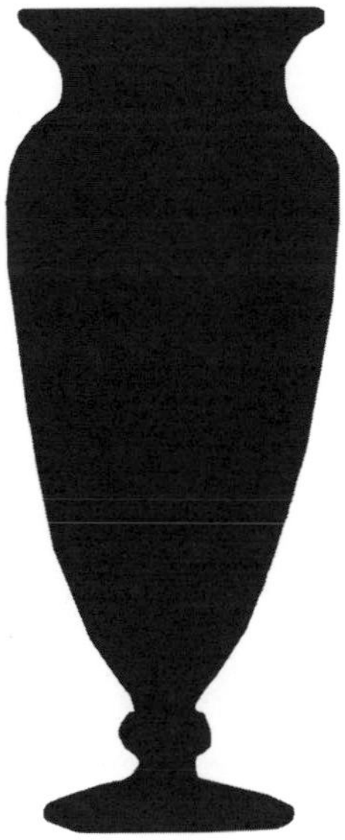

Shape #2031

Shape #2032

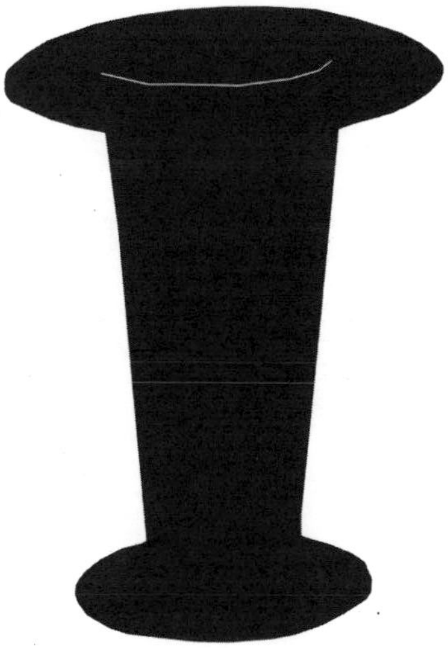

Shape #2033

Shape #2035

Shape #2036

Shape #2037

Shape #2038*

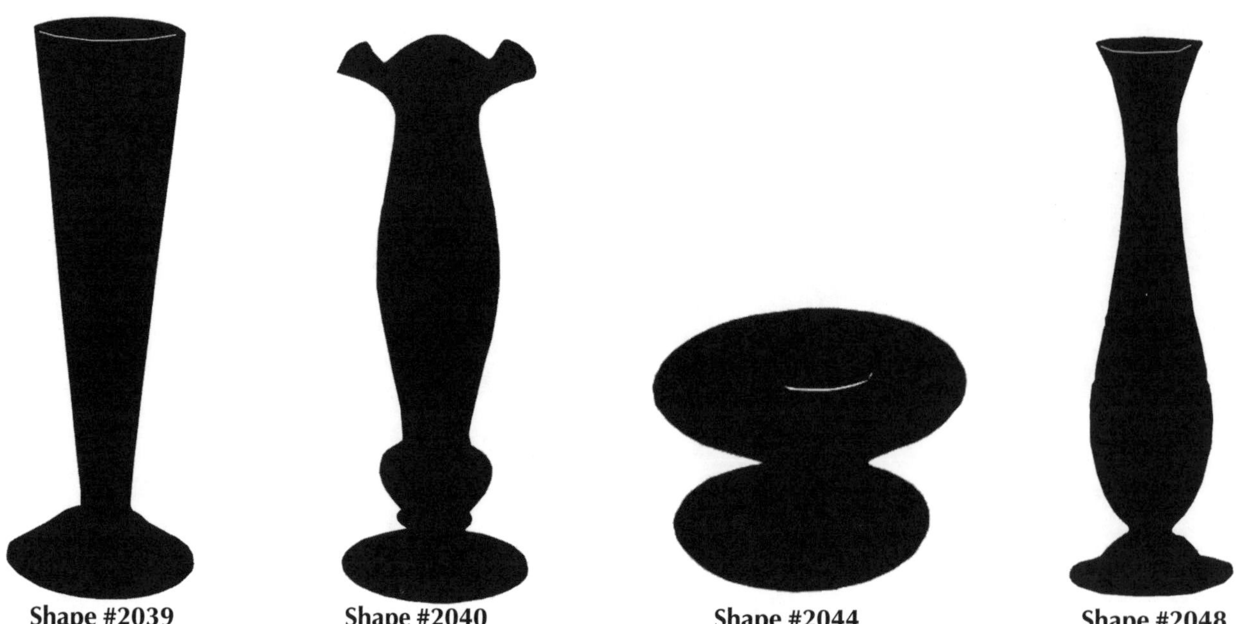

Shape #2039 Shape #2040 Shape #2044 Shape #2048

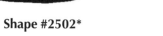

Shape #2502*

Shape #2503*

Shape #2601

Shape #2602

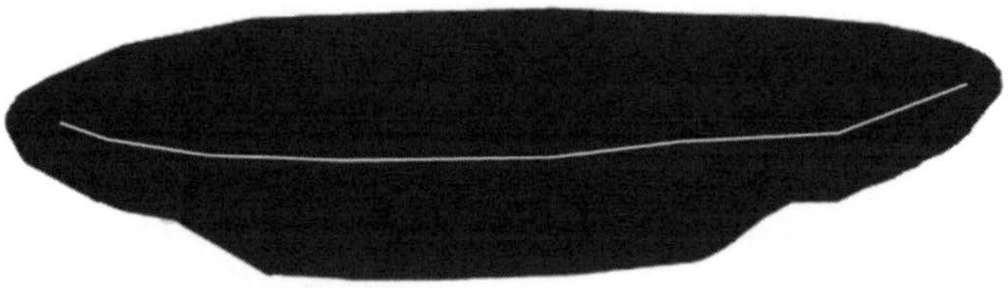

Shape #2603

Shape #2611

Shape #3000

Shape #3001

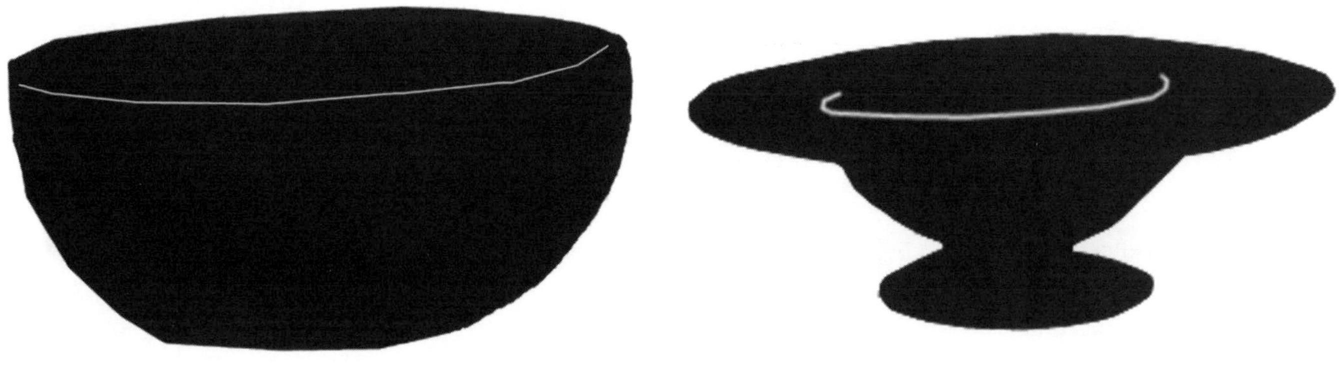

Shape #5000

Shape #5002

Shape #5005

Shape #5008

Shape #5009

Shape #5011

Shape #60 & #60000

Shape #20120

Shape #20121

Shape#20122

Shape #20123

Shape #20124

Shape #20133

Shape #20133
Shape#20136
Shape #20139
Shape #20150
Shape #20155
Shape #20161
Shape #20164
Shape #20167
Shape #20170
Shape #20177

Numbers shown on the following pages are noted in catalogs as Console Sets and After Dinner Sets and are not shape numbers.

After Dinner Set #4000

Console Set #2500

Console Set #2506

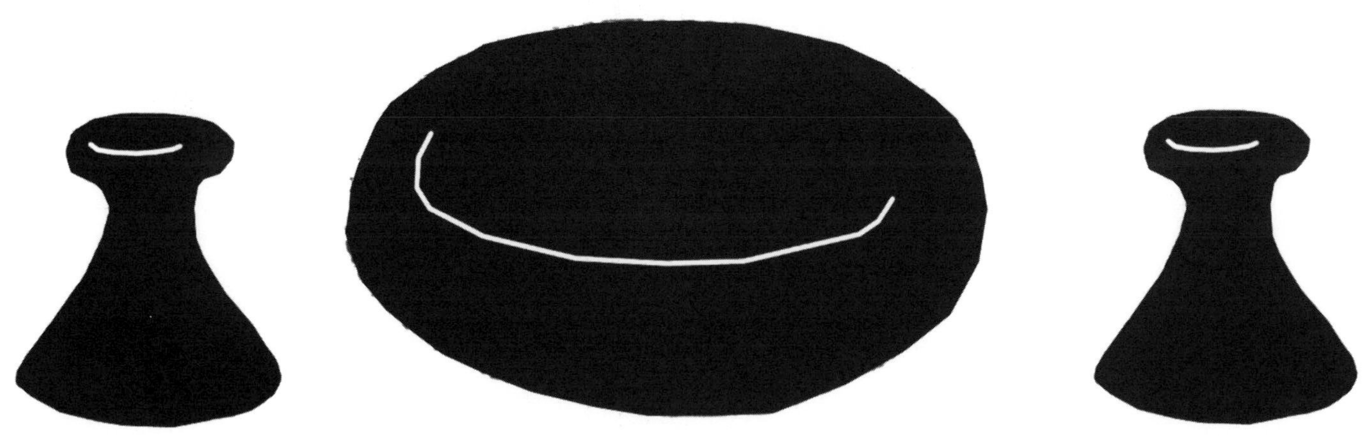

Console Set #2600

Console Set #2650

Bibliography

Farber, Samuel. "Durand Glass." *Antique Journal*, August 1960.

Lagerberg, Ted and Viola. *Collectable Glass Presents the Technique of Emil J. Larson Featuring Durand Glass, Book III.* Des Moines, Iowa: Wallace-Homestead Book Co., 1967.

Pepper, Adeline. *The Glass Gaffers of New Jersey.* New York: Charles Scribner's Sons, 1971.

Revi, Albert Christian. *American Art Nouveau Glass.* Camden, New Jersey: Thomas Nelson and Son, 1968.

INDEX

A

B

C

D

E

F

G

H

I

J

K

L

M

N

O

P

Q

R

S

T

V

W

Y

Z

DURAND
THE MAN AND HIS GLASS

1998–99 VALUE GUIDE

BY EDWARD J. MESCHI

This section of the book is dedicated to providing current values for the Durand art glass shown in color on pages 33–80. Values are listed in order by the figure numbers assigned each piece in the color pages. These figure numbers correspond with captions on pages 113–125.

Neither the publisher nor the author can accept responsibility or liability for losses incurred by persons using this guide, whether due to typographical errors or other reasons.

PAGE 33

Fig.	Value
1.	$ 2225

PAGE 34

Fig.	Value
2.	875
3.	1025
4.	2000
5.	850
6.	450

PAGE 35

Fig.	Value
7.	850
8.	1000
9.	950
10.	975
11.	975

PAGE 36

Fig.	Value
12.	1350
13.	1075
14.	825
15.	1000
16.	950
17.	1075
18.	850

PAGE 37

Fig.	Value
19.	1650
20.	925
21.	1350
22.	1475
23.	1175
24.	2250
25.	975
26.	975
27.	1225

PAGE 38

Fig.	Value
28.	1550
29.	1325
30.	1850
31.	575
32.	1225
33.	850
34.	1175

PAGE 39

Fig.	Value
35.	1075
36.	1125
37.	1000
38.	400
39.	1900
40.	600

PAGE 40

Fig.	Value
41.	725
42.	1325
43.	1325
44.	1325
45.	1125
46.	750
47.	1325

PAGE 41

Fig.	Value
48.	1450
49.	1000
50.	1250
51.	1250
52.	1150
53.	875
54.	875

PAGE 42

Fig.	Value
55.	1475
56.	1525
57.	1575
58.	1425

PAGE 43

Fig.	Value
59.	875
60.	1250
61.	800
62.	1750
63.	1800
64.	200

PAGE 44

Fig.	Value
65.	1050
66.	875
67.	925
68.	1025
69.	925
70.	1150

PAGE 45

Fig.	Value
71.	1400

72. 1200
73. 1600
74. 1200
75. 900

Page 46
76. 1250
77. 1425
78. 1325
79. 1275
80. 1225
81. 475
82. 875
83. 1025

Page 47
84. 3200

Page 48
85. 2550

Page 49
86. 3150

Page 50
87. 2100
88. 1425
89. 1675
90. 1425
91. 2250
92. 725

Page 51
93. 1350
94. 2100
95. 1425
96. 1300
97. 1800
98. 1950
99. 1200
100. 675
101. 1500

Page 52
102. 1900
103. 1300
104. 2150
105. 2000
106. 1300

Page 53
107. 1400
108. 1900
109. 1600
110. 1500
111. 1400

Page 54
112. 1050
113. 1400
114. 1800
115. 1400
116. 675

Page 55
117. 1200
118. 2100
119. 800
120. 1600
121. 1050
122. 800
123. 1400
124. 1800
125. 1500
126. 1900
127. 1200

Page 56
128. 1200
129. 1000
130. 600
131. 1200
132. 900

Page 57
133. 975
134. 1250

Page 58
135. 1175
136. 1275
137. 1275
138. 1050
139. 1200

Page 59
140. 2300

Page 60
141. 1500
142. 2200
143. 2100
144. 2300
145. 950
146. 1550

Page 61
147. 3200

Page 62
148. 1675

Page 63
149. 1575
150. 1800
151. 2150

Page 64
152. 2675
153. 1900
154. 1500
155. 500
156. 1350
157. 2675

Page 65
158. 1800
159. 1800
160. 1250
161. 1500
162. 1350

Page 66
163. 1250
164. 1575
165. 1150
166. 1875
167. 1125
168. 1075
169. 1750
170. 575
171. 750

Page 67
172. 1400
173. 900
174. 1500

Page 68
175. 1525
176. 2125
177. 1375

Page 69
178. 1750
179. 1900
180. 2600
181. 1900
182. 2500
183. 2000
184. 2000
185. 1300

Page 70
186. 950
187. 1200
188. 1250

189. 1200
190. 600
191. 925
192. 950
193. 900
194. 950

Page 71
195. 1375
196. 900
197. 1900
199. 675
198. and
200. 2200 pair

Page 72
201. 1100
202. 400
203. 650
204. 650
205. 850
206. 1025

Page 73
207. 1525
208. 1375
209. 1325
210. 1250
211. 1200
212. 825
213. 275
214. 575
215. 295

Page 74
216. 2475

Page 75
217. 2800

Page 76
218. 900
219. 1050
220. 1250
221. 575
222. 900
223. 975

Page 77
224. 275
225. 275
226. 325
227. 125
228. 275
229. 275
230. 675 pair
231. 525
232. 125
233. 100
234. 275
235. 375
236. 325
237. 150

Page 78
238. 925
239. 1150
240. 375
241. 900
242. 1050
243. 1175
244. 825
245. 525
246. 450
247. 675

Page 79
248. 275
249. 325
250. 175
251. 325
252. 200
253. 175
254. 325
255. 125
256. 175
257. 225
258. 225
259. 175
260. 275
261. 300
262. 225
263. 275
264. 350
265. 350
266. 175
267. 125

Page 80
268. 925
269. 1425
270. 1175
271. 1275
272. 825

Page 81
273. 725
274. 1250
275. 1250
276. 1175
277. 725
278. 825
279. 475
280. 750
281. 400

Page 82
282. 1275
283. 925
284. 1575
285. and
286. 1650 set
287. 1075
288. 1350
289. 575

Page 83
290. 1375
291. 975
292. 2300
293. 1250
294. 1375

Page 84
295. 150
296. 275
297. 275
298. 295
299. 375
300. 275
301. 295
302. 175

Page 85
303. 1025
304. 625
305. 525
306. 100
307. 125
308. 125
309. 100
310. 225
311. 125

Page 86
312. 575
313. 1525
314. 425
315. 475
316. 225
317. 175

Page 87
318. 150
319. 125
320. 125
321. 325
322. 225

323.	250

Page 88

324.	275
325.	225
326.	275
327.	100
328.	125
329.	125
330.	100
331.	125

Page 89

332.	325
333.	525
334.	675
335.	1350
336.	575

Page 90

337.	1050
338.	1050
339.	1175
340.	1375
341.	275
342.	1050
343.	775
344.	675

Page 91

345.	650
346.	1175
347.	1050
348.	1875
349.	725
350.	875
351.	400
352.	400
353.	325
354.	175
355.	175

Page 92

356.	1300
357.	1250
358.	1050
359.	1050
360.	2000

Page 93

361.	725
362.	1175
363.	1075
364.	775
365.	775
366.	350
367.	1375
368.	525
369.	525 pair
370.	425

Page 94

371.	175
372.	200
373.	600
374.	900
375.	325
376.	325
377.	285
378.	925
379.	525

Page 95

380.	575
381.	575
382.	175
383.	725
384.	175
385.	525
386.	625
387.	1100
388.	75
389.	120
390.	75

Page 96

391.	1350
392.	1250
393.	1250
394.	675
395.	125
396.	125
397.	150
398.	175
399.	125

Page 97

400.	125
401.	125
402.	125
403.	175
404.	125
405.	325
406.	275
407.	325
408.	400
409.	325
410.	175
411.	275
412.	275
413.	275
414.	275
415.	275
416.	100
417.	225
418.	225
419.	425
420.	125
421.	350

Page 98

422.	1350 each
423.	1450
424.	725
425.	450

Page 99

426.	1725
427.	1675
428.	975 pair
429.	1825
430.	2000
431.	350

Page 100

432.	1200
433.	1200
434.	1125
435.	800
436.	1025
437.	1325
438.	575
439.	600
440.	750
441.	925
442.	650
443.	650

Page 101

444.	1250
445.	200
446.	875
447.	1375
448.	1275
449.	1300
450.	875
451.	950
452.	2200
453.	225

Page 102

454.	2725
455.	2575
456.	725
457.	275
458.	300
459.	450
460.	1375

461. 1250
462. 1225

PAGE 103
463. 1875 set
464. 790
465. 750
466. 1450

PAGE 104
467. 3300
468. 3500

PAGE 105
469. 1275
470. 1450
471. 1325
472. 1075
473. 1225
474. 1175
475. and
476. 2150 pair

477. 925
478. 575
479. 1325
480. 2175
481. 3150

PAGE 106
482. 1500 pair
483. 875 pair
484. 675
485. 1325 pair
486. 650 pair
487. 500 pair

PAGE 107
488. 1200
489. 875

PAGE 108
490. 325
491. 525
492. 375

PAGE 109
493. 95
494. 925
495. 225
496. 575
497. 625
498. 575
499. 375

PAGE 110
500. 875
501. 875
502. 75
503. 825
504. 325
505. 175
506. 1375 pair
507. 425
508. 925
509. 475
510. 575

PAGE 111
511. 425
512. 425
513. 1650
514. 350
515. 250
516. 700 pair

PAGE 112
517. 375
518. 475
519. 575
520. 625
521. 425
522. 375
523. 575

Notes